NEMONE

A young woman barrister's battle against prejudice, class and misogyny.
Her controversial marriage.

Nemone Lethbridge has asserted her rights to be identified as the author of this work in accordance with Section 77 of the Copyright, Designs and Patents Act 1988

All rights reserved. No part of this publication may be reproduced, stored in a retrieval system or transmitted in any form or by any means, electronic, mechanical, photocopying or otherwise, without the prior written consent of the publisher.

First published in the UK in 2021 by Milo O'Connor
All enquires to milo.oconnor@outlook.com

Graphics www.lissakdesign.com

© 2021 Nemone Lethbridge

Acknowledgements

I can never thank Michael Dover enough for the hours he has spent editing and correcting my manuscript, for his kindness and constructive criticism. Without Michael's help I would never have got this show on the road. I must also thank my dear friend Elli Petrohilos who typed the manuscript and put me right on all matters Greek. To Anthony Adewumi who helped at the early stages. To Katie Gollop QC who makes marvellous things happen. To Mark Lissak who did the graphics, restoring many old precious and damaged photographs. To my grandson Finlay O'Connor who researched the fate of the Goebbels' children. Finally, to my son Milo O'Connor who gladly took on the double task of agent and publisher.

To my sons and grandchildren.

CHAPTER ONE

<u>NEMONE</u>

1 March 1932: I was born in India, a child of the British Raj. The lights failed that night in the Quetta Military Hospital, and I came into the world by the light of a hurricane lamp. My mother had refused anaesthetics during her labour, not wishing to have, as was her right as the wife of an officer, what was denied to the wives of the soldiers.

My parents engaged a nurse for me, a large affable girl of mixed race. She was kind and competent enough I'm told, but on her nights off, to supplement her wages, she would service the soldiers from the nearby cantonment. One morning she was found on a mountain road with her head stoved in, and, as it is said, multiple injuries. At the inquest (which returned a verdict of murder by a person or persons unknown) a client said in evidence 'There's some as calls her the buffalo, some as calls her the hephelant, but I always known her as the warthog'. No one claimed the body.

After that my mother decided to dispense with nurses and nannies and to look after me herself. Ayahs she would not entertain, having seen too often the spoilt, brattish product of their gentle regime. Her decision was regarded as eccentric in the world in which she lived. 'What an oddity' said the other army wives. 'Can't play bridge; won't drink gin; looks after her child herself'.

My father took me on his knee. He smelled of pipe tobacco and had a prickly face.

> *Hutti tutti, little donkey*
> *Hutti tutti, little donkey*
> *Hutti tutti, little donkey*
> *Bismillah, grumpy old camel*
> *Bismillah, grumpy old camel*
> *Bismillah, grumpy old camel*

At this point he threw me into the air. As he dangled me, I shrieked with laughter. So I dangled my children and later my grandchildren who also shrieked with joy. "Again, again" until this day.

I had no birth certificate, which has caused me much hassle with bureaucrats ever since. (A baptismal certificate from Holy Trinity Church, Simla, never quite fits the bill.) This problem I share with many immigrants from the sub-continent who are routinely refused entry to the United Kingdom for lack of documentation. What need of papers? – they know the village where they were born; they know they are the children of so and so. Isn't that enough? We children of the Raj knew that we were British even though for generations our forebears had been born anywhere other than the British Isles. It took an Act of Parliament to give us what we had always taken for granted.[1]

My father was, at the time of my birth, a captain in the Bengal Sappers. He was born in Bangalore, as his father, Colonel Sydney Lethbridge, another loyal servant of the Raj, had been before him. The name Lethbridge is a corruption of 'leatherbreeches', itself a translation of the Old Norse *Lodbrog*. The founding father of the family, Ragnar Lodbrog, a Viking who was based at Scara Brae in the Orkneys[2], is reputed to have sacked London, Dublin and Paris. He met his death at York where his enemies persuaded him to take off his leather armour after which they threw him into a pit filled with poisonous snakes. The family are immensely proud of this charming fellow. I named my eldest son after him. My father succeeded a line of Asian-born ancestors going back to the days of the East India Company – 'John

Company' they would have called it – for whom they provided what was in effect a private army. However, had you asked any one of these sub-continental Lethbridges where they came from, firmly they would have replied, "Devon, of course". They would have seen no paradox in the answer: the country churchyards of Devon are replete with Lethbridge graves.

My maternal grandfather, Herbert John Maynard, known as 'Bertie', was the only member of my immediate family to have been born in England. His father, Frederick Waite Maynard, a gentle aesthete, was a founding member of the Medici Society. He married Mary Margaret, daughter of David Gravell who printed and published Hansard, the official record of Parliamentary proceedings. Frederick Waite Maynard died when his wife was only twenty-four and mother of three young children. She became headmistress of Fernbank, a girl's boarding school on Wandsworth Common and all too quickly mutated from tragic young widow to a gruesome old dragon who sought to dominate all those around her. Her grandchildren remembered her without affection. It was her habit, when they displeased her, to fix them with a basilisk stare and address them as 'dog'.

Bertie, a lonely, introverted child, avoided, whenever it was possible, the clutches of his alarming mother and escaped into the ancient world. Athens, Sparta, Marathon were more congenial, more real to him than the suffocating female regime at Fernbank. Attending Merchant Taylor's School as a day boy, he regularly spent his dinner money on books. His mother seemed not to notice how hungry he was or how thin. She took sole credit for his achievement when, at the age of sixteen and proficient in Latin, Greek and Hebrew, he won an open scholarship to St John's College Oxford. There, on Buttery Staircase, he shared quarters with Gilbert Murray and Walter Alison Phillips, both in time to become, respectively, eminent classical scholar and historian. The three men were of a similar cast of mind: agnostic in religion, rational in philosophy, admirers of Edward Gibbon and Sir James Frazer, gentle in their personal relationships, true sons of the Enlightenment. They enjoyed a lifelong friendship, as close when continents separated them as when they shared digs in Oxford.

Bertie had set his heart on an academic life. He had, however, a perverse fondness for taking exams. Having heard that the most difficult in the public sector was the entrance examination for the Indian Civil Service (more challenging, so it was said, than the Foreign Office entrance) he decided to give it a try, just for the hell of it. Of some three hundred and fifty entrants he came out sixth. This he regarded not as a success but as a humiliating failure for which he had to make a grovelling apology to his mother (she of course had expected him to come first). It was as much to escape her recriminations as to satisfy his longing for adventure that he decided to accept a twelve-month posting to India. He promised the old gorgon that he would return at the end of the year and take up a fellowship offered by St John's. In the event he broke his undertaking (the first and last time in his life he did such a dastardly thing) and stayed in India for forty years. An assistant commissioner for an area the size of East Anglia at the age of twenty-two, he combined the duties of travelling magistrate, administrator and arbitrator. Later he became Financial Secretary of the Punjab (a post roughly equivalent to that of Chancellor of the Exchequer) and Vice Chancellor of the University of Lahore.

After five years' service in the subcontinent, Bertie was granted six months furlough. This he decided to spend, not in the confines of Wandsworth Common, but in visiting the classical sites of Europe and North Africa. It was in Egypt that he noticed two American girls, Josephine and Alfreda Eppes, who were making the grand tour. Family legend has it that at the foot of the great pyramid at Giza, Alfreda, the younger of the two, fell off her donkey. Remounting with great elegance and composure she impressed Bertie to such a degree that, there and then, he determined to marry her. Having pursued the girls round the Eastern Mediterranean for two months he finally ran them to ground in Venice where, in the basilica of St Mark, he made his proposal. It was accepted. Bertie and little Freda were married the following year in the drawing room of Appomattox Manor, the family house in Virginia. It was 4 August 1896.

Bertie spoke nine languages, Freda, who had never been to school, spoke one. But the English she spoke was a delight; the closest thing to the language of Shakespeare, so he maintained, that Bertie had ever heard. It could be that, having settled in Virginia while the Bard was still alive, the Eppes family had lived in such isolation that the language they spoke remained uncontaminated by contact with the outside world. In the event this unlikely marriage was blissfully happy. The shy introverted young man, starved of affection as a child, burgeoned in the warmth of Freda's unconditional love. Freda, unselfish, unspoiled as she was, adored her scholarly husband and crossed the world to make a home for him. That first home was the Charing Cross Hotel in Lahore. From there they moved up to Simla (the summer capital of the Raj) in the Himalayan foothills, as soon as the heat of the plains became too much to bear.

1 December 1904. It was here that my mother, Katharine (Nikki), was born. She spent her early childhood at Armadale Cottage with her siblings Elizabeth (Buffy), John Gravell (Dobby) and Josephine (Babs). It must have been an idyllic childhood, centred on cricket, ponies and dogs.

There came however the sad moment when hard decisions had to be made about the future of the family. It did not occur to any of these Anglo-Indian families that the children might be educated on the spot: the only possibility was to split the family, to undertake the long journey home and send the children to English public schools. In the case of the Lethbridges, mother opted to stay with her husband in India while the Lethbridge boys (my father Jack and his younger brother Robert) were sent first to prep school in Norfolk and then to Uppingham. In Robert's case his childhood was particularly miserable: the outbreak of the First World War meant that he could not at any stage rejoin his parents in Bengal but had to spend lonely holidays in an empty boarding school. He did not see his mother or father for four years, which must have left emotional scars. He never married and in later years took in a big way to the bottle. The Maynard children were more fortunate. Freda went home with them and took a house at Bovey Tracey in Devon where the Edwardian idyll of cricket, ponies and dogs continued much as before. While Jack went to prep school and then on to Rugby, the girls were educated by a series of governesses and finally at Sherborne. There the connection with the Raj remained unbroken; the head girl was, at the time, a Sikh named Amrit Kaur.

My father went to war in 1915, straight from school, having been commissioned at Woolwich. I have a booklet compiled by a pious member of the Lethbridge clan, detailing the thirty members of the Lethbridge family in active service that year. My seventeen-year-old father (heartbreakingly grown up in his uniform) has an expression of gentle eagerness which I never saw on his face again. His mother sent him off to war with a big carton of cigarettes for good luck. It is ironic that, having survived two world wars, and various horrors on the North-West Frontier, it was, in the end, the cigarettes that killed him. He was deeply scarred by three years in the trenches at Ypres and on the Somme. Of his year at Uppingham he was the only survivor save for one other man who was shot through the head and lived – but totally blind. Rejoining his regiment in Northern India after compressing a three-year mechanical sciences tripos into two at Jesus College, Cambridge, at the Army's expense, he was too full of anger, too melancholic to throw himself into the polo and shooting parties enjoyed by most of his contemporaries. On leave he preferred solitary excursions into the jungle or the foothills of the Himalayas.

Freda returned to India in 1920 with Buffy and my mother. The plan was that the girls would be presented as debutantes at Viceregal Lodge, do a couple of seasons and then, either to make suitable marriages or to be 'returned empty' to England as social failures. Josephine, who was essentially studious, stayed in England to complete her education, which she did at Somerville College, Oxford where she read PPE.

My mother, although what was expected of her was conventional enough, was never a conformist and had in her a streak of wildness. She and her sister Buffy, older by eleven months only, after a number of escapades where they swapped identities in order to confuse their suitors, were nicknamed 'the Jakko Monkeys' after the hill behind Simla where they rode together and tormented the lovesick subalterns.

When presented at Viceregal Lodge in August 1925 they refused to wear the satin confections by Worth worn by the other debutantes. They turned up as two little Japanese geishas who would not curtsey but who "kow-towed banging their heads on the floor. The aides-de-camp and the other girls' mothers were horrified but the Viceroy was highly delighted and asked them to come back and do it again. Afterwards with one on each arm, he escorted both in to dinner".[3]

It was thought in Simla that my father would, of the two Jakko monkeys, choose Buffy, who was a beauty. It was, however, Nikki, the tomboy, whom he married. After the wedding at Holy Trinity Church my parents put their wedding presents into an auction and set off on their honeymoon, on foot, across the Himalayas towards the forbidden frontier of Tibet. It was to my grandparents' chagrin that the same presents appeared in the auctioneer's window in the Mall under the legend 'The elegant effects of Captain J.S. Lethbridge R.E' for Mrs Hawksbee[4] and le tout Simla to gawp at: "Strange young man. Disgraced? Cashiered? No. Gone to Tibet. And what a peculiar gal."

My grandmother had already had problems with the Simla wives: "She is not one of us" someone said when she first arrived. "An American. Never been to school."

"But what about Lady Curzon?" ventured another. "<u>She</u> was American."

"Ah but Miss Leiter was an heiress." My grandmother, of course, hadn't got a penny.

My mother carried me to the parade ground to hear the band play. When it struck up, so she used to tell me, I shivered with excitement. Military music in the open air; even now I feel the prickles start on the back of my neck when I hear it and my stomach tightens.

Oh be kind to our web-footed friend
For even a duck has a mother
She lives in the swamp

Where it's awfully domp
And so do her sisters and brother

This was the North West Frontier. The town was Quetta, later cradle to the Taliban. My father was there following a course at the Staff College. From the cantonment the desert ran northwards, rising inexorably towards Kabul and on to Russia. This was the location of Kipling's Great Game[5] and, because it was believed that a Russian attack on Afghanistan was imminent, it was from this place that my grandfather and his colleague Michael McClagan were seconded, in 1896, to Moscow to learn the Russian language.

I remember from my pram an austere treeless landscape where the hills are much paler than the sky. It is a landscape which haunts me still. I have seen glimpses of it since but never returned to the original: on Salisbury Plain at midsummer, in the Cyclades, where a bone-white hillside stretches parched under an indigo sky; most nearly on the northern tip of Corfu where one looks across the narrow Ionian Straits to the pale mountains of Albania. I go there sometimes in my dreams then wake, disappointed and resentful; homesick almost.

Shortly after we left Quetta, my father having been posted to the hill station of Chakrarta, the town was shaken by an earthquake. More than 30,000 people died. Among them was a baby called Imogen Wakefield, who was killed when the ceiling of her nursery collapsed into her cot.

Chakrarta in the monsoon. I was ten months old. My mother would push me over rough mountain roads in a big, black pram more suited to Kensington Gardens than to a hill station in the Himalayas. I remember that sudden bump under my back as we hit a particularly large stone or went down a pothole. She must have been soaked in spite of her huge black umbrella, while I lay snug as a bug in a rug under layers of waterproofed gabardine and oilcloth. Sarah Jane, my brown velvet doll, rode beside me in the pram. She used to have black curly hair but after she fell into a mud pie my mother cut it off and made her braids. Her face was flat and worn away by constant kisses. She was my familiar and, a couple of years later, when I had solved the mystery of speech, I used her to negotiate delicate matters such as second helpings: "Sarah Jane would be awfully sad" I would say, "if she couldn't have another tomato". Meanwhile, the clouds rolled sullenly down the mountainside through forests of weeping purple rhododendrons. I am haunted by that colour, the most mournful and evocative in the world. Thirty years later I recognised it in the willow herb and Himalayan balsam which grow along the banks of the river Taw and gathered great armfuls of it to place round my father's coffin in the Devon cottage where he died.

I knew the landscape long before I recognised the people. I was aware of the kindly presence of my parents before I knew their faces. The first time I saw them as distinct human beings was on the day we drove, in a small black jalopy, to the top of an escarpment in the foothills, got out of the car and I ordered them "Let's all shout hooray".

I adored my mother, and the adoration was mutual. I was her second child. My parents' first daughter Charmian died in infancy. She had spina bifida, as the result, so it was thought, of my mother having contracted malaria in early pregnancy. She was advised not to carry another child until the malady left her. Every time she got chilled or over-tired the sickness would return, bringing with it fits of shaking and burning fevers. It was seven years before the sickness finally ran its course and departed. Perhaps it was this long delay that caused the intensity of her emotion towards her second child.

My parents called me Nemone, a slightly complicated decision which has caused me problems all my life, not least at school where I was known as 'Lemonade'. Somewhat pedantically they took the Farsi word *nemone* which may be translated variously as criterion, touchstone or benchmark (I see the work of my Godfather, Sir Aurel Stein, archaeologist and scholar in this). More romantically, they looked to the Greek *anemos* after the windflowers which sprang from the blood of the dying Adonis. My first great love, to whom I shall refer in this memoir as 'The Flying Dutchman' refused to use it, saying that it was a silly name and meant nothing. I was too over-awed by him to argue. He always called me Susan.

My mother and I used to share our dreams, our nightmares even. Living as we did in one another's minds we were both unsure which were hers, which were mine and which we held in common. Both remember a tiger which chased us to a gate which we could neither open nor climb; there were rocks over which we had to struggle, first spiky and rough, second smooth and slimy, both equally frightening; there were evil men with aeroplane wings. Later our dreams divided, becoming unique to each.

To the predatory, the children of Warren Hastings, the concept of Empire meant the ruthless pursuit of a luxurious life and of riches beyond the dreams of avarice. To others it meant striving towards a perfect system perfectly administered, a new Antonine age. An example: Alfred Lethbridge, a cousin of my grandparents' generation, was, at the age of twenty-four, put in charge of a district the size of Wales. A famine broke out. What an opportunity for a dishonest man to make a fortune! He went into that famine with a personal overdraft and came out twelve months later with that overdraft slightly increased. He lived all his life on his pay and died a retired Indian army Colonel in straightened obscurity, in a small Hampshire village.

The Maynards, the Lethbridges, the Tollingtons, the McClagans, the Lorimers, the Wakefields: these were the Antonines, marked by their crystalline voices, their incorruptibility, their love of Northern India. Their children lived in an Edwardian dream of innocence: the ponies, the ayahs, the adorable dogs; the smell of dust and marigolds, and, standing sublime in the distance, the ever-present and eternal snows.

Then it was gone. Many carried, when they left, the irremediable scar of homesickness and loss which would haunt them for the rest of their lives. In some cases, it would even precipitate their deaths.

JIMMY

18th May 1918: It was at the point where the Edgware Road bisects the Holy Mile[6] that Annie O'Connor's waters broke. As the tall policeman circumnavigated Marble Arch on his bicycle officiously blowing his whistle, his helmet reaching a good two feet above the heads of the pedestrians surrounding him, the notice pinned on the back of his uniform announced 'TAKE COVER! HUNS APPROACHING!'

As the great grey Zeppelin slid overhead, the people scattered in every direction, like minnows in a millpond avoiding a pike. Only one person in the crowd noticed Annie's distress. He was a kindly costermonger who helped her up on to the back of his cart, turned his horse's head to the West and clip-clopped off to Queen Charlotte's Hospital. Five minutes later the Zeppelin deposited its bombs somewhere to the northwest near Queen's Park. Sixteen hours later Annie delivered her firstborn son and called him James. He was a furious howling baby, red of face and red of hair. In her pain and confusion Annie muddled the dates and James' birth was recorded on official documents variously as having taken place on 19th, 20th, and 21st May 1918.

It is hardly surprising that Annie had no cards, no flowers, no congratulations, no visitors; no toys or layette for the baby. After a brief respite between Queen Charlotte's clean white calico sheets, she was ready to take her baby home. The lady almoner gave her a bundle of woollen vests, a dozen terry nappies and a few words of advice on the virtues of thrift, temperance and moral rectitude. But Annie's attention was distracted from the homily by the sight of a fine tweed jacket carelessly draped over the chair next to a neighbouring patient's bed. The owner was most probably wetting the head of his latest child in the pub nearby. It was an opportunity too good to miss. "Seems fair enough" Annie thought to herself "poor little devil's got no shawl".

So Annie took her baby home wrapped in the stolen jacket;

home to Kilburn (County Kilburn, as the Irish ghetto was known in those days), home to the slops bucket on the landing, to the bed bugs in the furniture and under the floor boards; to the streaks of dried blood, her blood, on the walls; home to her drunken, tubercular husband recently returned from the Somme. He, having gone to war as a volunteer, was so outraged by what was done and suffered in the name of King and country that he swore that if he ever made it back to Blighty he would never work again.

> *'I don't want to join the Army*
> *I don't want to bleeding go to war.*
> *I'd rather hang around the Piccadilly Underground*
> *Living on the earnings of a high-born lady!'*

James O'Connor was true to his word for the next thirty years. Except at Christmas, when he would sign on as a temporary postman. He would bring home sacks of mail, open the letters, extract postal orders where there were any, and burn the letters on an open fire. As they grew older, the children would help their father in this ritual which, for them, was the high point of Christmas. This was especially so when a good mood took their father and he would deprive the bookmakers of a portion of the proceeds of his crime and he would buy the children sweets.

Young James (Jimmy for the rest of this memoir) had three siblings. There was recalcitrant dark-eyed Maria, born in 1914, who never bonded with the father who was absent during the early years of her childhood. She left home as soon as she was able to do so to escape his terrible rages and even more alarming and inappropriate displays of affection. There was Timothy, born the year after Jimmy, who suffered from tuberculosis. He lived out his short life (dying at the age of thirteen) in a hospital in Pinner run by the Sisters of Charity of St Vincent de Paul.[7] The nuns took him to Lourdes every year praying for the miraculous cure which never took place. Annie said "Timmy was a little saint. He never knew nothing bad. God took him home early because he was too good for this world."

The fourth child was Kathleen, known as Kitty. She died of meningitis at the age of four. Annie regarded her as a genius because she could dance and sing

> *"Horsey horsey don't you stop!*
> *Just let your feet go clippity-clop,*
> *Your tail goes swish,*
> *The wheels go round,*
> *Giddy up! We're homeward bound."*

"She was too clever to live," said Annie "her brain just exploded. It burst. So God took her home. She had big beautiful blue eyes. Not horrible black ones like Maria."

Kitty was buried at Kensal Green in a pauper's grave. The pit remained open until the last of twelve tiny coffins was put in place, raising the grave to the level of the ground surrounding it. It remained unmarked until James, noticing a couple of suitable pieces of timber on a building site in Maida Vale, took them, trimmed them and, with a poker heated in the living room fire, inscribed the resulting artefact with the name KITTY. He was busy banging the cross into the pile of grey-yellow clay which now covered the common grave when a passing bureaucrat caught him in the act.

"Are you an authorised monumental mason?" the fellow asked. "No, I didn't think you was. Are you aware that the by-laws do not permit the erection of any structure made from any material other than granite, marble or obsidian?" He seized the cross and flung in on to a pile of rubbish lying nearby.

"Piss off out of it, you fucking little jobsworth" roared James, swinging a great left hook at the man, breaking his jaw. For this act James appeared before the Marylebone Magistrates' Court the following week where he was sentenced to twenty-eight days hard labour. He felt no resentment, only a quiet sense of satisfaction that justice had been seen to be done.

St Vincent's, Pinner, was as much hospice as hospital. The ward where Timmy spent the last nine years of his life was open to the elements at each end like a cowshed. Children with every kind of disability were accommodated there: short limbs, no limbs, cerebral palsy, microcephalus, macrocephalus. Jimmy used to arrive every Friday evening to spend the weekend with his brother. He would bring with him a load of empty jam jars which he had cadged from the grocery shops along the way up from Kilburn which, having been washed and sterilised, would serve as chamber pots for the children. He would also bring cakes, sweets, chocolates – anything edible he could lay his hands on by sleight of hand or petty larceny. Many of the children had been abandoned by their parents and had no visitors save the young thief from the Irish ghetto. The good sisters never questioned the provenance of the goodies he brought. They believed that he was a saintly little boy like his brother.

When Timmy died his funeral was arranged by the sisters with proper reverence and discretion. The O'Connor family attended on their very best behaviour. James wore a well-cut blue suit and an immaculate silk shirt displaying exactly four inches of dazzling white cuff. Annie was there in a felt cloche hat fixed with a long diamante pin, fox furs and six-inch heels. They looked the epitome of a respectable Irish couple aspiring to the middle class. Jimmy arrived late, wearing a wolf cub's uniform and carrying a great sack of cakes which he had stolen on his way up to Pinner-on-the-Hill.

When the obsequies had been completed, much strong tea drunk and soda bread eaten, the O'Connor family departed, each to live a life the good sisters could scarcely have imagined, even in their worst nightmares. The nuns washed up the cups and plates and agreed between themselves that the afternoon had been a great success and wasn't poor dear sainted Timmy blessed in having such a lovely family to mourn him.

The O'Connor family's allegiance to the Catholic Church was less spiritual than tribal. Baptised at the Church of Our Lady of the Holy Rosary, Homer Row (a turning off the old Marylebone Road) in the first week of his life, Jimmy became part of the ancient Irish tradition whereby, after the birth of a baby, mother stays at home while father does the ecclesiastical business. I have been reliably informed by a retired midwife who knew the culture well that, on occasion, father would so thoroughly wet the baby's head on the way to the church that he would forget the name chosen for it. So an intended Fergus would end up as Finbar, an intended Seamus, Sean. At least on this occasion James remembered his own name and handed it on to his son. This having been done he felt that his duty to the child (and to the Holy Roman Catholic and Apostolic church) had been accomplished. The boy would, of course, go to a Catholic school. The rest would be left to Lady Luck and the University of Adversity. Save for pitching up for the baptisms of Timmy and Kitty (and their funerals) James did not enter a church again until in 1950, he arrived for his own funeral in a cheap wooden box.

Hunger stalked the Irish Diaspora. From the dying days of the 1840s when the potato famine drove the smallholders from their rotting fields to the advent of two world wars which brought employment, briefly, even to the poorest of ghettos, starvation was replaced, at best, by subsistence. Within three generations the handsome, strong peasant farmers of County Cork had shrunk into the urban proletariat, half a head shorter than their great grandfathers, lungs riddled with tuberculosis, limbs twisted by rickets, brains and livers rotted by alcohol.

The only element which gave identity or cohesion to this sad community was its religion. Only the hope of heaven could reconcile these poor women to the loss of their infant children, their numbers decimated by scarlet fever, measles and diphtheria. Only the cluster of handsome churches which arose round the city 'built with the pennies of the poor'[8] could give the community self-respect.

A few of the immigrants made good their escape via the basic education provided by the Catholic schools, unsubsidised by public money until after the Second World War. Moving towards the periphery of the city they did well in the church, the army or construction. For the rest trapped in the shanty towns of Kilburn, Paddington and Rotherhithe, the only escape from the ghetto (as Jimmy was to observe in his years of reflection) was by boxing or by crime.

The O'Connor clan arrived in London in dribs and drabs during the hungry 1840s. They settled in North Wharf Road, a collection of hovels between what would become Paddington Station and the Regent's Canal. Shortly afterwards they were joined by the Ball family with whom they were to intermarry. While the black-haired O'Connors gradually moved north to Kilburn the red-headed Balls stayed put in Paddington until the outbreak of the Second World War. Jimmy remembered his grandmother Ball, an alarming old lady who worked as a female dustman for the Paddington Borough Council, collecting rubbish with her horse and cart. Famously she stood no nonsense from her inebriate husband. It was said that she was twice the man he was. On Sundays, when he stayed longer on licensed premises than she liked, she would burst into the pub with his dinner on a plate, bang it down on the counter and then, with a mighty left hook, knock him clean out. Sadly Annie, her daughter, inherited none of this spirit and became the victim of many more beatings than Granny Ball ever administered to her unfortunate husband.

For the Kilburn O'Connors in the 1920s the cupboard was often bare. What food there was was rarely more than bread and dripping. Boiled bacon and cabbage was a luxury. Jimmy, with his mixture of Celtic charm and Cockney cheek, became adept at cadging from his neighbours. One day a kindly Italian woman, whose husband sold ice cream from a tricycle on Oxford Street, took pity on the hungry urchin and gave him a bowl of minestrone soup. Jimmy was transfixed. That dark briny viscous emulsion, with its tiny pieces of carrot and celery, its miniature submarines of Arborio rice, became for him the platonic ideal of all that food could be. In later years when (occasionally) he ate at the Tour d'Argent or in the Riviera's finest, he found nothing which could match its sublime perfection.

At the age of seven Jimmy decided to change his life. While Annie wept over her sick children and James sought to drown his own personal demons in the pub, he would become a grafter. Money. That was what was needed. He would get it. Money would solve his problems and those of the family, oh yes. He would get it for sure. He would put bread on the table.

So Jimmy went to work. Leaving the house at 3:30 in the morning, he did a milk round for Job's Dairy. Then another for United Dairies. Then a paper round for a newsagent in Kilburn, then going south to Maida Vale, he collected or delivered prescriptions for the local chemist. There seem to have been no restrictions under health and safety legislation forbidding the handling of drugs by children. No doubt the retailers were happy to avail themselves of cheap child labour.

By the time he arrived at school at nine o'clock, Jimmy was exhausted and would spend the rest of the morning dozing in the back of the class. Frequently late, he was often kept back in the afternoon in detention; it was during these late sessions that he acquired a basic literacy.

Monday morning at the Sacred Heart School, bQuex Road, Kilburn:[9] Miss Daley, the form mistress, took the register and checked on the children's attendance at their devotions the day before.

"James O'Connor?"

"Present Miss. Mass, confession, communion, Sunday school and Benediction Miss.'

'Which mass did you go to?"

"Ten thirty Miss."

"You're lying O'Connor. I was at ten thirty and I didn't see you there."

"Sorry Miss. Had to help me mum, Miss." Then, under his breath "Stupid fucking cow. I've got me living to get." There was a snigger from the class.

"Oh what a bleeding shame. You'll do thirty minutes detention after school this afternoon. Come to my office at four thirty."

So it was well after five when Jimmy crossed the Edgware Road to catch the number 9 bus to Piccadilly. As he stepped on to the platform of the old Routemaster a small figure emerged from the stairs of the tenement nearby: "Alright Jim?"

"Alright Bill."

It was Billie the Orphan, a ragged little urchin with the face of an old man. It was said that he lived on the stairwell of the Guinness flats but Jimmy felt that it would be insensitive to ask him too much about his private life. He had once seen him emerging from a back alley with his lip split and bleeding to be followed by a fat policeman with a smirk on his face. Since then Billie had been considered persona non grata in Kilburn and followed his avocation (that of a pickpocket) elsewhere. The two boys sat together on the top deck of the bus, smoking tiny roll-ups in the palms of their hands and talking, respectively, of the glories of Victoria Station (Billie) and Jermyn Street (Jimmy) until finally they emerged from the dark greasy mist of North London and were decanted into the jolly inferno of Piccadilly Circus. There, for a time, they went their separate ways.

Jimmy crossed to the south side of Piccadilly and made his way to Jermyn Street. There he entered the Cavendish Hotel. He had already established a valuable contact there. At the reception desk a tall, elegant old lady was examining the register of guests. Her style was that of a previous decade, her bearing that of a duchess, her voice that of a fish wife: "you little devil! Where've you been? You're bleeding late."

"Sorry Miss Rosa. Had to help me mum."

"Don't break me bleeding heart."

The old fox terrier at her feet danced on his back legs and set up a joyful yapping as the old lady handed Jimmy the lead. Its diamante collar sparkled in the lamp light. "Go on then. Give him a good half hour. He's been driving me bloody mad."

Boy and dog raced into St James's Park in the gathering dusk and circumnavigated the reedy lake before the rain came pelting down.

Peabody Buildings Victoria: a whiff of damp rags and sewage only a stone's throw from Buckingham Palace. The two boys sat on the stone staircase to avoid the driving rain, Kippie the fox terrier, snuggled between Jimmy's knees to keep warm. The evening had been disappointing for both boys. Jimmy's intended shoplifting had been hindered by the presence of the wet dog while Billie had found Victoria Station crawling with British Transport Police and had beaten a strategic retreat. The young pickpocket eyed Kippie's jewelled collar.

"Give us your dog, Jim, just for a week. I'll learn him to be a good ratter."

"Bloody 'ell, Bill, you're joking me. This dog don't eat rats. He takes nothing but minestrone, the finest minestrone soup."

"He don't have to eat the bloody rats Jim, just kill 'em. You get tuppence a tail round the flats for them."

"Leave off, Bill. Me dad give a monkey for this pedigree dog off of the Prince of Wales." "Then borrow him to me, just for the week."

"In your dreams, mate." Then, getting to his feet "rain's stopped. I'm off to work. See yer." Billie looked so disconsolate that for a moment the older boy's heart was softened. "Look mate. I can't give you the bleeding dog. But how about a nice goldfish?"

The old man led his horse through the mean streets of Kilburn. On the back of the cart stood a large glass carboy. "Old clothes for goldfish" he cried, "old clothes for goldfish."

Jimmy looked out of an upper window. "Here mate. Just a tick." Seizing his father's favourite blue serge suit, he raced downstairs and into the street.

"Here we are, then. Give us a couple of nice fat ones."

The old man fished two large goldfish out of the tank on the back of his cart and deposited them in a jam-jar of water. Jimmy handed over the suit.

When James senior came home from the pub and found out what had happened, he went berserk. Jimmy shouted "I just thought I'd teach you a fucking lesson." He didn't wait to hear the reply, so James wreaked his vengeance on the nearest person to him, Annie, innocent as she was. He blacked both her eyes, broke her jaw, kicked her in the ribs and then seizing his long old-fashioned razor, hacked off her beautiful red hair. Without a glance at the damage he had caused, back he went to the pub.

When he was certain that the coast was clear, Jimmy crept back home.

"Don't cry, Mum," he said, "I'll take you up the hospital."

"I can't go there," sobbed Annie "who's going to give him his dinner?" So, as many times before, she washed her face in the sink, put her blood-stained dress into a bucket of cold water to soak and waited at home for the next beating.

Jimmy picked up the shining auburn snake of hair from the floor and put it into an Oxo tin. This he kept under his pillow until, in 1939, he finally left Kilburn and went to war, gladly.

NEMONE

It was time to go. Hitler was on the rampage in Europe and my father was called back to the War Office in London to work on re-armament. I can recall much later his fury and despair at the thought of having to go through it all again; at the fact that our masters appeared to have learned nothing from the catastrophe of the First World War; at the fact that Britain had no armaments – just two war planes and two tanks or something silly like that. Ironically, although the situation was dire, the War Office still allowed him six months to get back from India.

The family set out for home by sea, taking in Australia and New Zealand on the way. "Completing our girdle round the earth, halfway across the Pacific, between New Zealand and Panama, we passed an island called Ducie" my mother wrote. A very small island almost lost in the vast ocean. Gazing at this remote dot from the deck of our ship, Jack, who could see "Further through a millstone than most" said "If I had my way, I would get off here and spend the next ten years on that island." But we went on and the little island disappeared among the waves. To the east of us was a cloud, a Hitler cloud, black, unavoidable, heavy with darkness and sorrow, the colour of war ... Little Ducie dropped over the world's edge and was no more.'[10]

Our ship, the *Rangitikki*, stopped off at Panama. We bought a proper straw hat for Sarah Jane, my brown velvet doll. On our way across the Atlantic we made friends with two little old French ladies, Miss Thevenard and Mrs Wood. Auntie Tikki and Auntie Wood became frequent visitors to my grandparents' house at Gilston Road in London and a part of the extended family. Auntie Tikki could make a dancing doll out of a pocket handkerchief. He could sing too, but in French, of course, and his name was Alphonse.

I cannot remember docking at Tilbury; the train journey so often described with a shudder by my mother; the shabby little back gardens along the tracks; the mud, the rain-swept streets, the gruesome army digs infested by regiments of cockroaches against which the only prophylactic was cucumber peel, cut into strips and distributed at every crevice or dark corner. During the next five years I can recall a few pictures in cameo, nothing more. It is as though the mind, conditioned by the jewelled kaleidoscope of golden India, could not register the sombre tones of England. There was the birth of my brother Peter shortly after we arrived. There was the picture of him aged about eighteen months, I suppose, flaxen haired and chubby, toddling through Kew Gardens. I wondered whether his cheeks rattled. In the same gardens I remember bowling my hoop between the drab flowerless rhododendrons and being told to "stand back" by men in bowler hats. A gigantic old lady, apparently with no feet, glided past as though on ball bearings. "That's her Majesty Queen Mary" they said. Once I heard my mother's sharp intake of breath when a voice on the wireless said "there is now no hope for the men aboard the *Thetis*." Somehow her understanding of the plight of the submariners, slowly suffocating on the ocean bed, conveyed itself to me and I burst into tears.

I have a composite memory of my grandparents' house, 18 Gilston Road, The Boltons, in South Kensington. It was a tall house standing back from the road with a high wall and a green wooden gate. There was a bird bath in the shape of a shell. There was London Pride growing in the flowerbeds but little else. My mother said that the London air was so dirty it killed all the proper flowers. I remember breakfast, which was eaten at a long mahogany table without a cloth. In the middle of this stood a glass bowl – Venetian probably. It had glass water lilies floating on the surface and was the most beautiful thing I had seen in my life. I remember with fascination watching my grandfather eating a soft-boiled egg and waiting for it to drip onto his moustache. He followed the egg with three black biscuits, dog biscuits I was sure. It was explained to me that they were charcoal biscuits which helped his digestion. I didn't believe it. After all, I knew he was a dog lover. I remember a magnificent lavatory with a crystal handle. You approached it up mahogany steps and in the china bowl there were huge blue poppies. I remember walking round the Boltons, a quiet traffic-less street, and watching the sparrows picking over the piles of manure deposited by Harrods's dray horses. I remember wondering how the naked lady in one of the gardens managed without her arms and whether she wasn't awfully cold.

Apart from these flashes I remember nothing between Alphonse dancing on the deck of the *Rangitikki* and, four years later, the outbreak of the Second World War. By this time I was seven years old.

JIMMY

Jimmy's fortunes took a turn for the better when he acquired a change of clothes. As a ragged street urchin he had attracted the attention of every policeman in the West End. Even with Kippie, with his jewelled collar as escort, he was denied access to the lush premises he hoped to plunder. He had little difficulty in persuading Miss Rosa to give him an old page's uniform from the hotel. A distinguished dog like Kippie with his royal connections deserved a well-dressed walker.[11] Now resplendent in green and gold with dazzling white gloves, Kippie with his sparklers alongside him, he could work Piccadilly without let or hindrance. One day he attracted the attention of one Micky Maserati; manager of the Swallow Club in Soho. Maserati took a liking to the cheeky little leprechaun and was impressed by the Jermyn Street connection. He decided to put Jimmy on his payroll.

So every evening, after returning Kippie to the Cavendish Hotel, Jimmy was to report to a certain Italian restaurant in Frith Street where he would collect a silver canister of minestrone soup for Mr Maserati's dinner.

"Can you borrow me a farthing until tomorrow?" Jimmy would ask the chef.

"There you go," the chef replied, "but mind you don't leave the country."

Walking through the narrow rain-swept streets of Soho hugging the warm container to his chest, he managed one swig of the delicious soup, then another, till nearly a third was gone. It was his first meal of the day. With the farthing he had borrowed he was able to purchase enough boiling water from the owner of a pavement coffee stall to top up the container to the brim before delivering it to his new guvnor. Then, changing from his green page's uniform into a blue, he worked the evening shift at the Swallow Club.

It was on one of these evening expeditions that Jimmy noticed a group of smartly-dressed women taking shelter form the rain under the overarching porch of a building nearby. He approached them, still hugging his soup. Then he saw her. 'Ullo, Mother. What are you doing here?"

"That's alright, Jim. I'm just waiting for a friend." One of the women standing by started to giggle.

"Don't give me all that bollocks, Mum. You ain't got no fucking friends."

Neither mother nor son ever mentioned this meeting but inevitably it led to a certain constraint between them. To make a moral judgment was not in Jimmy's nature but more than ever he grasped the necessity of getting money. Money and food he took straight back to Annie, hoping to keep her at home. Items he could not dispose of gainfully himself (such as the jewellery or watches he occasionally swiped from hotel rooms with Kippie providing cover) he gave to his father to fence. This improved James's temper and eased some of the pressure on Annie's fragile shoulders.

Jimmy was thirteen when he left school. Somehow, against the odds, he had acquired basic literacy. He had already a natural aptitude for figures. Moreover, he was filled with restless energy and ambition. The circumstances of his birth, the difficulties of his life, in no way cast him down. He felt no envy towards the rich and fortunate, just an immense desire to associate with them, to be like them. There was in his nature a kind of innocent snobbery. He was thrilled that, among the nuns who cared for Timmy, was the Duke of Norfolk's sister; that the little dog he walked in St James's Park had associations (however remote) with Royalty. Some of the aristocratic patina which surrounded them might, with luck, rub off on him. His circumstances should have made him political – but politics never entered his head.

Kippie died and not so long afterwards Rosa Lewis departed for the great bawdy house in the sky. The West End lost something of its glamour. Jimmy and Billie decided to emigrate to Notting Hill. They felt that there might be richer pickings to be found there than there were in Kilburn; besides, the police presence was less conspicuous there than it was round Piccadilly.

Bypassing the great bourgeois mansions of the Bayswater Road they struck into the varied hinterland of Kensal Rise and Notting Dale, of Portobello Market and Latimer Road. This was an area of small grubby mews where the costermongers kept their ponies and stored their barrows overnight, of rag-and-bone men; of rats and cockroaches; of pawnbrokers' shops almost as decrepit as the clientele they served. In Portobello Road the boys were befriended by the great market families, the Ratchfords and Kanes who had worked the territory for a hundred years. Here they learned market skills, loading carts to capacity; displaying fruit on stalls in the uniquely English way, each piece balanced at a steep angle so that it is shown to its best advantage and each barrow becomes something approaching a work of art, backlit with paraffin lamps and, at Christmas, decorated with long strips of silver lametta.

At close of trading in the evening they bought what flowers remained for a few coppers and sold them on the curb the next day. 'I loved selling beautiful fresh flowers' Jimmy wrote later.[12] 'Wrapping them up, I used to stroke them: gladioli like the neck of a swan.' They learned to dye white carnations different shades of blue and sell them to the punters at the Boat Race; when a Test Match was played at Lords or the Oval, they wired broken rose buds to make buttonholes which they sold at the gates to the spectators. Then of course there was crime, when the opportunity came to commit it. First there were the quasi-criminal activities such as playing the three-card trick or 'Find the Lady' or running errands for street bookmakers. Next the boys, whose dexterity and cheek had not gone unnoticed, were adopted by a gang of 'jump-up merchants' who specialised in stealing from lorries and carts. One of the lads would be instructed to distract the driver or drayman: "your engine is leaking oil, guv." or "your 'orse's bridle's loose" while the adults unloaded as much as they could carry from the back of the vehicle. This went on successfully for a number of weeks. The boys did not resent the fact that their share of the proceeds of crime was miniscule; they felt proud to be associated with proper professional thieves.

However, all bad things have to come to an end: the gang were apprehended at the shabby end of Ladbroke Grove attempting to steal a load of Woodbines destined for a pub nearby, the Hero of Alma. The boys made a rapid getaway into the backstreet while the adults, who were less nimble on their feet, were arrested and remanded to the Inner London Quarter Sessions where they received six months apiece.

The lads would have to go it alone. To Jimmy this was an opportunity to maximise their profits; to Billie it was a source of anxiety.

"We'll go for the big time" said Jimmy, "We'll do a smash and grab."

"But we ain't got no transport" demurred Bill. "Anyways, neither of us can't drive." "Leave off moaning. Right now we do better as a couple of plumber's mates for the wages we get. I've got a plan."

One of the traders in Portobello Market was due to take his annual holiday, picking hops in Kent. The boys offered to look after horse and cart: they'll try the rag-and-bone game they said. A deal was struck. Billie liberated a sack of oats and a bale of hay from a mews nearby. Jimmy did a reconnaissance of the location, deciding finally on a pawnbroker's shop off Westbourne Grove. So, one September evening after the shops had closed, they approached their target at a brisk trot. They halted, jumped off the cart, smashed the window with bricks wrapped in long football socks. Sweeping their pathetic haul of pinchbeck trinkets into an old mail bag, they urged the pony into a reluctant canter. Alas, after ten yards or so poor Dobbin cast a shoe, came to a halt and refused to go further. At the same moment outraged citizens appeared from every direction, followed by the police. The boys fled, spilling their ill-gotten gains into the gutter.

They raced into a cul-de-sac nearby and tried to scale the high wall at the end. Jimmy got over, but someone caught Billie by the legs and pulled him down into the street. He was later sentenced to twelve months in an industrial school, as young offender's institutions were known in those days. Jimmy thought it prudent to make his way back to Kilburn. He realised that he would now be persona non grata in Notting Hill, having blown all the credit he had with the market families.

Furtively he made his way north, sloping through the alleys and narrow back streets which lead to the Harrow Road. Crossing the canal by the iron bridge known as the Halfpenny Steps, he felt a sudden cloud of fear and desolation overcome him. It was more than a sense of guilt over Billie's capture. Billie, who had not wanted to undertake the crazy enterprise in the first place.

He, at least, would have a warm bed to sleep in the coming winter and three meals a day; things he had never had before. It was rather the realisation that 'the race is not to the swift nor the battle to the strong'[13] that there had been too many lies, too much deception, too many thefts. He had been too lucky for too long. He knew in his heart that one day he would suffer for something he had not done. On the distant horizon there waited for him some unimaginable horror.

CHAPTER TWO

JIMMY

It was in the baker's shop in Kilburn High Road that Jimmy met Mary Davey. He had gone there to cadge some stale bread for his mother. Seeing the pretty girl behind the counter with her sparkling blue eyes and shining brown hair arranged in neat Marcel waves, he was embarrassed by his errand.

"I'll have the best cake you've got" he said "Don't never mind the dosh. It's for me Mum." He pointed to an amazing specimen in three shades of pink icing, decorated with white sugar roses. The girl looked at him curiously. He looked very young. Although he was smartly dressed, he was very thin, gaunt almost. She guessed he had little money. The Welsh thrift she had inherited from her ancestors condemned his extravagance while her natural Welsh warmth of heart thought it sweet that he should so love his mother.

As Jimmy painfully counted out the change from his pocket, Mary prayed that he would have enough to make his purchase. When he slapped the penultimate half penny on to the counter he grinned triumphantly. "Don't never like to carry too much on me. There's a lot of thieves about."

"Too true, I don't know what the world's coming to" she answered, putting the cake into a white cardboard box and tying it up with silver ribbon. "There we go, let's hope your Mum likes it."

"She will. She likes everything I bring home." Jimmy's heart was thumping. "Come for a drink love? Tonight? At the Warrington?"

"You're joking me. I don't never go out with men with red hair. They're dangerous."

But go she did. Within a month she was pregnant. Within three, as her respectability demanded, they were married. Neither family attended the ceremony at the Willesden Register-Office. Only a little Jewish chap in a skull cap who Jimmy saw in the street outside and gave three bob to act as their witness.

Their son James William was born on 19 September 1935. Mary was twenty-two; Jimmy exactly sixteen years and four months old.

Poor Mary. The marriage never stood a chance. While Jimmy loved his pretty wife and his sturdy little boy, he had no idea of how to show his affection. To be seen in public with them he regarded as positively effeminate: but, while in the pub, he talked about them incessantly. Of Mary he would say "She's got a face like a film star, legs like a Shetland pony and she idolises me" of little Jim "He's a little cracker. Brave as a lion: strong as an ox."

The older men at the bar found this all very tedious. More boring still were his dark hints about the dozens of beautiful women who were breaking their hearts for him and whom he thoroughly despised. But Billie the orphan felt a desperate envy for what Jimmy had and what he knew he could never obtain.

The Davey family was not impressed by Mary's choice of husband. They were everything the O'Connor's were not: respectable, hardworking, and devoted to one another. Mary's father, a builder, took Jimmy to work with him as a hod carrier. Jimmy, while enjoying the sheer physicality of the job, showing off his considerable strength and joining in the badinage of his work mates, was disgusted by the wages he earned. Two pounds fifteen shillings for a six-day week. He had done better moonlighting as a schoolboy, running errands for the rich families in Maida Vale, delivering the morning milk and newspapers. His discontents mounted; as he was to write in later years, he had nothing but larceny in his heart.

The young couple took rooms in a tenement off Carlton Vale. The address sounded much grander than the reality of the place. The post code was Kilburn, but Jimmy insisted that they lived in

Maida Vale. There was a bed and a cot for little Jim, two chairs and a table where an old copy of the News of the World served as a tablecloth. There was a gas ring in the corner, a butler's sink on the landing, a water closet in the back yard four floors down. The crystal set on the windowsill provided the only entertainment. There was of course, the usual infestation of vermin.

It is hardly surprising that, within a few weeks, Mary was pining for the Welsh warmth of her mother's kitchen where doting grandparents would indulge little Jim and where, as he grew from baby to toddler, he could play with numerous little cousins. As for Jimmy, he regarded his home as a depot – a dump almost – from which to escape at the slightest excuse. All his life he was to feel only truly at home in the pub; only truly at ease in the company of men.

Christmas 1938. It had been arranged for Jimmy, Mary and little Jim to eat Christmas dinner with the Davey family and to stay on overnight. Jimmy resolved to be on his best behaviour. Earlier in the day he had dropped off a couple of crates of beer and a stolen box of toys (still in their Hamley's wrappings) for the children. Then, on the corner of Kilburn High Road he met, purely by chance, Billie the Orphan.

"They're having a lock-in up the Alma" said Billie. "All the Faces will be there. Are you up for it?" If conflict there were in Jimmy's mind, that conflict resolved itself within a matter of seconds. He'd skip Christmas dinner with the Daveys and go to the Alma. He'd find a way to make it up to Mary later.

Dusk was closing in, damply fragrant with the aroma of fog, woodbines, roast potatoes and gravy as the two boys approached the Alma. A great blast of warmth hit them as they pushed open the door of the saloon bar. The party was well underway. As Billie had promised, the Faces were out in force: Tricky Dicky from Kensal Rise, Red-faced Tommy and Puffing Billy Berman from Whitechapel, Wally the bent boxer from Fulham, known as the bookmaker's friend. There was a group of specialist shoplifters known as the Forty Thieves who had dropped in, so they said, "to kill half an hour" on their way home from work in Harrods but who stayed all night. There was

George 'Taters' Chatham, the renowned cat burglar; there was Freddy Foreman from the Elephant. All faces Dickens would have recognised, or Damon Runyon.

Several hours and many pints later, Billie took the stage. He was working his way up to the position he was to hold for the rest of his life, that of Court Jester to the Mob.

> "Any old iron" he sang, "any old iron, any, any, any old iron,
> You look neat – talk about a treat!
> You look dapper from your knapper to your feet.
> Dressed in style, with a brand-new tile
> And your father's old green tie on.
> Oh, I wouldn't give tuppence for your old watch chain,
> Old iron, old iron!" [1]

As Billie embarked on the verse
"I shan't forget when I got married to Selina Brown.
The way the people laughed at me, it made me feel a down.
I began to wonder, when their dials began to crack,
If by mistake I'd got my Sunday trousers on front to back..."
Jimmy slipped out to the lean-to lavatory at the back of the pub. In a corner he saw a pile of green and gold carrier bags; this must be the place where the Forty Thieves stashed their booty. He shook open one of the bags and the beautiful blonde mink coat with its albino satin lining gleamed with a soft pearly opalescent glow. "Have I had a tickle here!" he said to himself. He took off his camel overcoat and put on the mink. It had absorbed something of the ammoniac stench of the latrine where it had been stored but no matter. "Hoisters can't be choosers" he chuckled as he replaced his own coat over the mink, locked the door of the lavatory and then squeezed himself through the narrow window into the yard behind the pub. Skirting the crates of empty beer bottles he made his way, via a maze of back alleys to the Harrow Road, then, via the Half Penny Steps across the canal, into Kilburn, just as the sullen grey dawn was breaking over Boxing Day London.

Mary was asleep in their narrow bed, little Jimmy curled up in his cot. "Here's your Christmas box". Mary sat up in bed.

"You pig! You Bastard! You spoiled my Mum's Christmas dinner."

"Ah, but look what I brought you darling."

"You've been thieving. I don't want no bent gear."

"But just look at it darling. I bet Mrs Simpson ain't got a fucking coat like this."

"Fuck Mrs Simpson and fuck your fuckin-coat." shouted Mary. She grabbed the coat and ran out on to the landing where she stuffed it into the dustbin. As Jimmy raced after her to retrieve the coat she turned and ran back into the room, bolting the door after her. She got into bed and wept bitterly.

Jimmy stood, non-plussed, on the landing. He was too proud to knock and plead to be let in. After a few moments he shrugged and said to himself "Women! Ain't it bloody marvellous! Well, at least I can earn myself a few bob." He took the coat, still smelling faintly of urine and woodbines, out of the dustbin, put it on under his own and made his way towards his parents' flat in Kilburn. Not having the contacts to fence so luxurious an item, he sold the mink to his father for five pounds.

A couple of days later he returned to the room in Carlton Vale. The woman who lived next door saw him arrive. "Sorry Jim," she said "she's done a moony. Hopped it. Gone back to her Mum. Your stuff's in the junk shop round the corner."

Mary had left before but had always come back when asked to. Nicely. This time it was obviously serious. Not a stick of furniture remained. Not a cup. Not a saucer. Not even the kettle. Only, on a dish by a hole in the skirting board, a small piece of cheese left out for the mouse.

NEMONE

From the time we arrived home from India, my father had worked in the War Office in Whitehall. There he struggled with the problem of trying to re-arm the United Kingdom before the inevitable outbreak of war. The Munich accord gave a brief respite, but my father did not doubt for an instant that Hitler would strike within a matter of months, if not weeks.

In the late summer of 1939, believing that London would come under immediate attack he moved the family from Kew to Harrietsham in Kent. He took a small bungalow with a rough paddock and an empty chicken house. As I recall he stayed up in London (it being too far to commute) but visited us from time to time. War was finally declared on 3rd September.

At the beginning of the autumn term Peter and I were sent to school in the village nearby. The school was a tall building called Clock House surrounded by an unkempt shrubbery. Aged six I was already reading fluently and writing moderately well but I never got the hang of sums. At the start of a maths lesson I could feel a shutter of boredom and annoyance come down in my mind. I remain virtually innumerate to this day.

We started on the scriptures. Blood and thunder, ripping yarns; the plagues of Egypt, Sampson and Delilah, Cain and Abel, Judith and Holofernes; the Old Testament was fine by me. I liked singing the Psalm 'I'd rather be a Dorky Bird in the House of the Lord than dwell in the tents of the ungodly.' However, the plight of the Children of Israel, wandering in the desert for forty years, bored and depressed me. Their predicament became, in my mind, inextricably bound up with that of Alice in Wonderland forever searching for a way out of that wretched rabbit hole.

The New Testament, apart from the story of the nativity, seemed less interesting. I did, however, like singing the carol

We three kings of Orient Tar
Bearing gifts we travel afar
Field and fountain
Moor and mountain
Following yonder star. Oh!

And better still

Gladly Wood the cross-eyed bear. – Poor bear with his handicap!

The New Testament also contained some silly ideas. Love my enemies? Why? I <u>hated</u> mine: the Germans with whom we were now at war, the sad girl at the back of the class. In the Old Testament there was plenty of smiting and the chopping off of heads. Smiting was far more my style.

I decided to murder the sad girl at the back of the class. She annoyed me. I saved up one of my sweets (Peter and I were given three sweets per day), a green boiled sweet, as I remember. I picked some white berries from a snowball bush: (I had been warned that they were poisonous and on no account eat them.) I pounded them into a mush and then soaked the sweet in it.

I sought out the poor sad girl and gave her the sweet. "Is this for me?" she asked, astonished. Her little eyes filled with tears. I watched her eat it. I was overcome with terror and remorse. I hugged her and told her that I would be her friend. Thank God she suffered no ill effects. Had she died, or suffered serious harm, I would at the very least have been taken into care and criminalised for life. [2]

Peter and I crossed the Pilgrim's Way and climbed the steep escarpment of the North Downs. We sat down on the summit which stretched away as far as the eye could see, covered with wild flowers in miniature, poppies, harebells, vetches, trembling grasses, all of Lilliputian size. Above us larks ascended and tumbled down again, filling the air with their ecstatic song. We had not come on a nature hunt however; we had come to watch the Battle of Britain.

My mother made no attempt to curb our adventurous spirits, to keep us at home. "When you hear the air raid warning" she would say, "look for a nice dry ditch and lie down in it. Stay there until you hear the All Clear."

High above the larks in the bright blue ether, the sky was engraved with thin white swirls of vapour which moved in ever changing curves as the airborne protagonists circled one another. (Peter and I called this 'treacling' because it reminded us of the patterns made by the syrup which we trickled onto our breakfast porridge.) From the relative safety of our prickly hiding place we discussed the relative merits of Spitfires and

Hurricanes. Peter supported the former I the latter. This was such super fun. Oh! How we were enjoying the war.

The adults however, enjoyed it somewhat less. We knew no fear; they must have been consumed by it. My father moved the family again, this time west to a village called Norton Malreward in Somerset. It was not far from Bristol. The owners, a stockbroker and his wife, seemed so eager to let their house, overeager as it appeared in retrospect. My father was agreeably surprised by the price. Norton Court was a large handsome house in pseudo-Georgian style. It had high-ceilinged rooms, a separate nursery wing, pantries and sculleries lined with slate, and capacious cellars. There were stables in which the local Home Guard, as though ready to fight the Napoleonic Wars, kept their horses. The furniture was hideous and veneered. I remember a dressing table in one of the bedrooms which was shaped, so my mother said, like Mrs Stockbroker's enormous bosom.

To Peter and me the garden seemed enormous. There were lawns and areas of rough grass; potting sheds where we could play hide and seek; a disintegrating greenhouse which no-one ever told us was too dangerous to play in; there were Cedars of Lebanon to climb. Beyond the garden stretched meadows which we were free to run in and, beyond the meadows, woods. We found a hollow tree trunk where we made a den. There we tried to collect and drink dew from acorn cups and ate hawthorn buds which country children call bread and butter. We called the den 'Calfskin' after a Viking ancestor's homestead at Scara Brae in the Orkneys.[3]

One morning, it must have been in December 1940, the month of enormous moons, we were woken at four thirty by the blazing white light of the moon. We decided to get up and have a picnic. Down we went to the pantry where we found a wicker basket fitted with enamel cups and plates. We also found some nice green apples and packed them up. We filled the flask with water from the tap. Off we went, our feet crackling on the frosty grass, to eat our chilly banquet.

Another day, running well ahead of my little brother, I entered the wood alone. Deep in the thicket I came upon a great heap of boulders where a thin stream of water (too small to be dignified with the name waterfall) trickled down the rocks to the rill below. I stood there, silent, looking around me. No birds sang. But I could hear something: a breathing, a strange murmur, a heartbeat almost. I could not tell from whence it came. A dryad perhaps? No, too deep in tone to have been a dryad. A monster? No, it did not have the malevolence of a monster. I stood amongst the waist-high ferns, perplexed; finally in awe. I could not understand what was happening. The experience was so strange and so strong I did not speak to anyone about it: anyway, I would not have known what to tell them. It was only by reading that I learned that the experience was not unique. First, I recognised what had happened when I read in *The Wind in the Willows*, how Ratty and Mole searching for Portly, the lost baby otter, chance upon the demi-god Pan.[4] Later I found the less specific but no less striking encounters with the supernatural in *The Prelude*.[5] Whatever it was that happened that day, it left me with a reverence close to awe for the created world and a loathing for those who desecrate it.

Back with Peter again, in the corner of a meadow only a couple of hundred yards from the house, we found a huge pile of timber, old motor tyres and other flammable materials. "A giant's rubbish dump" we said. We thought no more about it. All too soon the adults found out what it was and why Norton Court had come so cheap.

We enjoyed, in the fifth decade of the twentieth century, more freedom than most children do in the second half of the twenty first. We went where we pleased. No one asked us where we were going or to stay within earshot. "Be back in time for tea" was the only instruction. My mother, who as a child had, with her siblings, run wild on Dartmoor, thought this the only rational way to bring up children. We would learn from our mistakes; become self-reliant. She did not fret over possible dangers; charm would get us through. There was virtually no traffic on the roads; no one had heard the word 'paedophile'. It is possible that, wondering each day whether we would all be alive at the end of year, lesser dangers seemed unimportant.

JIMMY

3 September 1939: the grey exhausted voice of Neville Chamberlain announced the outbreak of war. In the Hero of Alma the old boys huddled round the wireless to catch the latest news. Each felt a stab of pain and fear as he heard the announcement followed by a sigh of relief at the realisation that they all were too old to go to the front.

In the corridors of the War Office, between blasphemous imprecations and mutterings of "We told you so" each staff member tried, in his own mind, to minimize the discrepancy between the armed strength of Germany and our own. My father felt some satisfaction at least in the fact that he had already relocated the family well away from London.

Jimmy felt no dismay, rather a burst of excitement – of exaltation almost – at the realisation that here was his road out of the ghetto, the gateway to a world of infinite possibilities; of heroism; of high romance; a world where he would no longer be numbered among thieves and pickpockets but would rub shoulders with moustachioed fighter pilots or glorious creatures from the Brigade of Guards.

After an abortive attempt to join the RAF (he was told to wait until he received call up papers) Jimmy volunteered for the Army. He travelled to Sutton in Surrey where he took the oath of allegiance and thence to Croydon where he received his documentation and uniform. He also gave the recruiting officer Mary's details: he hoped that the financial stability and the respectability of being a military wife might soften her heart and achieve their reconciliation. Impressed by Jimmy's obvious enthusiasm the recruiting officer gave him two chevrons, making him a corporal on the spot.

Crossing the river at London Bridge, Jimmy took the underground north. Emerging at Kilburn High Road into the pale September sunlight he made his way towards his parents' flat. In his freshly pressed uniform and walking with a slight swagger, he felt sure that all the pretty girls in County Kilburn were looking at him with admiration.

Admiration was not the sentiment expressed by James Senior when he saw his son in uniform. "What the fucking hell d'you think you're playing at?" he roared. "You must be fucking mad."

"I'm off to fight the Nazis," said Jimmy, "it's me duty".

"It's your duty to stay here and look after your fucking mother. I'll cut your fucking arms off. Who's going to put bread on the bleeding table?"

Annie began to cry. "Don't cry Mum" said Jimmy. "I'll make it pay. You know I will. Promise. Everything I nick I'll bring straight home. Like I always do."

"Don't give me all that bollocks" bellowed the patriarch. "You're nothing but a fucking waste of space."

Jimmy didn't wait to continue the argument. Out in the street he wondered whether to go straight to the Alma or whether to make one last attempt to make up with Mary. She at least would be sure to admire his uniform, for once it was Mary who won. As he walked up the road to the Davey's house, rehearsing his speech, the beautiful women he used to boast about in the pub slipped from his mind. Even his rosy-cheeked sweetheart from Wiltshire who had recently borne him a child.

Two weeks later Jimmy was walking the rain-washed cobbled streets of a small seaport town in Normandy. If this army was to march on its stomach, then Le Havre was to be the pantry of the British Expeditionary Force. Nothing here was as Jimmy had imagined it to be. The vehicles rumbling out of the dockyard were not the tanks and armoured personnel carriers of his imagination but were lorries stuffed with cases of tinned food, crates of beer and hundreds and thousands of cartons of cigarettes. In an instant Jimmy's dreams of military glory mutated into a great flush of greed. To hell with patriotism: here was the chance to make a fortune.

Jimmy was not alone in thinking this way. Those who were to service the parasite economy were already pouring into town like wasps buzzing round an open honey pot. There were sleek Brylcreemed gangsters from Paris, fearsome Apaches from

the Anglo-French team made themselves a fortune. Everyone was happy. The horrors which were already occurring in Eastern Europe seemed a distant unreality; the possible advance westwards of the German army a silly fiction. France was tucked safely behind the Maginot Line and all would be well.

As Jimmy sauntered round Le Havre in his neatly tailored uniform and handmade shoes, stopping off occasionally at Madame Samuel's to enjoy a class of red wine and check his accounts, he felt invincible. He took up with one of the Algerian girls and before long had promised to marry her and, when the time was right, to return with her to North Africa. When she pressed him to set a date, he arranged for Father Paddy Byrne to perform a marriage service. He sent toys, discreetly stuffed with paper money, to little Jim. In the eyes of the Davey family he was transformed from ogre to distant benefactor. Even his father, who received some part of the largesse, softened his heart towards him. Annie no longer felt compelled to walk the streets. He would have subbed his sweetheart in Wiltshire if only he could have remembered her address. But he made a mental promise to himself that, when the war was over, he would drive down to Swindon, find her and put things right for her and their daughter whose name he could not remember either but whom he always regarded as Kitty Number Two.

Jimmy was twenty-one. He was bursting with arrogance and physical energy, rolling in money, feeling no sense of guilt or responsibility towards anybody. He had his women and children exactly where he wanted them: fond, but at a distance. As he wrote later 'I would say that those few months in France must have been one of the happiest times of my life; so much so that I refused to come home to England on leave and gave it to a man who had a wife and four kids.'[6]

Down the long perspective of the years, I see him like MacHeath, in his hubris, caught for a moment in an eerie shaft of light before the long dark shadows fall.

'Here I stand like the Turk
With my doxies around;
From all sides their glances my passions confound.

For black, brown and fair my inconstancy burns.
And the different beauties subdue me by turns.'[7]

It was a winter of smoke and mirrors; of playing gangsters, playing soldiers. To Jimmy it seemed possible that it would go on forever. Then, in the spring of 1940, the rumble of distant warfare, monotonous, almost inaudible, increased in a crescendo to a roar like an approaching tsunami. The German Army swept northwest across Europe, obliterating first the Low Countries, then Belgium, then, rolling into Northern France, menaced the Channel ports.

Jimmy's private army melted away like a wraith at sunrise. Suddenly he found himself subject to proper orders from proper officers. He was instructed to load up a convoy consisting of three lorries with supplies and drive East to Rouen, there to meet a contingent of troops who had run out of everything. Easier said than done; every bridge had been sabotaged and the roads were packed with refugees hoping to make their escape via the northern Channel ports from the doomed continent of Europe. Above these terror-stricken hordes roared German fighter planes, constantly strafing them with machine-gun bullets.

In the marketplace at Rouen the shopkeepers refused to serve the starving refugees. They appeared to feel no pity towards these wretched people, twice in a generation driven from their homes and thrown upon the mercy of their inhospitable neighbours. Instead, they cursed "les braves Belges" calling upon ancestral hatred. Jimmy was outraged. With his crew he held the shopkeepers to account at gunpoint, ordering them to supply the civilians. This the shopkeepers did, sullenly, but without argument. When a weeping woman approached him, begging for food for her children and offering her body in return, Jimmy said "I don't want your fucking body, sweetheart. Save it for your husband, boyfriend, whatever. Here, take the lot."

Together Jimmy and his mates tipped the entire contents of the lorries on to the pavement. Then, holding the crowd back until the poor woman had picked up as much as she could carry, left the Belgians to take the rest. "Let's get the hell out of here" he said. Boarding the empty lorries, the motley crew drove southwest at speed, seeking what they imagined would be the safety of the Atlantic ports of Brittany.

During the preceding months Jimmy had accumulated something in excess of twenty thousand pounds. In today's money this would have amounted to a sum approaching half a million. He had designed a briefcase lined with tin which a local blacksmith crafted for him. It incorporated a long thin metal chain which could be fixed to his wrist by means of a single handcuff. Half his fortune Jimmy placed in this container.

Before he set off with his convoy towards Rouen he visited Madame Samuel. She had been working on a body belt for him intricately sewn with internal pockets to hold different currencies and denominations. She was embroidering his initials on it as he entered the cafe. He thanked her for her collaboration. He had already given her, as had been agreed, one quarter of his ill-gotten gains. She asked for another twenty-four hours to perfect the body belt: Jimmy explained that time was of the essence and that he must take the belt right away, whether it was finished or not. They shook hands and said a formal farewell, exactly as if their relationship had been wholly legitimate.

He did not see the Algerian girl (or indeed attempt to do so). So, she got nothing. Jimmy argued to himself that: 1. He didn't want to alert her to his desertion; 2. He'd probably be seeing her in a few days anyway; 3. She was doing very well for herself and probably would do even better when the Germans arrived.

"Bloody Norah!" exclaimed Jimmy "We're going the wrong way." There were three mighty thumps as, in quick succession, the village square was hit by three shells. Two of the lorries in the convoy were blown right off the road and never seen again. At the same time something hit Jimmy on the upper arm. He felt as though he'd been struck by a heavyweight boxer. He felt no pain, just a sense of disorientation as he struggled to control his vehicle and to keep it on the road. Then, all of a sudden, out of the fog of dust and debris, appeared a little figure. Jimmy's heart seemed to miss a beat as he saw it. With its eager innocence of expression he thought it must be Timmy, or his ghost. As the look changed to an expression of canny neediness, he gasped "My God! It's Billie the Orphan." But, when the little fellow ran up to the lorry, he realised that he did not know him after all.

The lad said "I know <u>you</u>. You're Ginger Connors. Take us with you."

"Sorry, mate. I don't know where the fuck I'm going."

"Don't say that, Ginge. We all fink you're extra brainy."

"Who's <u>we</u>, then?" asked Jimmy, half laughing.

"All the 'ard nuts round Notting Hill. We all fink the world of you."

No young man could resist such flattery. "Alright then. Jump up. We'll steer by the stars and see what happens."

Flaming June. The Meteorological Office was to record that month as the most perfect of the century: cloudless skies, flawless sunlit days, nights cooled by temperate breezes from the Channel. The summer afternoon glowed with green and gold as Jimmy struck southwest through the meadows of Normandy. He paused by orchards where the ancient trees were half crippled by the weight of their load of rough green cider apples; skirted fields knee deep with jade-green wheat, circumnavigated medieval villages half hidden behind thick hawthorn hedges.

As he drove, Jimmy gradually became aware of pain throbbing through his chest and shoulder, of feverish heat coursing through his veins. His arm had swollen to twice its normal size. Earlier he had not noticed that he was bleeding; now he felt his shirt was hard, dry and stiff as brown paper. His mind started to wander, sometimes to hallucinate. He was confused as to the identity of the little chap sitting beside him: if it was Billie the Orphan, so shrewd, so streetwise, why did he boast so idiotically about the crimes he had committed? If it was sainted Timmy, how had he turned so bad?

The little fellow chatted without pause, never stopping to draw breath. His name was Artie Tubbs. He lived with his Nan in Golbourne Road. He'd done a stretch in an industrial school.

He did a bit of ducking and diving; a bit of dipping and hoisting. One day he would do some serious villainy. He supported Chelsea and thought that QPR was rubbish.

Up to this point in time, Jimmy had never exercised his considerable intellect in the pursuit of anything other than sex or money. Now, of its own motion, his mind started to explore new and unknown paths. While he acknowledged the ineffable beauty of the created universe, he was experiencing immediately the unspeakable cruelties of the creatures who inhabited it. How could he reconcile the one with the other? Irène Nemirovsky, herself a refugee in Northern France at that time, later to die in Auschwitz, noted the glory of that summer and wondered how such halcyon days could witness Armageddon.[8]

Dusk fell. A chill damp breeze suggested the proximity of the ocean. The sun, setting over the western horizon, left behind in the sky long horizontal stripes of crimson and gold. These gradually faded to grey as the lorry reached the brow of a little hill. Below lay the estuary of the River Loire and the wide, darkened harbour of St Nazaire. Black and huge as leviathan, at the point where the waters of the harbour decanted themselves into the Atlantic, an enormous Cunarder lay at anchor. Around buzzed a swarm of tiny vessels; tugs, dinghies, weekend pleasure boats, all weighted down to the gunwales by a crowd of desperate refugees, all seeking to escape from the doomed continent of Europe.

At this point it seems that Artie took charge. Jimmy, who, by this time, was suffering from a raging fever, had no recollection of this part of the journey. Artie spotted a coracle which was not yet full and, with the assistance of a handful of banknotes from the briefcase, persuaded the owner of the boat to ferry the two of them to the waiting liner. Once aboard, another fistful of money induced a member of the crew to find them a cabin. Half conscious, Jimmy tumbled into the only bunk, while Artie curled up, like a little dog, on the floor beside him.

17th June, 1940: Both were fast asleep, when, in the early hours of the following morning, the *Lancastria* slipped her moorings and slid quietly out into the black obsidian rollers of the Atlantic.

Above his head the cabin door was flapping like a sail. "Bloody hell" said Jimmy, "What's the fucking door doing in the fucking ceiling?" He had been thrown violently out of his bunk and was lying on a flat surface which must have been one of the walls of the cabin. At the same time a rush of black water obscured totally the small round porthole.

"Let's get the hell out of here" he said to Artie. Together they scrambled out of what had become a hatch into the corridor outside.

Up on deck they were met by a scene of pandemonium. Passengers were pouring out of every orifice of the ship which was shuddering and swinging from side to side. Some bright spark was shouting "Left, right! Left, Right" in a vain attempt to get the passengers to steady the ship by running from side to side. Lifeboats fell into the sea the right way up; others fell upside down or capsized. Smoke was blowing from the interior, adding to the impression of hell.

"We'll have to jump for it before she goes down" said Jimmy.

"But I can't never swim" answered Artie, trembling.

'Don't you never worry, son. You'll be fine. Just pretend you're in the Serps. Just do doggie paddle."

They jumped. As he hit the cold water Jimmy felt his septic right arm burst, releasing its poison. He struck out with a steady crawl, away from the ship. He heard a despairing cry of "Ginger" as Artie was caught by the undertow and pulled down beneath the sinking ship. He was never seen again. At the same time a squadron of German fighter planes roared overhead, circling the wreckage and machine gunning the survivors in the water. Patches of oil floating on the surface caught fire, burning many of those who escaped the bullets.

Jimmy swam on. The briefcase floated beside him, still attached to his wrist by its chain. He did not look back. He did not want to think about Artie. Behind him he could hear the sound of singing. At first he thought it must be a radio, then, as the singing became ever more ragged and discordant, he realised that it was the poor souls trapped on board the ship. They were singing:

>"Roll out the barrel
>We'll have a barrel of fun
>Roll out the barrel we'll get the Boche on the run
>Sing boom – te – arrah
>We've got nothing to fear
>Sing boom – te – arrah
>The gang's all here."

    He became very cold and started to vomit. He turned on his back to rest, his head pillowed on a piece of floating debris. The singing ceased and was followed by a profound silence. A rubber dinghy floated by, loaded to the gunwales with survivors.
    "Give us a lift" called Jimmy
    "Sorry mate, we're full up" replied a voice from the darkness, like a grumpy bus conductor. As Jimmy stretched towards the side of the boat the man threatened him with an oar.
    Jimmy slipped back into his chilly cradle. Night fell. The dinghy disappeared. Above, the full moon blazing in the heavens was reflected by the patches of oil still blazing in the sea. Twelve hours passed.
    Day was breaking when Jimmy was picked up by an anti-submarine trawler, HMT *Cambridgeshire*. The brief case had long gone, swept away by a huge wave, strong enough to break the thin chain which had secured it to his wrist. As he was pulled up the side of the vessel his trousers slid over his emaciated loins and disappeared into the depths of the ocean, taking with them Madame Samuel's money belt. Lying on the deck of the *Cambridgeshire*, Jimmy was as naked as the day he was born. And as penniless.
    Survivors of the catastrophe said that the ship had been hit by a number of bombs dropped by JU 88s. Captain Sharp described how a bomb had gone straight down the funnel, although this was disputed by other members of the crew. What is certain is that she went down in twenty-two minutes. Of the 6,500 passengers and crew on board, 4,000 perished

and 2,500 survived. The death toll was greater than those of the *Titanic* and *Lusitania* combined. A government D-notice forbade any mention of the disaster in the press or on the radio.

CHAPTER THREE
JIMMY

In his mind's ear Jimmy could hear the voice of Vera Lynn pleasantly wailing about the White Cliffs of Dover. He lay on the floor of the hold of the Cambridgeshire, his mind in a strange half world between consciousness and delirium. A kindly member of the ship's crew massaged his icy back and shoulders then brought him a mug of fresh water and some cold boiled rice in a tin. Gradually his phenomenal physical strength started to ebb back into his body but with it, returned the heat and throbbing pain from the infected wound in his arm.

Somewhere south of the Lizard the minesweeper made contact with a little merchant man, the *John Holt* of Liverpool. Jimmy and a couple of other survivors from the *Lancastria* were transferred to this ship while the *Cambridgeshire* slipped back into the vast grey expanse of the Atlantic to resume her convoy duties. The *John Holt* made a right turn into the channel and, hugging the coast, made its way east past the austere coastline of Cornwall and the tumbled dark red cliffs of Devon until finally she docked at Plymouth. Jimmy felt the gentle thud as she touched the quay. Head spinning with the fever induced by his sepsis, and naked as he was, he raced up onto the deck and leapt ashore. A delicious, warm, homely smell enticed him, and he pounded down the dockside to a little coffee stall. There he seized a tray of Cornish pasties, ran back to the ship and distributed them among the crew 'there you are chaps' he said 'get stuck in'. A minute later he was seized by two red caps who had observed this audacious robbery. He remembered nothing more until he woke up in hospital in Plymouth.[1]

From Plymouth he was transferred, with other wounded survivors, to an emergency military hospital in Sutton. There he was delighted to discover that one of the patients on his ward was Paddy Byrne. Paddy was suffering from terrible burns and was wrapped from head to foot in bandages. "Paddy, you old scoundrel! You look like a bloody Egyptian mummy." He laughed and took both his hands. Paddy burst into tears. It seemed that he too had lost all his money. In his case, robbed by one of his comrades. "Never mind the money" said Jimmy "at least you've got your bloody life. Get yourself fit and we'll soon be out of here."

"I don't think so" said Paddy, "look at the state of me."

"Leave off" replied Jimmy, "You wasn't never no oil painting anyway. Come on, we'll act mad. You be Lazarus and I'll feed the ducks."

"Do yourself a favour Jim. They'll put you in Broadmoor and you'll never get out."

"Not on your Nellie, Pat. We'll recover miraculous, put a nice little team together just like old times. We'll have some good tickles."

"Leave off, Jim. It's too late for me. I've been through two bloody world wars, done the Foreign Legion and got nothing to show for it. I'll never see money like that again."

Jimmy was astonished to hear himself say "Money? What's fucking money? There's more to life than fucking money".

Paddy refused to be comforted. "No there ain't" he replied, "I'd sooner be dead than live in fucking poverty". He turned his face to the wall.

Two nights later dead he was. There seemed to be no more fight in him. Without a struggle he slipped away; without another word to Jimmy or anyone else on the ward.

*   *   *

Late summer 1940. The heat wave continued. London seemed

strangely silent and derelict. In the parks the grass had been bleached to pale brown, the borders filled with dead flowers and rubbish, the fountains bone dry. When war had been declared, some eleven months previously, there had been a frenzy of activity. Anti-aircraft batteries had been put in place, air raid wardens and Home Guards recruited, air raid shelters opened, barrage balloons floated, gas masks issued to all civilians. Windows had been shrouded with opaque black material and streetlights extinguished. The wrought iron railings surrounding the great mansions of Mayfair and Belgravia had been torn down, sent for scrap and replaced by rickety wooden fences. Many children were evacuated to the country and their schools closed. Yet while war raged on the continent of Europe and in the Atlantic, on the Home Front, as it was known, nothing happened.

As the months passed, things gradually started to return to normal. Happy to risk the bombs which never fell, people deserted the chilly air raid shelters to sleep in their own warm beds. They became less obsessed about carrying gas masks now and switching off lights. Many of the children who had been evacuated to the country came home. [2] Whatever the risk of danger, they preferred the friendly little streets, the companionable tenement blocks of East London to the eerie silence of the empty fields, the unlit country lanes, the unfamiliar food of rural England. [3] The dangers of which they had been warned in September 1939 seemed increasingly unreal.

*   *   *

At the end of August 1940 Jimmy was discharged from hospital. He was given no indication of what was required of him, he was simply told to go home and wait for further orders, so he made his way back to London. Late in June Mary had been informed by the War Office that her husband was missing. She had heard nothing from Jimmy himself since he left Le Havre.

His legs aching after weeks of enforced idleness, Jimmy trudged the shabby streets of Kilburn. There was little to suggest that this was a city at war, only the general atmosphere of dilapidation and neglect and the presence of the great bloated barrage balloons floating above the rooftops suggested abnormality. Jimmy could not see a single face he knew. Where were the swaggering youths, the pretty girls, the grizzled faces? His spirits sank. He felt like a stranger in a strange land.

Finally, Jimmy knocked at the door of the Davey's modest terrace house. There was no answer. Irrationally he felt annoyed. Surely they should have guessed he was coming home and waited in for him. Disgruntled, he turned south and made his way towards Paddington.

"Bloody hell, it's me fucking hero son! What have you got for us then?" Jimmy and his father were surprised by the strength of affection that overcame them where previously there had been little but suspicion and fear. They hugged each other while Annie wept quietly in the corner. Then Jimmy said "Here Dad, fetch us that brown waistcoat I sent yer". James senior fetched the waistcoat and Jimmy started to unpick Madame Samuel's meticulous stiching.

When the money in the lining was revealed the old man shouted "You diamond geezer! Now I know you's my son".

Jimmy told his story. His father nearly cried when he heard what had been lost with the *Lancastria,* but took comfort from the treasures that were excavated from the various presents which Jimmy had sent home from France. They chatted for an hour or so and Annie made tea. Then Jimmy asked "You seen Mary and me boy? They wasn't at home when I called."

"Nah" answered the patriarch. "I never seen them. She's most likely got herself a new fellow by now." A great flood of jealousy and rage swept over Jimmy. Slamming the door behind him he took the road to Kilburn.

When she opened the door and saw her husband, Mary fainted. Not through guilt or fear but because she thought she'd seen a ghost. Soon the family were gossiping happily and dismembering the presents. When Jimmy took a knife to little Jim's teddy bear, the lad roared with grief. But as soon as the contents were laid out and explained to him, he took comfort. "Don't worry son, Teddy's going to get you a lovely Hornby train set".

"When?" demanded the toddler.

"Now" answered Jimmy. "We'll go down the West End. Go to Hamleys. Mary, fetch his coat." As father and son boarded the number 9 bus in Edgware Road heading for Piccadilly Circus Jimmy took his boy's hand in his. He felt that there might be something in this family life after all.

*   *   *

Two weeks later, on September the 7th 1940, the Blitz on London began.

NEMONE

Although the East End took the worst of the bombing, the fact that Buckingham Palace received a direct hit on the 13th September made it clear that even Kensington and environs were vulnerable to attack. My grandparents decided that it would be prudent to leave Gilston Road and move to the greater safety of Somerset. So late in the autumn of 1940 they moved into Norton Court in the village of Norton Malreward, not far from Bristol. No bombs would fall so far from the centre of things, or so they thought.

My grandfather had long retired from India. He had spent much of the 1930s travelling the length and breadth of Russia making use of his fluent Russian and studying the effect of the revolution of 1917. My grandmother went with him, always carrying her little spirit stove and possessing a wealth of appropriate experience derived from many years in camp. She could do more to transform the uncomfortable into the tolerable. She could transform a Siberian railway carriage into a cosy-cat corner. There they remained, crossing and re-crossing that vast bleak continent until 1937 when, furious at my grandfather's condemnation of the regime, Stalin expelled them both. Now my grandfather was writing up his scholarly researches[4] and arrived at Norton with his papers and books. To us children he seemed remote, always working, working, but we adored our American grandmother Freda.

My grandmother Alfreda Horner Eppes was born at Appomatox Manor, near Jameston, Virginia. She was the eighth daughter and ninth child of Richard Eppes and his wife Mary Josephine Horner. The family, which came originally from Romney Marsh in Kent, had been granted a parcel of land in the state of Virginia by King James I and had lived there since the beginning of the 17th Century. The present house, built in 1763, became famous a hundred years later as Union General Ulysses Grant's headquarters during the Civil War. From June 1864 to April 1865 he directed the course of the war from the house. On two occasions the President of the Union, Abraham Lincoln, as Commander-in-Chief of the Federal Army, visited Grant in the drawing room of Appomatox, to discuss the progress of the war. The house is now a national monument open to the public and administered by the National Parks Service.

As slave-owning aristocrats the Eppes family naturally supported the Confederate cause during the Civil War. Ravaged by successive battles as the fortunes of war marched opposing armies back and forth across the rolling, once fertile countryside, the state of Virginia was in physical and economic ruin by the time the war ended in 1865, with farms torched or pillaged and the slaves, the economic capital of the larger farmers, set free.

As large landowners the Eppes family were hard hit and were reduced to the status of subsistence farmers as the state slowly recovered from the depredations of a long and bloody conflict. Sometime in the mid 1870s there were no presents for the children at Christmas. My great, great-grandfather found a litter of piglets on one of the farms on the estate. Each pig was washed and brushed and brought in a basket to the drawing room. Each had a ribbon round its neck and there was one piglet for each child.

There was however a darker side to this idyll. Richard Eppes wrote a definitive account on how to run a slave estate, a book which was recently donated by my second cousin Elise Eppes to the library at Richmond, Virgina, on condition that it was not opened for one hundred years. All my childhood I was told, gently but persistently, how well treated the slaves had been and how Paulina, the cook, loved the family so much that she stayed on after abolition. It could be, of course, that she had nowhere else to go. Paulina, however, was dearly loved by the children and died, still living at Appomatox, during my mother's lifetime.

When Bertie arrived in Virginia to marry Freda, thirty years after the end of the Civil War, financially things had hardly changed. At the end of August 1896 he wrote to his mother: [5] 'Everything bears traces of ruin and decay. The very rails of the local railway line are rusting, there are melancholy remains of numerous wharfs along the riverbank showing what a great emporium of trade the place once was: the roads are neglected and inches deep in sand. Negroes form the majority of the village population. They do not love work and practically no satisfactory labour is available...' [These villagers were, of course, recently emancipated slaves. Each family had been given a smallholding sufficient for its needs: one can hardly blame them for not wanting to go back to work as labourers where once they had suffered as slaves.] "On one of the Eppes' three estates, which consists of more than 1,000 acres, only 40 are under cultivation. They really would have nothing to live on but for their property in a scrip which comes from mother's side of the family. The farming barely returns the outlay upon it; and the fisheries, once a considerable source of revenue, have ceased to be productive. I admire the way in which notwithstanding all these disheartening circumstances Richard Eppes works on the two farms across the river, and all practically for no return at present."

No degree of hardship, however, could shake the family's belief in its innate superiority, in its pride in its ancestry, its withering contempt for new money, money made in trade.

4th August 1896. My grandparents married at noon in the drawing room of Appomatox Manor. The family was in mourning after the death of Dr Eppes, Freda's father, so the ceremony was simple and brief. The mantelpiece had been arranged as an altar and it was all over in several minutes. Freda wore a pale gold dress made of pineapple fabric with which I used to play as a child, and which was kept in our dressing-up box at home. After the wedding, lunch was eaten and the young couple left by boat, at about three in the afternoon, to enjoy the briefest of honeymoons. By the end of November, they were settled in India where they would remain for forty years.

* * *

1940, Norton Court, Norton Malreward, Somerset. It was Christmas. Preparations had begun some weeks before. The cake and the mincemeat for the pies had been made already and the plum pudding with its cargo of silver trinkets and sixpences already tied in its cloth for ritual boiling. The evening before, the jelly, made from an Appomatox recipe, which remains secret among the surviving members of the family to this day, was made and put to set in the ice cold pantry under a linen cloth. At the same time Peter and I settled ourselves by our grandmother's chair to hear her read the Christmas book before we left to hang up our stockings.

"Twas the night before Christmas
And all through the house,
Not a creature was stirring,
Not even a mouse..."

No one went to church, no one mentioned whose birthday it was. The family, steeped in the writings of Sir James Fraser and Gilbert Murray, were firmly agnostic and regarded all organised religion with courteous hostility. Feasting for its own sake was the order of the day.

The aunts began work at nine o'clock in the morning preparing the Brussels sprouts and peeling the muddy potatoes and parsnips. (We had been joined by Buffy, still unmarried and still a grey-eyed beauty, and by the youngest sister Josephine.) On Christmas morning, my mother was, by agreement, excused heavy duties as she was expecting another baby. She probably chopped the herbs; that certainly was her invariable duty when staying in other people's houses for the rest of her life. Expert she was too. Her party piece was to sharpen a knife to a razor edge using the stone kitchen doorstep.

The turkey, with its stuffing of bacon, sage, parsley and chestnuts went into the oven at eleven o'clock precisely. This was still a land of plenty, certainly for country dwellers. Shortages were months away and ration books still further. The turkey, butter and cream came from a farm nearby, the vegetables from the kitchen garden, the eggs from the hens in the paddock. The only thing missing was the wine – but that was hardly of concern to us children. We had our jug of homemade lemonade which we regarded as a special treat.

Josephine was set to work making the brandy butter. She had a large earthenware crock and a wooden spoon, beating, beating, until she had achieved that divine emulsion of unsalted butter, icing sugar and brandy, soft, light and ethereal as a cloud. Meanwhile Buffy was blanching almonds in preparation for the game of snap-dragon to come. She poured a kettle of boiling water over the nuts in a bowl, then, when the water had cooled, slipped the pale ivory-coloured almonds out of their rough brown skins with her long elegant fingers.

The family sat down to dinner sometime in the early afternoon. Grown-up meals are inevitably boring for children, so after half an hour or so, Peter and I were allowed to get down and play with our presents. This was much more interesting than sitting still watching the adults feeding their faces. We were called back later to see the lights go out and the pudding carried in from the kitchen with its blue halo of flaming brandy. We were not expected to eat it; the flavour was too dark for our childish palates. We were, however, allowed to dig for the trinkets. Buffy got the ring which meant she would be the next one to marry; Peter got the money bag and I had a nice silver sixpence. Our pudding was a helping of Appomatox jelly and ice cream which we ate from our little bowls.

Dinner ended with a game of snap-dragon, a game which originated not from Appomatox, like so much of our Christmas tradition, but from the Officers' Mess at Roorkee in the Punjab. A large silver tray was brought to the table piled high with raisins and the almonds which Buffy had so carefully blanched that morning. Brandy was poured on the pile and the whole thing ignited. The game consisted of snatching the almonds and raisins from the flames and consuming them. I cannot remember who won the game or whether there was a prize, but it certainly seemed hilarious.

When dinner was finished there were games: sardines and hide-and-seek for the energetic; charades for the well organised; consequences for the sedentary. Even my father smiled. No one mentioned the War: it was as remote as Agincourt.

*   *   *

It was pitch dark. I had been woken by a moaning, a low wailing sound. It was the air-raid siren warning of an impending attack. For a moment I lay in bed relishing the feeling, not of fear but excited anticipation. I whispered "Peter! We'd better get up." Before Peter had time to answer, the walls of the room turned from black to dazzling orange and gold as though the sun had tumbled out of the sky and was rolling round the garden below. But it was not the sun. It was the giant's rubbish dump which Peter and I had found in the meadow. It was the Bristol decoy, set alight deliberately to give the impression, from the air, of a burning city and so divert the bombers from Bristol nearby.
[6] As we scrambled down the narrow steps which led to the cellar below, the first bombs fell. The whole edifice shook, sturdy as it was. Even underground I heard a roaring, a bellowing, and a reverberation. It must have been the Minotaur, so I thought.

The cellar, with its barrel vaults, was bitterly cold. It smelled of damp and earth, the smell of the grave. Even so, some clever grown up had already done her best to humanise it: hurricane lamps hung from hooks in the ceiling diffusing their soft yellow glow. There were pillows and blankets in abundance, books for the children to read, even plates of bread and cheese. The three generations gathered and made themselves at home. During a lull in the bombing, Buffy popped upstairs and made everyone tea.

There was clatter on the staircase. A crowd of big boots appeared. It was the Home Guard, complete with their rifles (carefully uncocked), and come to join us in our homemade air-raid shelter. They had unlocked the stables and untethered the horses so that if the worst came to the worst, they could make a gallop for it. Buffy sparkled at the men and made them all tea. We played I spy and consequences, we ate the bread and cheese and my mother read us 'Peter Rabbit' until the sounding of the all clear.

The following night and many nights thereafter the same was repeated. One night however, my grandmother, having decided to forgo the chill of the cellar for the comfort of her bed, left it for a moment to answer a call of nature. When she returned the bed was covered in lath and plaster; the ceiling having come crashing down in fragments. Moments later she appeared in the cellar cool as a cucumber in her embroidered silk kimono. "I've changed my mind" she said – nothing else, "I've come to join you". No one realised what had happened until the next morning: Peter and I, running with our string carrier bags to collect the metallic fragments scattered over the lawn, saw a great hole in the roof. (On a subsequent occasion we picked up an unexploded incendiary bomb and carried it proudly home to put in the toy cupboard where my horrified mother found it after a couple of days and put it into a bucket of sand.)

21st March 1941. One night we were told, to our disgust, that we had to spend the night at school "Because Robert Katharine is coming"(in those days it was not possible to determine the sex of an unborn baby). My father had come down from London specially to welcome this person, whoever it was. Coming home from school the following afternoon, we found my mother in bed with a basketwork cradle beside her. In it we found the blitz baby, Katharine Charmian; crumpled face, clenched fists, but nice enough to eat.

Later that week Peter and I developed measles. Buffy came down from London to cope with the crisis, bringing with her

Jane Seymour, an itinerant midwife. Four feet ten tall, child size in build, black-eyed with a brown Asian complexion; we adored her the moment we set eyes upon her. Was it because she was so small that she could not threaten us, or was it that she was never judgmental? Maybe. One thing is certain however, she was one of those childless women who have complete empathy with the children of others, like Aunty Tikki, like Dickens' Louisa Bounderby.[7] We named her 'Nursey Girl'. She immediately took control of the household and, in years to come, she would appear like Mary Poppins and cope with every family crisis. She became the embedded family trouble shooter and lived out her last years in a caravan on my mother's land in Devon, where she died. Oddly enough she chose to look after the measles children despite her vocation while Buffy took over care of mother and baby. Peter and I were banished to the nursery wing, separated from the rest of the household by a sheet, wrung out in Jeyes fluid, which hung over the communicating door. Nursey Girl rigged up a pulley at the bedroom window so we received our meals in a basket hauled up and down as by the monks of Meteora.

The first three days of our banishment were spent in the dark. It was believed at the time that daylight would damage our eyes and we were not allowed to read. It was a wonderful excuse for Nursey Girl to tell us the most blood curdling-ghost stories, which she did in a constant stream. When the curtains were finally drawn back, we ran riot. The bedroom became an ocean and the beds pirate ships. We had to jump between them and everyone who touched the floor was drowned. We were supposed to be ill but never felt better. After a few more days we started to climb out of the window, shin down the drainpipe and go for impromptu picnics at Calfskin, now almost invisible among the bluebells and pink campion of mid-April.

The fiery decoy had failed to achieve its purpose. The Blitzkrieg had moved away from Norton Malreward and concentrated on Bristol itself. I remember driving with my mother through the city centre and up Whiteladies Road after one of these attacks. In the middle of the vast, rough, grey desert, which had once housed a thriving community, stood a solitary house. It had been sliced in half, precisely, neatly, as if with a cheese wire. The interior was unscathed. One could see the sofas, the comfortable chairs, the bedrooms with the beds neatly turned down, the bathroom with a roll-top bath standing on its clawed iron feet, the kitchen with its wooden plate racks and iron range. It was just like my dolls house when I opened it, I thought.

*   *   *

For a moment I must retrace my steps to the beginning of January 1941. Peter and I had to go to school. We were sent to the Sacred Heart Convent at Chew Magna. I surmise that there was no secular establishment within a reasonable distance. My parents could not have otherwise swallowed their principles and sent us to a Catholic school. My mother had adopted her own father's philosophy in every particular. He was of that Oxford school of classicists, who regarded ancient Athens as the apogee of civilisation and, like Gibbon, equated religion with barbarism. My father's beliefs were less structured; he was less militant in his agnosticism (if that is not a contradiction in terms). Nevertheless, his mother had been a strong influence on him. She had the high principles and intellectual rigidity of the Irish Protestant. She had died before I was born, but I knew her face from the photograph in its silver frame which stood on my mother's dressing table. I had a clear picture of her in my mind's eye: Susannah Slater, from County Offaly, with her long curly auburn hair, dwelling in the perpetual Celtic twilight of the Wood of O, one of the townlands of Ballyconnell. She would have turned in her grave had she known that we were being handed over to those ignorant, corrupting and idolatrous nuns.

The convent, as I remember, lay in a valley surrounded by black water which could have been a lake or a slow flowing river. There was a little bridge made of trellis work like the one on willow-patterned plates. There were rustling groves of impenetrable bamboo. My mother told me to take no notice of what the nuns told me because it was all superstition. I must have taken her at her word as I remember nothing of the education I received there. Nevertheless, I found the place immensely seductive.

The day I saw the chapel for the first I was overwhelmed by its intoxicating glamour: the red votive candles, the golden tabernacle with its mysterious curtain; the Host exposed in a monstrance of metallic filigree; the strange sour smell of burning charcoal, the musky aroma of incense. There were statues. Jesus pointing to His glowing heart, St Theresa of Lisieux with an armful of roses, Mary Queen of Heaven with her crown of stars. I collected my pocket money and bought a postcard of the Child Jesus standing in a field of golden corn. I propped it up by my bed among the china ducks and animals. My mother said "What is this hideous thing?" and took it down. I said nothing. It was already too late. I had resolved, at the age of eight, that one day I would become a Catholic.

The infant Jesus was already part of my pantheon of familiars, joining Sarah Jane in her Panama hat, the stately Kings of Orien Tar, the Dorky Bird and Gladly Wood, the cross-eyed bear, gently ambling his way through the starry cosmos of childhood.

CHAPTER FOUR
JIMMY

Jimmy's flirtation with domesticity was short-lived. While his affection for Mary and Little Jim was warm and genuine enough, it could not supersede his craving for stronger meat. Using the proceeds of his French adventure he purchased two tipper trucks and, in partnership with an old school friend, he contracted to collect rubble from devastated buildings in London and drive it down to Wiltshire. On land near Swindon it was used as hardcore in the construction of a new military airfield.

This contract provided a decent living and a measure of stability for the family. Mary was happy and Jimmy was redeemed in the eyes of her parents. However, without a great wad of bank notes to wave around – to humiliate the men standing around and to entice the girls – Jimmy felt positively naked. In his Greek island years he learned to call this wad the *Kavaja*. It was inevitable that he should return to crime.

Using the disagreeable commute between London and Swindon as an excuse with which to pacify Mary, he took a couple of rooms in Swindon. Here, after a legitimate day's work, he could wash, shave and change into decent clothes before setting out on a criminal reconnaissance and survey in the neighbourhood. It looked promising. He rented a lock-up garage in which to store the goods he hoped to steal. He had intended to contact his country girlfriend and their daughter, his other family who he often mentioned – as did young Jim who longed to have a half-sister, but I doubt that he ever did. Certainly, when I asked him about it, he would become evasive. If indeed they did make contact, certainly nothing came of it.

Jimmy was selective in the crimes he committed. He would not do a domestic burglary but regarded commercial premises as fair game. He recognised a hierarchy among the criminal fraternity. At the summit were the expert technicians such as Jock the Fitter, the friend with whom he grafted. "He was an ex-borstal boy and carpenter. He could open a safe like a can of sardines. He used to pop the rivets off the back like nobody's business." [1] On the middle rungs of the ladder were the robbers and jump-up merchants like the ones with whom he and Billie the Orphan used to work as lads in Notting Hill. At the bottom were petty thieves and shoplifters. Sex offenders were totally beyond the pale.

Throughout the winter of 1941 Jimmy and Jock the Fitter worked their way systematically round the mid-West Country appropriating other people's property. Together they were responsible for a minor crime wave, facilitated by the blackout and the lack of police on the beat. They stole in Bristol, Gloucester, Cirencester and Taunton, stashing the proceeds of their larceny in the Swindon lock-up. Every now and then they would pop back to London. Jimmy would visit Mary and Little Jim and catch up with the faces in the Alma.

On 11 March they found themselves in Bath, twelve miles south-east of Bristol, which was, at the time, enduring nightly air raids. Parking their car near the railway station and carrying torches specially dimmed for use by air raid wardens, they set off to explore the darkened streets and see what they could steal.

Every window was darkened, every streetlight extinguished. A quarter moon, intermittently obscured by scudding clouds, cast a faint pearly light on the grand Georgian facades of the city. To the northwest an orange glow in the sky indicated the presence of fires still smouldering after the nightly bombing raid on Bristol. (Or perhaps it was, in part, caused by the lighting of the Norton Malreward decoy, still burning in the field behind the house where Peter and I cuddled together in the cellar while our mother read us 'Peter Rabbit' by the light of a paraffin lamp.)

Finding the city centre, the Abbey precincts and the glossy shops in Milsom Street too conspicuous, too well-secured, to risk tampering with, they turned back to the more modest streets near the river. There, in a side turning, they came upon a small jeweller's shop, Messrs Leslie and Company. The shop front was protected by a wooden shutter made of slats which was itself secured by a mortice lock and two padlocks. It took less than two minutes to deal with these, using a jemmy and a pair of bolt cutters. The display area inside had obviously been cleared of its most valuable items: all remained on the black velvet shelves was a tray of rings and few old-fashioned fob watches.

"Hardly worth the bother of nicking" said Jimmy as he swept the items, including a gold watch and chain, into the pocket of his great coat. They pulled down the shutter and were just replacing the padlocks with insurance locks of their own when they heard steps approaching. A faint yellow beam of light moved across the shop front.

"Good evening, guv" said the policeman, "working late, are we?"

"Too true" answered Jimmy, "no peace for the wicked."

"Take care, then. Mind how you go." And the constable was on his way.

Having had so lucky an escape, Jimmy and Jock decided not to push their luck further in Bath but to return to Swindon-. There, the same night, they robbed a wholesale tobacconist in Commercial Road of its contents. This they sold the following day to a local J.P., a fine fellow who considered himself a pillar of society. Jimmy and Jock decided to take a break and caught the Cheltenham Flyer back to London.

Happy as he was to see Mary and Little Jim, Jimmy felt that his first priority was to dispose of the treasures he had stolen. Larger items had been left at the lock-up in Swindon; smaller ones he kept on his person. By this time he had accumulated quite a substantial horde of jewellery and felt that this was the moment to sell it on. The obvious recipient was a man called Izzy Farrer, a professional jeweller, club owner and notorious receiver of stolen goods. He owned a basement club and spieler* in

Oxford Street which had become a meeting place for members of the underworld.

When Jimmy and Jock arrived at the club they found, to their disappointment, that the guv'nor wasn't there. "Nor won't be for a two stretch" said the club's manager, a man named George Sewell, himself a small-time receiver and fence. "Poor old Izzy's in the shovel. Never mind. I'll help you out."[2] Sewell was eager to do business with them but Jimmy was reluctant to engage. He doubted that Sewell had enough substance to enter into so large a deal. So he sold him the watch and chain from Bath for a trifling sum while holding back the greater part of the horde. This, to Sewell's fury, they said they would sell elsewhere.

"Sorry, mate" said Jimmy "you ain't got the powder and shot."

The two villains left him fuming with frustrated greed and wounded pride and made their way back to North London.

It was a moonless night. As Jimmy and Jock navigated the darkened streets of Kilburn it was possible to distinguish between buildings, pavement and sky only by the relative depth of their blackness, deep slate grey for the sky, dense pitch black for the houses. Bombs had fallen earlier and air was still thick with dust, irritating the nostrils and tasting thick on the tongue. On the corner of Hampton Road the dim beams of their blackout torches caught horizontal white stripes bisecting the darkness. They could hear the murmur of men's voices. Now they could distinguish the white police tapes which cordoned off the turning.

"Nitto! It's the Old Bill." Warned Jimmy "We'd best beat it."

Beat it they did. Before long they had found their man and concluded their business in the Alma. Jimmy had his *Kavaja*.

Meanwhile, back in Swindon, disaster struck. Jimmy and Jock had failed to pay the rent of the lock-up. The landlord broke in and found two stolen motor cars and other contraband. He called the police. Both men were arrested and charged with larceny and receiving. They appeared at Winchester before the Hampshire Assizes. Jock, who pleaded not guilty and fought but lost the case, was sentenced to eighteen months imprisonment. Jimmy, who did a deal – a plea bargain we would call it today – received nine.[3]

He had instructed Counsel to make a plea in mitigation of sentence on his behalf. However, when the fresh-faced young barrister came to visit him in the cells before the case was called on, he was filled with dismay.

"I don't want no fucking chinless wonder with an Oxford accent speaking for me" he said to Jock, who was awaiting sentence at the same time. "I'd sooner do it myself."

"Go for it, Jim" said Jock. "Break their bleeding hearts."

Up in the Court the judge, Mr Justice Charles, sat below the great circular replica of King Arthur's round table, a tiny, incongruous figure in a mythical setting.

"Permission to speak, my Lord?"

"I don't see why not."

"My Lord" said Jimmy "in my opinion this nice young man" (indicating his counsel) "this nice young man ought to be overseas fighting for his King and Country, not wasting his time here on a lowlife like me. May I have your permission, my Lord, to dismiss him and speak for myself?"

The judge, not known for his humour or compassion, permitted himself a tiny smile. "Since you put it so eloquently" he said "you have persuaded me. Mr Falconer, you hear what your client says. You are free to go and serve your Country."

"On yer bike mate" muttered Jimmy, sotto voce.

The poor young man blushed scarlet, gathered up his papers, bowed to the judge and shuffled out of Court.

"Well, O'Connor, what have you got to say?"

"My Lord. I was in the British Expeditionary Force but I wasn't no hero. The only thing I can say in my favour is that I did volunteer to go overseas. I was on a ship that was bombed. I have a wife. I have a son. I think that crime is a mug's game. You know it's a mug's game, Sir.

There is only one thing I ask you. I don't want to delapidate in gaol but I know I'm going to. Would you make it as light as you can, Sir?"

The judge laughed, smiled and nodded his head. He duly

passed a sentence of nine months.

"Thank you, my Lord. Very fair if I may say so." While he was speaking Jimmy suddenly realised that what he was saying was true. He remembered the stupid fiasco of the Swindon lock-up. A mug's game indeed. It was almost a Damascene moment. He realised that there must be a better, a more intelligent way of making a living. Unfortunately, it was to be many years before he could put this discovery to the test.

Friday 18 April 1941. *The Kilburn Times* reported the proceedings of a coroner's inquest into the death of George Alfred Ambridge, age 62, a coal merchant of 2 Hampton Road, Kilburn. It appeared that he had been the victim of a burglary and had died of head injuries. Verdict: "Murder – by Persons Unknown."

From the Assize Court Jimmy was taken up the hill to Winchester prison. There, to his chagrin, he was put under the care of Dr Christie, the prison psychiatrist. This news, on the grapevine, was round the prison in a flash.

"I didn't know that you was a nutter, Jim" said Jock as they met in the exercise yard. "I never seen you feed the ducks."

Dr Christie questioned him every day, not about his health but about the death of George Ambridge. Jimmy was outraged.

"I ain't no fucking murderer" he shouted "I admit I'm a thief but I ain't never killed nobody."

"You're plainly a man of violence" replied the doctor. "Only last week you made a brutal and unprovoked attack on your own friend."

"He shouldn't have taken the mickey. Some things ain't funny."

"Did you take pleasure in killing George Ambridge? Or did you just hit him too hard?"

"Bloody hell. I'm telling ya. I didn't never kill him. Never met the man. Never seen him."

Dr Christie persisted. "You're a Kilburn man?"

"Of course. I'm a Kilburn man. Lived in Kilburn all me life."

"You know most people in the area?"

"I know the faces. What are you getting at?"

"You have local knowledge?"

"Of course I got fucking local knowledge. D'you think I'm

stupid or something?"

"Far from it" replied Dr Christie, "you know who's got money in the area?"

"Dunno what you're on about."

"You know who's worth robbing, don't you?"

"Now you're talking stupid."

"From your connections, from your local knowledge, you believed that George Ambridge was a wealthy man..."

"Nah"

"...an old miser who had a horde of money and valuables hidden in his house."

"Nah"

"That's why you killed him."

"I never killed nobody."

The interrogation went on for days, then weeks, then months. Finally Jimmy lost his cool. "I don't know what you're trying to do" he shouted "Are you a fucking doctor or a fucking policeman?"

Dr Christie knew that he was going nowhere.

"I'm trying to do you a favour laddie. I'm trying to save your life. You've got a stark choice in front of you: it's either Broadmoor or the hangman. There isn't a third way."

"Well I ain't mad and I ain't killed the man."

"Look laddie, I like you. I'm trying to save your life. At least think it over."

"Thank you for your concern Dr Christie, but I ain't going to confess to something I never done. No way."

Dr Christie gave up the struggle. On the "grounds of overcrowding at Winchester gaol" Jimmy was transferred to Cardiff. Then, after a few weeks, he was moved again, this time to Wandsworth. It was January 1942.

Meanwhile back in Kilburn, the investigation into the death of George Ambridge had been taken over by Detective Inspector Nat Thorpe. Following usual police practice Thorpe pulled in all the known law breakers he could find in the area. He arrested and interviewed a number of men whose evidence, because of their background or way of life, was likely to be compromised. Henry Waterton, a man with criminal convictions, was treated as a suspect. He accused Les Allen, himself a professional thief. George Sewell, treated as a suspect, who relied on police good will towards the spieler, the illegal gambling club in Oxford Street, accused a man named Frederick Andrews, himself of bad character. Sewell subsequently accused Jimmy himself. These men were all called as witnesses for the prosecution.

Thorpe visited Jimmy twice in Wandsworth and interviewed him. Jimmy would have been within his rights to refuse to see him; but so confident was he in the truth of what he was saying that he willingly agreed to see the officer. Thorpe however had no more success than Dr Christie in obtaining a confession. He left, frustrated, and Jimmy thought that that was the end of the matter.

It was the morning of 14 January 1942. Jimmy was due for release. Mary had come down to Wandsworth to meet him. He walked across to reception to change into his civilian clothes. He was thinking that he'd go for a drink at the Alma and see a few Faces, then move over to Covent Garden and finally over the water to the Elephant to catch up with what was going on in South London. He combed his hair, looked in the mirror and realised that he was missing his diamond tie pin and cufflinks.

"Where's me bloody gear?" he asked the Officer in charge of releases that morning. The officer replied with a smirk "You won't be needing it. I have to inform you that Scotland Yard is at the gate to see you."

So it was. Thorpe was outside with an escort. As Jimmy stepped through the wicket gate he snapped the handcuffs on his wrists.

"I am arresting you for the murder of George Ambridge" he said. No caution, no formalities. Mary, who was waiting nearby, saw what was happening and burst into tears. As Jimmy put it elegantly in his memoir, she "was screaming and hooting."[4]

Jimmy was taken to Willesden Police Court and remanded to Brixton Prison. He felt no fear, only a sense of indignation that his life had been rudely interrupted. He was sure that this was all a horrible mistake, confident that he would be vindicated. Nothing seemed quite real: everything took on a strange, uneasy dream-like quality, exacerbated by the presence of his fellow prisoners, a motley crew of oddities, misfits, rag tag and bobtail.

Each man seemed to have his own value system, his own moral compass; most were terrific snobs. "There is a snobbery amongst murderers" Jimmy wrote.[5] The man who had killed his wife despised the child murderer who had killed the 'Babes in the Wood.' The Man who killed the 'Babes in the Wood' despised the cockney who killed an old man. The man who killed the old man despised the man charged with killing five prostitutes. Trevor Evans, who was awaiting trial for murdering his landlady, despised everybody. He was a professional conman. He claimed that he had once posed as an Admiral and inspected the fleet. Now he was conning himself.

"They'll never hang me, Jim" he said "Not at my age. I'm sixty-five". But hang him they did.

The greatest snob of them all was a man named Gordon Cummings, a young supercilious fellow who said that he was an officer in the Air Force, a gallant fighter pilot. He also claimed that his father had been a housemaster at Eton. He had murdered five prostitutes and dismembered their bodies. He was absolutely convinced that he was of a different breed to his victims and to "the poor illiterate bastards" as he called them, who were remanded with him. He was far too grand to be hanged. But hanged he was.

One little guy never spoke to anyone during the whole ten weeks he was remanded with Jimmy, He spent his whole time reading westerns. It was said that the warders had to snatch a book from his hand when they dragged him to the scaffold.[6]

"One right nutter had killed three people because they had refused him membership of the Chiswick Tennis Club." Jimmy wrote[7] "I used to get him at it. I said 'Now look here, they're keeping you in this prison for nothing. You've done nothing wrong. You go and tell the Governor you've got to meet Winston Churchill. You've got a special assignment. You're going to the

Middle East. Your real name is Colonel Vadistock. Give him the code number M.I.21. Tell him to have a car here at four o'clock and you're taking me with you. I've come into this prison especially to select people for the Secret Service. I have chosen you and am promoting you to Colonel.'"

Every day this fellow drove the Governor to distraction. In the end he sent for Jimmy and said "Turn it up, Connor."

"Turn what up, Governor?"

"Don't keep sending that character along to see me. He's driving me mad."

"You've got to have a laugh" answered Jimmy "do something to pass the time away."

The day of the man's trial arrived. To no-one's surprise he was back in Brixton by early afternoon.

"I've had a right result" he said emptying his personal possessions from his locker."Yeah – I'm going home. They said I wasn't fit to plead."

"Brilliant" said Jimmy. "I'm really happy for you."

Of course the poor man was on his way to Broadmoor where, forty years later, he died.

Every day Jimmy used to walk round the exercise yard with these characters. He tried to choose someone different to talk to each day. Some achieved a kind of immortality in his plays, most notably 'Her Majesty's Pleasure' which producer Tony Garnett described as "the Marat-Sade with jokes".[8]

There came a time when the joking had to stop. One a bleak March morning in 1942, Jimmy was driven from Brixton Prison to stand his trial at the Old Bailey.

Does it exist, the spirit of place? Where gigantic emotions – whether of terror, misery or disgust – have been unleashed, do those emotions disappear once those who felt them are gone, have slipped into the ether, have disappeared? Do they evaporate, like steam from a boiling kettle? When time has passed, when the writhing victims of torture have been replaced by jolly busloads of tourists, does the Tower of London, in its essence, revert to a pleasant watermeadow by the Thames, the Colosseum to a friendly Italian marketplace?

The Old Bailey is built on the site of Newgate Gaol, on ground soaked with centuries of blood and tears. Where today motor bikes are parked on a traffic island in the middle of the street outside the Court, public executions took place while the local populace hung out of every tenement window to cheer Jack Ketch as he carried out his obscene trade.

Victorian reformers, Edwardian architects and planners have tried to expunge the noisome stench of Newgate, to exorcise its shrieking ghosts. The new building, in its pleasant neo-Baroque style has a dome surmounted by a statue representing Justice, not so much threatening as friendly and fair, despite the sword and scales she carries. Inside, the principal courts are lined with pleasant light oak and soft-green leather. The great hall is decorated with friezes in the Art Nouveau style and reasonable platitudes. The court administration is efficient, courteous and affable. Security is provided by gentle giants from the City of London Police. It is all a thousand miles away from the corrupt regime of John Gay's Peachum.

The judges, largely drawn from blue-chip prosecuting chambers in the Temple, are immensely proud of their court. They frequently refer to it as if it had a personality of its own: "Juries in <u>this building</u> understand … Juries in <u>this building</u> will not tolerate…" they will often say.

There is a close association with the City of London, within whose boundaries the building stands. In Court number 1 the central chair (almost a throne) on the bench is reserved for the Lord Mayor. The judge sits to one side. VIP seats are reserved for distinguished guests and foreign visitors. For many years the black night-club singer Hutch was a daily presence there.

On the first morning of each session the judges parade from court to court carrying, rather self-consciously, posies of flowers supplied by an expensive City florist. This ritual harks back to the days when they carried bunches of medicinal herbs, such as rosemary and rue, prophylactic against gaol fever, endemic in the dungeons of Newgate. They are accompanied by officials of the City of London, some carrying swords, all wearing ceremonial dress. An irreverent visitor once remarked in my hearing "Do the Valkyries often ride in this place?".

Sleet rattled on the metal roof of the prison van as it made its way north from Brixton towards the Old Bailey. Handcuffed to the wall, Jimmy sat in the back, trying to think his way through the situation in which he found himself.

It was a little disturbing perhaps that, of his fellow prisoners on remand in Brixton, only one had returned there after his trial. and he was the poor fellow who went to Broadmoor. The rest, despite their boasting, their noisy protestations of innocence, simply disappeared. Sunk without a trace. Never spoken of. Never mentioned. <u>His</u> case was completely different. There was no evidence against him. He had nothing to worry about. No worries at all. Nothing to worry about. No worries at all. Hadn't his solicitor, Morrie Marks from Whitechapel who had visited him in Brixton, told him so? Morrie came highly recommended by the Faces "one of our own" they said. He'd told him that he'd walk out of it. No jury would believe that bunch of low lives, most of them suspects themselves in the case, that Thorpe had dug up. They probably wouldn't turn up to give evidence anyway. No one likes to be called a grass. And he'd instructed the best defence advocate in the country, a King's Counsel and a member of Parliament. "An old and dear friend of mine." Nothing to worry about. No worries at all. "This time next week you'll be back in the arms of your very lovely wife."

The van turned into Newgate Street and drew up outside the high wooden gates of the prison yard. This was it. Jimmy stepped out of the van straight into a deep puddle. The rain came down in sheets. Then down the rattling iron steps to the cells, not so very different from the dungeons below old Newgate.

The Court was to sit at half past ten. At a quarter to, Morrie Marks, his Homburg hat balanced at a jaunty forty-five-degree angle on his head, bounced into the cell where Jimmy was waiting.

"Let me present your barrister" he boomed. "Mr Hector Hughes, KC, MP very eminent Leading Counsel. Best in the country. Nothing but the best for Morrie's clients. Eh Hector?"[9]

Jimmy shook hands with the eminent personage. He smelled

faintly of last night's whisky. "What d'you think of my case sir?" he asked.

"What do I think about your case? I'll tell you exactly what I think about your case. It's a disgrace. An absolute disgrace. It should never have been brought. I shall tell the Attorney General so next time I see him. I know him. We go back a long way. We belong to the same club".

"But what about the evidence" asked Jimmy. "What about the watch and chain? We've got to deal with that, haven't we? Mr Marks was getting a statement from the jeweller in Bath, weren't you Morrie?"

"Not necessary" bellowed the solicitor. "Prosecution has to prove its case. *You* don't have to prove anything."

"Quite so" said the eminent barrister. "We can't touch the business in Bath. If the jury hears that you're a burglar they'll eat you alive. I advise you – in the strongest terms, though of course it's a matter for you – not to give evidence."

"Shtum and Krum" said Morrie tapping his nose. "Shtum and Krum"

"If that's what you say –"

"That's exactly what I say. If you were my own son, I'd say the same."

"But how about me war record? How are they going to know that I volunteered?"

"Don't worry about that, dear boy. This case isn't anything to do with the war. Besides, the judge knows already. It'll be in his papers. Whatever happens, it'll be in your favour."

"Well, if you say so…"

"I do say so. Most emphatically I say so. Now just give me your autograph if you'd be so kind."

"What's all that about then?"

"It's just to confirm that you've had the benefit of your Counsels' advice" explained the solicitor, "it's standard practice."

So Jimmy signed Counsel's brief and that, said John, was that.

In the Central Criminal Court, Court Number One, The King against James O'Connor and Buller Redhead, before Mr Justice Croom-Johnson and a jury. The judge, a slightly malevolent presence, was already seated on the bench when the jury filed in. There were more than the twelve required to try the case, to allow for possible challenges or objections. None were made.

The jurors all seemed much of a muchness: white, elderly, slightly resentful. A couple of women were on the panel, but neither was called upon to serve. The jury was hardly representative of Jimmy's peers, as Magna Carta demands, but the panel was, of necessity, limited by the fact that so many of his contemporaries were absent on war service.

A second man stood in the dock with Jimmy, Buller Redhead. They had been at school together and had remained in contact in later life. I know nothing of the case against Redhead because he was acquitted (he did not give evidence) and I have seen no papers. Jimmy always maintained that Redhead was innocent – as he was. It is probable that initially he was charged because of his friendship with Jimmy, however slight that friendship may have been. He does not feature again in this memoir.

Detective Inspector Thorpe sat in the well of the Court, nervously biting his nails. He seemed like an impresario who had brought his play to the West End but feared that neither the public nor critics would like it. Morrie Marks had been correct in one of his observations: many of the scoundrels Thorpe had interviewed failed to turn up to give evidence. Peer pressure and the fear of breaching the unwritten code of conduct adhered to among the criminal fraternity proving stronger than any of Thorpe's threats or inducements. He hated the thought of losing the case: he feared the condemnation of the judge, the scorn of his superiors, scorn for a copper who couldn't get his own witnesses to court.

The witnesses who did give evidence were anodyne. Sir Bernard Spilsbury, the pathologist, said that the victim had died of head injuries and had eaten a meal of fish and chips a couple of hours before his death. Nellie Metcalfe, one of Jimmy's girlfriends, said that she had dyed his hair from red to black sometime during the winter of 1942. Neither could establish a link between Jimmy and the murdered man.

It was George Sewell who did the damage. Deferential, moderate, polite, he was the perfect prosecution witness. Thorpe was able to breathe again. Sewell could anticipate every question asked in cross-examination and answer it with a kind of sorrowful diffidence.

"Yes, I have to admit I'm no angel. I've been a bit light-fingered in the past. Yes, I do run an unlawful gaming club. No, I couldn't operate without a bit of help from you know who. But I never do no harm to no one. The one thing I can't never tolerate and that is violence."

He was asked about the watch and chain.

"Yes, I remember a gold fob watch and chain. It was quite unusual. I brought it off of Ginger Connors. That's the name I know him under. He's the gentleman sitting there. I sold it on. No, I didn't never ask him where it came from. In my world it ain't done to ask. No, he didn't never mention nothing about Bath. But he did say maybe it came from Kilburn, from the poor old fellow what died. He was boasting like. With a nod and a wink. But –"(this with an ingratiating smirk, first at Thorpe and then at the dock) "he never meant to kill the geezer. He don't like violence no more than I do. Maybe he just hit him too hard. Shame, really."

The rest of the trial was a fiasco. It lasted for a day and a half. Hector Hughes huffed and puffed about the burden of proof, but his heart did not seem to be in his closing speech. The judge's summing up was sarcastic and dismissive. The jury retired and were out for less than two hours. Sewell's evidence had been fatal. They came back and found Redhead not guilty; Jimmy guilty of murder.

"Let the defendant Redhead be discharged" ordered the judge. Buller, looking totally confused, spun round in the dock, glanced at Jimmy then stumbled out of the Court and out of our story.

The clerk of the Court rose to his feet.

"Prisoner at the bar" he said "You have been found guilty of murder. Have you anything to say before sentence is passed upon you according to law?"

"Yes I have" Jimmy said. He then addressed the judge directly. "I have not had a fair trial my Lord. You have been vindictive to me throughout this trial. The jury have only found me guilty because you told them to. I am not afraid to die but I do not want to die for a murder I didn't commit."

The judge did not reply. His clerk put the black cap on his head.

"James O'Connor." he intoned "You have been found guilty of murder. You will be taken from here to a place of execution where you will be hanged by the neck until you are dead. And may God have mercy on your soul."

"Cor fuck me, ain't it nice" replied Jimmy. Then to the attending prison officers. "He looks just like Will Hay, don't he?" He took a cigarette from his pocket and put it between his lips. Before he could light it the screws grabbed him and pushed him down the stairs into the dungeons below.

morning of his death.

As soon as he arrived in the condemned cell Jimmy was told to change into prison clothes. He was to be hanged in the suit he had worn for his trial. Two sets of prison clothing were laid out on the bed. There were two jackets made of grey cloth without buttons, two pairs of baggy trousers fastened with pieces of tape. There were two shirts, collars attached, white with black stripes, again without buttons. There were two pairs of black socks and a pair of carpet slippers. Everything was designed with the intention of frustrating any attempt to commit suicide. One set of clothes was labelled 'O'Connor', the other 'Redhead'. It had not occurred to anyone that Jimmy's co-accused might be acquitted.

Jimmy refused to change into the prison clothes. Neither would he sit down but spent the afternoon pacing the tiny cell while the warders watched and wondered how to deal with this recalcitrant fellow who seemed unwilling to die. At seven o'clock he was given supper, his first meal of the day, eight ounces of bread, half an ounce of butter and a pint of cocoa in a thick china mug.

"You've heard about the luxuries the condemned man gets" he wrote later "well, that's all cobblers".[1]

At ten o'clock the night shift came on duty. In charge was an officer named Fred Parsons, described by Jimmy as "a good screw". He was a sensible and humane man who hated condemned-cell duty and who avoided confrontation at all costs.

"Be a good fellow and get changed for the night" he said "you don't want to sleep in your clothes and ruin this good suit. I'll organise you a pint of beer."

This he did, and it marked the beginning of a kind of friendship between the two men. Jimmy sat on his bed and drank the beer. It must have been near closing time in the pub in Caledonian Road opposite the prison. He could hear the jingle of the pub piano and the customers singing Vera Lynn's hit song:

> "We'll meet again,
> Don't know where, don't know when,
> We'll meet again

Some sunny day."

Jimmy prayed. "Oh God, let it be true."

He asked Fred how long it would take him to die, whether it would hurt. The good screw tried to comfort him "don't think about things like that. You're a long way from being dead yet, Jim" he said. "Remember you've got your appeal coming up-. You'll probably be out of here before I am. Why don't we have a nice game of chess?"

Jimmy did not sleep that night but paced the tiny cell like an animal caged in the zoo. Fred sat half reading the *Daily Herald* and smoking his pipe until the air was as thick as a London smog. At six o'clock another screw brought in breakfast: a pint of porridge, six ounces of dry bread and a pint of tea.

That morning the cell was never empty. There was a stream of official visitors, the prison governor, the doctor, the Protestant chaplain to whom Jimmy, according to the traditions of his tribe, gave short shrift, and finally the Catholic priest Father – later to become Canon – Williams.

At midday he was told that his father had arrived to see him. Family visits were arranged in a cell like a box, prisoner and visitor separated by a sheet of glass. Three screws were present, two on the prisoner's side, one with the visitor. Every word was overheard and, if thought to be significant, noted down. No physical contact was allowed between prisoner and visitor.

James senior was suffering from the terminal stage of tuberculosis. His breathing was laboured, he was thin as a rake and white as a ghost. The two men looked at each other; neither spoke. Each felt an immense pity for the other as the shadow of death hung over both. Had it been permitted, they would have hugged each other. It was not permitted.

Suddenly another warder appeared. "Meeting's terminated" he said, "Chief medical officer wants to see you."

"Stay right there, Dad" Jimmy said, "I'll be back in a tick."

Dr Murdock had the reputation of being a hard man. He swore by the water-only diet as the cure for all ills. "Connor" he said.

"O'Connor" Jimmy replied "Leave the handle on."

"Connor – if you behave yourself, I'll get you cheese, jam, milk, a pint of beer a day and ten cigarettes."

"I <u>am</u> behaving myself. I don't want no favours, I want justice. Just give me what I'm entitled to, nothing more, nothing less. Now my father's waiting for me. He's more important than the fucking jam. You can stick it up your arse."

James senior was still in the visiting booth. They both tapped the glass panel between them, gave each other the V for Victory sign and went their separate ways.

The prison governor, Albert Ball, was bound by Home Office regulations to visit a condemned man every day. He came across to Pentonville from Wormwood Scrubs, which was still fully operational. He resented the extra duty imposed upon him. The visits cannot have been easy; Jimmy was rude, recalcitrant and ribbed him unmercifully. Mr Ball would arrive at the condemned cell looking miserable, his little gas mask slung over his shoulder.

"Afraid to die, guv?" I'm not."

The governor tried to be pleasant. "Is there anything I can do for you?" he asked.

"What d'you fucking think? Tell Mr Pierrepoint to get a rubber rope. I've got a very sensitive neck."

"Is there anything you want?"

"Yeah, a fuck."

Of course, there was no carrot with which he could bribe or stick with which he could punish his impossible charge and there was no way in which he could avoid the visits.

Annie and Mary came every afternoon. They would sit together in the visiting booth crying quietly and making stilted conversation about family illnesses and domestic matters. Jimmy sometimes wished that they would stay away. On one occasion several of Mary's relations came with them. There was no waiting room for visitors, so they had to wait in the corridor outside the visiting box while Annie and Mary made their visit.

They made little attempt to keep their voices down as they chatted amongst themselves. Quite clearly Jimmy heard one say. "No – the insurance don't never pay out when someone gets hung."

Jimmy leapt from his seat and shouted "Do me a favour. Take me back to me Peter. I'd rather die. I don't want no more fucking visits."[2] The warders grabbed him and took him back to the condemned cell. He had not said goodbye to Mary or Annie and left them weeping bitterly.

That night he and Fred Parsons played chess until they were too tired to move the pieces.

A couple of days later Jimmy received a letter. With a jolt he recognised the small neat handwriting. It belonged to Miss Daley from Quex Road Catholic School. She asked whether she could visit him. Jimmy felt a surge of embarrassment. He really did not want her to come. For years he had entertained the pleasant fantasy of pulling up at the school gates in a beautiful limousine and taking Miss Daley for a drink at the Ritz where he would flash his bulging wallet and boast about his success in life.

However, without waiting for an invitation, visit she did. Miss Daley had not changed: the years had been kind to her, she looked the same as she had a decade before when she had given the young street urchin many hours of detention, a pretty woman with the composure of a nun. "I'm so sorry to see you here, James" she said.

Jimmy was thrown. He reverted to childhood mode. "I'm sorry, Miss. Honest I never done it."

"I believe you. You were never a bad boy. Just a bit wild. You've got your appeal coming up. I'm sure you'll win it and be back home with your family. You've done nothing wrong."

"Oh, but I have miss. I've been a terrible villain. I deserved to be punished."

"Nobody deserves *this*" said Miss Daley, real fury in her voice.

To his great embarrassment Jimmy noticed that she was beginning to cry. "All the children are praying for you. We mention your name at every mass. Here, take this. Put it in your pocket". She handed him a picture of the Sacred Heart, the size of a cigarette card. On the back she had written "Dear God, thou seest all, though knowest all, thou canst all. I place all my faith in Thee". She was almost choking as she got up and said "Sorry James. I've got to go. Got detentions to supervise. God bless." In an instant she was gone. She did not return although she wrote again. Jimmy put the picture in his pocket, where it remained.[2]

Jimmy rarely mentioned religion, he regarded it as something essentially private, it was bad form to talk about it just as it was effeminate to demonstrate affection to those close to him. Accordingly, I was astonished when I read in his memoirs "The only thing which kept me going in the condemned cell was my upbringing as a Catholic child".[3] The closest he ever came to writing about his beliefs was in his play 'Three Clear Sundays' when the priest explains to Danny, the hero, that Jesus was condemned after an unjust trial which was part of a corrupt system.

Shortly after Miss Daley's visit Jimmy asked Father Williams to hear his confession. A little boastfully perhaps, he said afterwards, that it took at least two hours as he had done so much villainy. However, he was sincerely contrite and received absolution. As Jimmy had not been confirmed Father Williams then arranged for Bishop Matthew to come into the prison and confirm him.[4]

It must have been a surreal scene: the acolyte carrying the gilded cross, the Bishop in his flowing vestments and mitre followed by Father Williams, the 'dead man walking' between two prison warders as they processed through the derelict building to the chapel, which stood open to the elements, without windows, without roof, the floor covered with huge puddles of rainwater and broken glass.

After the service a celebratory cup of tea was drunk; the Bishop shook Jimmy's hand and wished him good luck with his appeal. Jimmy could not believe that it might be turned down. God would not allow it.

For a time, he was filled with a feeling of ineffable peace and serenity. Nothing could harm him now. All would be well. All manner of things would be well. Then the slamming of an iron door, the rattle of keys, brought the rage rushing back.

Jimmy had been in the condemned cell for forty days. His appeal was listed for 4th May 1942 before Lord Justice Caldecott,

Mr Justice Humphreys and Mr Justice Cassels. There was a cursory review of the trial: Mr Justice Humphreys expressed anxiety about some of the prosecution evidence – notably that of George Sewell – but after forty minutes Lord Justice Caldecott brought matters to a conclusion, saying that the conviction was well founded and dismissed the appeal. For the first time Jimmy felt a sense of complete despair. He refused to receive any visitors, including his family.

According to prison regulations Jimmy was entitled to one hour's exercise in the open air. Escorted by two screws he would walk in the small yard behind the main building; on the days when rain fell heavily, they would walk up and down one of the bomb-damaged corridors on the ground floor. On one such occasion he heard a regular thumping sound outside.

"Let's see what's going on" he said and pulled his two escorts (to whom he was handcuffed) to the broken window to look outside. Two men were digging a seven-foot trench in one of the flowerless borders.

"Sorry mate, you wasn't supposed to see that" said one of the screws, pulling him away from the window.

"Bloody hell" said Jimmy. "That's me fucking grave. Ain't it nice! You couldn't bloody well wait until I was fucking dead". A great tide of fury swept over him. "Well I'm not fucking dead yet."

That night he asked Fred Parsons to give him a pen and paper. He wrote a letter to the Home Secretary, Mr Chuter Ede, beginning with the words "I am writing for my life." He went on to explain that the evidence of George Sewell (when he told the Court that Jimmy had brought a watch and chain to his house and had implied that it came from the murdered man) was false. He said that the items had, in fact, come from the jewellers shop in Bath which he and Jock the Fitter had burgled during the winter of 1941. Jock was, at the time, still serving the sentence of eighteen months he had been given at Winchester Assizes. Jimmy found out later that he had been visited in prison by DI Thorpe as a result of the letter to the Home Secretary. He was questioned about the burglary in Bath but had refused to confirm or deny that he had taken part in it. Perhaps he was afraid that Thorpe would try to implicate him in the murder. Shortly after his release from gaol Jock was killed in a car crash while being chased by the police.

Days passed. Jimmy had no reply to his letter. One morning the prison governor arrived for his usual visit looking particularly miserable. He seemed to be trying to say something but had difficulty in finding the words. Jimmy almost felt sorry for him.

"Alright, guv" he said "I can guess what you are going to say. The execution has been fixed for 20th May, my birthday, that's a fucking nice birthday present."

Mr Ball nodded miserably. Before he left, he handed Jimmy a letter. It was from the War Office recalling him to his regiment. "I have to give you this" he said.

"Am I supposed to bloody laugh or cry?" asked Jimmy.

"Maybe it's a good omen" said the Governor with a tiny smile.

Three extra screws were added to the death watch. It was feared that Jimmy would cause trouble. Prison folklore was filled with horror stories about executions which had gone wrong. Recently Pierrepoint, the hangman, had been seen leaving the scene of his labours with a black eye. Not everybody went obediently to his death and Jimmy was exactly the type who would kick up a fuss. So it was thought. Jimmy took an instant dislike to these three warders. They were young men who somehow had managed to avoid service in the armed forces. They spent their time talking between themselves about their expenses and allowances and the pensions they would receive on retirement. Jimmy thought of the men who had gone down with the *Lancastria*, of little Artie and of Paddy Byrne.

One morning a man in a well-cut tweed suit wearing a Homburg hat came to the cell. He had an air of authority about him and sent all the screws away. He sat down on the bed. He smelt strongly of whiskey.

"Who the fucking hell are you?" asked Jimmy "you're half-pissed, aren't you."

"Sorry about the smell" said the visitor "but I couldn't come to this place without having a couple of large whiskies. My name is Alexander Patterson.[5] I'm the prison commissioner."

Perhaps it was the manifestation of human weakness, but Jimmy found something immediately sympathetic about his visitor. He told him the story of George Sewell and the watch and chain. Sir Alexander listened attentively.

"D'you think I've got any chance?" Jimmy asked.

"Look laddie. I can't guarantee anything, but I'll do what I can. In the meantime, is there anything I can do for you?"

"Yes sir. Get rid of these miserable bastard screws. All they do is moan about their increments and allowances. Send me a couple of youngsters, ex-service men. Not a couple of war-dodgers like this lot."

"Good as done. Good luck laddie and God bless you."

The miserable warders were duly replaced by three ex-army men who did their best to keep Jimmy's spirits up and who kept their own problems to themselves.

It was 18th May, two days to go. Jimmy did not want to see anyone - least of all Annie or Mary. He did however ask to see his father as he knew that he was dying. He had more or less given up all hope. He felt physically cold, as though the grave was already closing in on him. He sat on the floor, his back against the radiator, ironically right next to the hidden door to the execution shed.

Suddenly the outer door was pushed open and the head of the deputy prison governor poked into the cell. Jimmy thought that his father must have arrived.

"Come right in guv. Don't just stand there"

"Well, it's come, my boy" said the deputy.

"What's come?" He unrolled a parchment. "A respite. His Majesty has graciously granted you a respite."

"A respite? What the fucking hell does that mean? Penal servitude for life?"

"I suppose so."

"What d'you mean, you suppose so? It don't say nothing…"

At that moment James senior arrived, Fred Parsons was on

duty. There were tears in his eyes when he waived the rules and allowed the two men to embrace.

Within an hour Jimmy had left Pentonville and was on his way to Wandsworth gaol and to the beginning of a life sentence.[6]

*Appomattox Manor, City Point, Virginia
USA. Home of Eppes family.*

Confederate headquarters during American Civil War.

Steps of Appomattox 1890s. Family members and staff

Print Commemorating John Sydney Lethbridge's service on the Somme during WW1

Ypres League of Officers and Men.

Katharine Lethbridge, my mother. Cameronia Society Party Simla 1926.

Nemone aged 4 Kew Gardens.

Nemone, John Sydney Lethbridge and Peter Lethbridge - picnic.

Nemone, Lady Maynard, Cherry

and Cellophane (rabbit)

Black Dog Cottage

CHAPTER SIX
JIMMY

Encircled by a strange monochrome landscape, devoid of trees or cultivation, more lunar than earthly, from the peak of Hessary Tor one looks down, almost invariably through rolling clouds and driving rain, on the village of Princetown. At sixteen hundred feet above sea level it is reputed to be the highest and is certainly the wettest hamlet in Great Britain. The rain streams off the grey shining roofs of a jumble of small granite buildings which huddle under the flank of an unforgiving, dominating edifice, like peasant cottages crowding round the castle of their feudal warlord. Welcome to Dartmoor Gaol.

A few yards from the prison lies a graveyard. Two hundred and seventy-one small crosses, most without inscription. These are the graves of French prisoners captured during the Napoleonic wars who had, at first, been confined in the hulks moored in the Channel near Devonport and later, in 1806, transferred to the new prison being constructed in the middle of Dartmoor. The location was chosen because it was so remote and the terrain so hostile that it was thought unlikely that any prisoner would dare to escape, or, in the event of his having done so, that he would perish on the moors.[1]

A few hundred yards from the prison boundary lies another graveyard, known to this day as the American Cemetery. This is the last resting place of a number of American soldiers captured in the war of 1812 – 1814 between the United Kingdom and the United States.[1] When, after the treaty of Ghent, the

American prisoners were repatriated, the gaol lay empty until the 1850s when it was extended and used for civilian prisoners. What Jimmy saw in 1942 was largely a Victorian construction, illuminated by gaslight.

Jimmy had lasted less than a month in Wandsworth. Plainly his truculent reputation had gone before him, or maybe it was punishment for his rudeness to the prison governor at Pentonville, but instead of being lodged in the hospital wing for observation, as was the general rule for reprieved lifers, he was sent immediately to the punishment cells. Although he had lost two stone in the condemned cell the prison doctor put him on a diet of bread and water. The regime in the punishment block, known as 'chokey', was designed to break a man's spirit. All moveable furniture was removed from the cells; the bed consisted of a low concrete slab. Two blankets were passed in at eight o'clock in the evening and removed first thing in the morning. There were no books, no radio, virtually no human contact. Bread and water were passed in through a hatch; slops were passed out once in twenty-four hours in a zinc bucket. Jimmy spent the days pacing the tiny cell: two paces forward, two paces back; nights were dominated by hideous dreams. Before long, it was decided to transfer him to Dartmoor. He was the first prisoner in fifteen years to commence a life sentence there.

It was, of course, midsummer when Jimmy arrived at the village of Princeton but a November gloom hung over the moor, reducing everything to winter shades of sable and grey. The rain lashed down, soaking prisoner and escorts as they squelched the short distance from station to prison gate. "Why not visit sunny Devon? – it rains for six days out of seven" smirked one of the escorting screws.

On arrival Jimmy was, as procedure demanded, taken straight before the prison governor. This official sat at his desk inside a cage made of iron bars, designed to protect him from his disgruntled – or enraged – charges. "So, you're the tough guy from London, are you?" he said. "Well, we're mighty tough too, here in the West. As you will soon find out."

Find out he did. A flight of steps led from the governor's

office down to the punishment cells. By tradition a prisoner's feet must never touch these steps. Two or three screws would kick him from top to bottom. Jimmy soon learned to deal with this. He would leap from the top of the staircase to the floor below then race to his cell, turning as he reached the back wall, fists raised, to face his tormentors.

Total silence was to be observed in the punishment wing and obviously no smoking was allowed. The only chance to speak to anyone was when on one of the outside working parties: the prisoners were marched to a quarry nearby where they broke great blocks of granite, reducing them to manageable pieces of stone. Surveys have shown that the area is rich with radon gas, now known to be carcinogenic. Each blow of the hammer must have released it into the saturated moorland air. Armed guards stood over the prisoners as they worked, breathing the toxic fumes.

When the mist came down so thick that it was impossible for the guards to see where their charges might be, the working party was moved indoors. There, in a hall below ground level, wringing with damp, they were set to sew mailbags, seven stitches to the inch exactly, by flickering gaslight. Any failure to complete the allotted task, any mistakes – for example the wrong number of stitches – and the prisoner was taken before the governor for punishment.

On one such occasion Jimmy announced "I can't live like this no more. I'm going to die."

"Good luck" replied the governor. "Be sure you make a good job of it."

"I will. I'll make a very good job of it. And I'll take you with me. I'm going to kill you. You won't mind. After all, you told me you were mighty tough in the West."

The governor went very quiet. His face went white, then it turned red. No doubt he meant to roar but when he opened his mouth his voice came out as a squeak:

"Officers! Take this man to the hospital!"

In the hospital Jimmy drew a flock of ducks on the wall. He fed them twice a day and talked to them nicely. He accused the screws of trying to poison him. When he was given bread he washed it under the tap. The water, as it is in much of Devon, was peaty brown in colour. "I told you" he said, "that's the poison coming out." When he was given porridge, he smeared half on the wall for the ducks and poured the rest down the drain. He refused to wash or shave; his hair became matted and he grew a long red beard. He said he was Napoleon. This went on for three months.

The hospital orderly was a kindly old lag called Joe Kinsella. He had arrived at Dartmoor years before as a furious young man. He suffered terribly as a result of his intransigence. Now his hair was snow white and his manner compliant. He did not feel that he had sold out to the system, rather that he had learned to survive it. He had been watching Jimmy since his arrival and he grieved for him. One day he said "look Jim, a word in your shell-like".

"What's going on then?"

"Look, I know you're trying to work your way to Broadmoor."

"It can't be no worse than this."

"Well it can, and for this reason. You may get a soft bed and a pint of beer on Sundays but mark my word: with your conviction once you get in you will never ever come out."

"Look, mate" Jimmy said "I know you mean it kindly, but I can't stand another twenty or thirty fucking years of this. I'd rather be dead"

"You can survive it you know. I have."

"What am I supposed to do then?"

"I tell you. Get yourself an education."

How can I do that? Half of this load of fuckwits can't even spell their own names proper."

"You don't need the screws. We got a library of books. That's all you need. Now go and get a hot bath. I'll cut your hair. Then ask to see the doctor."

This is exactly what Jimmy did. At five to one he went into the doctor's makeshift surgery.

"Good afternoon, Napoleon. How are we today?"

"My name's O'Connor, Sir. No more Napoleon."
"How are the ducks?"
"They've all flown away, sir"
"D'you still want to go to Broadmoor?"
"No sir. Why should I want to go to Broadmoor?"
"Well, you threatened to murder the governor."
"No I never. I wish him nothing but the best. Long life, good health and happiness."

I'm glad to hear you say that. And in the nick of time. I have two magistrates coming at three o'clock. We have all the paperwork ready to certify you insane. Shall I send them away?"

"Yes sir. Please do that."

"Right you are. Now eat your lunch and report to number 15 working party."

Jimmy ate his lunch, a rice pudding, and by three o'clock was back at the quarry, breaking stones.

NEMONE

My father bought a house at Standerwick, a village in Somerset, three miles from Frome and twelve from Bath. To the east lay the escarpment of Salisbury Plain and the White Horse of Westbury; southwest lay Shepton Mallet and the Mendip Hills; further west still the wetlands of Glastonbury. The house, which dated in part from the sixteenth century, was built of blocks of local stone, plastered and then whitewashed. The roof was made of moss-grown pantiles which had replaced the original thatch. The house had once been a coaching inn on the road from Bath to Shepton Mallet, the Black Dog Inn. To this structure was added two farm labourers' cottages, forming together a long thin house, never more than one room wide, in the shape of the letter L. There was a large, neglected garden, a paddock with a muddy pond and an orchard full of old-fashioned apple trees, the Morgan Sweet, Tom Pud (or Put) and Sheep's Nose, the fruit of which are never seen on a supermarket shelf. A previous owner had called the house 'The Pantiles'. My parents changed it back to

Black Dog Cottage.

After the house and garden at Norton Malreward this cottage, with its surrounding plot which included a group of cottages, each let for the sum of five shillings a week (what the Greeks would call a *Ktima*), seemed small indeed. Later my parents bought the meadow which lay beyond the orchard. My father named it Czechoslovakia, because it was, so he said, his last territorial claim in Standerwick. It was let to a local farmer for grazing. The surrounding countryside was an idyllic playground to which Peter and I had unrestricted access. There was lush meadowland grazed by red shorthorn cattle, dotted with great free-standing elms and small coppices which gave shelter to pheasants and innumerable songbirds. At the village of Berkley nearby (Berkley pronounced Burrkley by the local people) there were substantial woods and a reedy lake. When we walked quietly there at night we could hear nightjars and nightingales sing. There was the river Frome with its glass-clear tributaries where we collected tadpoles and caught stickleback. There were pollarded willows by the water's edge, in one of which Peter and I made a secret tree house.

Venturing further afield, we found another Calfskin; this time not a tree trunk but a real cottage, roofless and half derelict but a perfect den for children. There was a hazardous staircase leading nowhere, there was a cast iron oven in the wall still in working order. We helped ourselves to flour and matches from the kitchen at home, made a fire of twigs and tried to bake bread which, to our chagrin, turned out as rock hard patties. There was an ancient orchard full of brambles and topsy-turvy apple trees. Beyond the orchard lay a marvelous wet land crisscrossed by narrow, deep streams of crystal-clear water where wild watercress and spearmint grew. We named it Rush Meadow and it was our great secret.

Black Dog was the first house my parents had owned. After seventeen years in army quarters or rented houses at last they had somewhere to put down roots. It was therefore ironic that, no sooner had the purchase been completed than my father was posted to the South Pacific. Japan had entered the war. He was to head an Anglo-American mission to study the suitability of various armaments for use in the island and jungle warfare to come.

So my father went off to war again. What was said between him and my mother I do not know; before the children they preserved their usual dry-eyed stoicism. As a child I never worried about Daddy: theoretically I knew that he could be killed at any moment but in my heart of hearts I knew that it would never happen. Self-centred little toad that I was, I was far more concerned about myself.

Peter and I were being sent to school. Peter was six when he was sent to Lord Weymouth's at Warminster as a weekly boarder. I thought it cruel; he seemed too chubby and small. I begged my mother to let us both go to the village school at Berkley nearby. She said that it was impossible. "Miss Clinkhard" (the headmistress) she said "is an idiot". "She has awful false teeth which one day will shoot out of her mouth and I will have to catch them". I was to be sent to Mandrake House in Dorset as a boarder. Full stop. No argument.

My mother explained that Mandrake House was a nice friendly place, small enough not to be intimidating. It was run by a husband and a wife whose own children went there "so it must be alright". Dr Mandrake was a child psychologist and had been much influenced by the progressive schools of the 1920s and 30s, such as Dartington and Bedales. There were no hierarchies, no prefects, no uniform and no inflexible rules. The Mandrakes had taken in several refugee children from Germany: they must be good people.

I was not convinced. I decided not to subject Sarah Jane to this nightmare and left her in her usual place on my pillow. With a heavy heart I packed up my china ducks and animals and a couple of family photographs. I felt that my world had come to an end.

I remember very little of those first miserable weeks. During the day I moved in a trance; at night I covered my head with the bed clothes and wept. I remember that Mrs Mandrake had funny hair in plaits curled round the sides of her head like earmuffs. I wondered how she kept them there and what would

a book token. It was for ten shillings and sixpence and I had hoarded it since March. I was keeping it to spend in the summer holidays. Now that I knew what I wanted I knew I couldn't possibly wait that long. I negotiated a trip into Wimborne where I bought it; two shillings change in my pocket. It was *The Odyssey* in W H D Rouse's translation. Every evening in the precious hour between end of school and bedtime I would read until a teacher shooed me into the dormitory. It took me just less than a month.

When I had finished it I wrote to my godfather, not, alas, encamped somewhere along the Silk Road but at the Travellers' Club. I told him what I had bought. He replied. He was pleased with me. I glowed. "The Odyssey is the best story ever told" he wrote. My feeling exactly. Shortly after this he died.[5] I was heartbroken. I had important questions to put to him and now I would never know the answers:

1. In a battle between Zeus Cloud Gatherer and the goggle-eyed Cyclops which would be a winner?

2. How do you stuff the winds into a leather bag?

3. How can you call Penelope a good woman when she forgot to feed Odysseus's dog?

I had however learned an invaluable life lesson; how to escape from the painful present into the sunlit uplands of the imagination.

It was the end of the summer term. Before me stretched eight weeks of pure unmitigated bliss. I waited with my trunk on the front steps of Mandrake House. I could hardly breathe with excitement. No anticipated tryst with a lover was ever to make my heart race as it did that day. When I finally saw my mother, smaller than I remembered her, her thin arms brown and her poor hands rough from gardening, I thought that I was going to burst. I rushed to her and buried my face in her cotton dress. I could not speak.

My mother said, "You little monster. Why don't you write?"
"I did write."
"Once. And you didn't tell me anything."
"Did."
"What have you been doing?"

"Nothing much."
"Are you happy?"
"It's alright."
"You little gooserwallah."[6]

Off we drove in furious silence. However, I could not sulk for more than a quarter of an hour. I told her about the comical water lilies and we both smiled.

When we arrived home that evening, Black Dog and its environs, the *ktima*, seemed to have closed in, to have shrunk. The densely cut and laid hedges of hawthorn and hornbeam were now opaque and impenetrable; the grass in the orchard which had not yet been scythed, stood waist high. The nodding grasses and the umbelliferous plants had already shed their seeds and now stood ghostly pale and translucent in the evening light. I rushed into the house to greet my grandparents and my little sister, baby no longer but a scrumptious little toddler in a smocked dress. Then I was away down the garden to inspect the livestock. There were the Chinese geese, Chang and Cooee, a belated birthday present from my mother; handsome birds with buff-coloured feathers and that distinctive chocolate stripe running down the back of their elegant long necks. There were brown maran hens and fat ducks which had arrived while I was away at school. There was a Bantam cock with iridescent feathers and his modest little white wife, Chanticleer and Pertelote. There was a fine marmalade cat who was supposed to keep down the mice within and the rats without but who did neither; he preferred fighting with lads of the village or sleeping exhausted by the battle on top of the Aga. The chickens and ducks had been bought with the intention of making the family self-sufficient but the marans laid very few eggs and no one could bring themselves to kill the ducks. The poultry lived out their lives in indolent comfort until a passing fox ate them all - except Pertelote, who somehow managed to escape the slaughter. She became somewhat humanised and would, whenever my grandmother sat out in the garden, come and sit on her lap, cuddling up like a kitten.

Having carried out my inspection, it was into the house for supper. My mother had made a vegetable pie, preparing it the day before and leaving it in the bottom oven of the Aga all that day to steep in its succulent juices. It was cooked in a deep stoneware dish; layer upon layer of vegetables according to the season. The penultimate layer was of tomatoes, the last of all, orange lentils, mixed with butter to make a crisp and delectable topping. This was my mother's tour de force: I would dream of it while lying in my cold narrow bed at Mandrake House and my tummy would rumble with hunger. We ate together, the three generations, at the kitchen table, warmed by the benevolent glow of the Aga. Even Katharine Charmian, now renamed Cherry, sat up at table on a kitchen chair augmented by a big red cushion.

Peter came home the following day, taller, thinner and sadder than before. We soon picked up our friendship, but it was never quite as it had been before we were sent away to school. Both now had our own preoccupations to brood upon: These we did not share with anyone, not even each other. Nevertheless, in the weeks which followed we made many happy expeditions to the tree house by the river, to Rush Meadow where we tried to work out how the wooden water gates and sluices worked and wondered how to flood the meadow; to Calfskin, where again we tried to unsuccessfully bake bread in the cast iron oven.

While we were away the household had taken on a cleaning lady and a gardener. The cleaning lady, Mrs. Pickett, was a stout little Wiltshire woman from Stanton Drew just over the county border; small, knobbled and gnarled as a result of the chronic malnutrition and rickets which afflicted generations of the rural poor. She told us that as a child, her principal diet was of turnips, which the family ate three times a day. Turnips and tea, nothing else. She was a dear soul but a rotten cleaner. My grandmother said that cleaners were good either above or below the knee: Mrs. Pickett was good at neither. She would rather wash around the cat's saucer than bend down to pick it up. When my mother complained that the cat wasn't catching any mice she said "Don't feed 'un."

"But he's a pet. I have to feed him" said my mother.

"That's nice for them as likes it" answered Mrs. Pickett.

She could put an end to any argument with this mysterious phrase. In the end she herself became, like the useless poultry, a household pet. My mother was incapable of sacking anyone.

Sadler, the gardener, was quite different. A Somerset man, a true son of the soil, a man of iron. In his huge hands he could use a billhook, a sickle, a scythe with the precision of a neurosurgeon using his scalpel. In those huge hands a garden spade had almost the power of a pneumatic drill. He knew where the underground rivers ran; he knew where he could double dig the rich black loam of a trench to a depth of two feet; he knew where the clay subsoil came so close to the surface that it was better to leave well alone.Like all country people who have known grinding poverty, he had no use for flowers; they could not be eaten. He would often put his great boot on some precious specimen of my mother's, grinning at her and saying "Do 'un good". When he was asked to mend a broken window he followed local custom by leaving his signature thumb prints in the putty. It was unlucky, so he said, to smooth it. He loved bonfires and contrived to make one every day. He could light a huge pile of wet garden waste with a sheet of newspaper and a single match; firelighters were unknown and white spirit was for decadents. Sometimes his wife would bar him from their cottage, smelling as he did of the "filthy old burn and bake", then he would have to sleep in a haystack, or, if the weather was clement, under one of the cut and llaid hedges he had woven himself.

By the time I arrived home from school it was late July. Sadler had already turned a great swathe of the paddock into what would become a vegetable garden, double digging it in trenches throughout, turning the grass and clover upside down at the bottom of each furrow so that it would form a band of natural compost. At this time most of the ground lay fallow waiting to be raked into a fine tilth before the autumn sowing began. Some crops had already been grown and harvested; peas, beans and early potatoes. The potatoes had already been stored in the loft. One day, going up the ladder to fetch some for the kitchen, my mother found that they had all disappeared. A thorough search by torchlight revealed that the rats had rolled them, half a ton of them, the length of the house, and no doubt for Samuel Whisker's own convenience. Not one was damaged. I've had a soft spot for rats ever since, brave, cheeky and resourceful.

My mother and grandmother, during the summer months, had been filling the stillroom with good things. The stillroom was the long low building, one storey high, which formed the foot of the L shape in which the house was constructed. In times past, when the house was a coaching inn, it must have been used for the brewing and storing of beer. The wide slate-lined shelves were now packed with glass Kilner jars of tomatoes, red, white and black currants, purple red and yellow plums, green gooseberries, apples pureed and spiced with cloves, runner beans sliced and packed in dry salt, pots of jam, medlar jelly, damson cheese and chutney. There were trays of eggs soaking in zinc buckets of isinglass to preserve them; (this process rendered them airtight). In later years these would be joined by combs of honey from our bees and by great flagons of cowslip, parsnip and dandelion wine. Of these latter, parsnip was the strongest. On one famous occasion later in the war my mother gave the postman a glass of the best parsnip; the poor chap fell off his bicycle and would have spent Christmas day in the ditch had he not been seen and rescued by a kindly passer-by.

I am not certain where my mother learned these skills. At the age of thirty she could not boil an egg. There was no domestic science on the syllabus at Sherborne, where she and Buffy were sent at the ages of twelve and thirteen respectively. There were two recipe books in my mother's kitchen. One of them, by Elizabeth Craig, *Economical Cookery*, told one how to feed a family of six for fourteen shillings and sixpence a week and explained how to make brown Windsor soup and other horrors; the other was Mrs. Beeton which, in an age of austerity, we read for fun rather than for practical purposes. "Take 24 eggs..." Well, I mean to say. The English tradition of preserving fruit and vegetables, of making jam and bread, had largely disappeared with the advent of cheap manufactured food and tinned fruit. These domestic arts must have come via my grandmother from the kitchens of Appomatox, where little Freda, who never went to school, spent hours, weeks and years with the beloved Paulina. She in her turn must have been practising skills brought by the Eppes family when they left Romney Marsh for Virginia in the first decade of the seventeenth century.

What we could not grow we foraged. Late summer is not ideal for hedgerow scavenging but tender leaves and shoots can be found where the long grass has been cut and a fresh shower of rain has encouraged a second growth. Young dandelion leaves, burnet and sorrel were good for salads; ladies' smock added a peppery flavour; the long green leaves of wild garlic made a subtle substitute for spring onions. The bright green re-growth of nettles made vile smelling but palatable soup. Each summer shower produced overnight a myriad field mushrooms and the occasional giant puffball which my mother cut in slices like a pumpkin and fried in butter. As August slid towards autumn the hedgerows blushed red with rosehips which were pressed into a cordial, prophylactic against winter colds, and elderberries which made dark potent wine. Finally, the blackberries ripened and my mother, Peter and I would pick baskets full of them which we ate with sugar and cream for supper, or which were made into pies or bramble jelly or, combined with cooking apples, bottled for winter puddings.

Blackberrying was a rough business. We would return home from the woods covered in long, bloody scratches which we showed off as proudly as dueling scars. Later in the autumn there would be sloes from the thorniest of hedgerow bushes (each hard, miniscule fruit to be pricked with a pin and infused for a year to make sloe gin). There would be wild damsons to make dense purple damson cheese; there would be hazelnuts which we would save for our Christmas table; there would be sweet chestnuts to roast over the parlour fire.

Peter and I made friends with an old gentleman called Mr. Rawlings. He had a long sensitive, humorous face rather like the actor Wilfred Hyde-White. He lived alone in a cottage in the water meadows on the way to Dilton Marsh. It was called Redbridge Cottage, after a nearby archaic standing stone of which no one knew the history. On his shiny dining table he had two silver shakers, one for sugar and the other for powdered cinnamon. When Peter and I were invited to tea he would make us cinnamon toast which seemed to us the most exotic thing we had ever eaten. When tea was finished he would sit at the piano and sing:

"Where have you been Lord Randall my son?
Oh where have you been my handsome young man?"
"I've been to my true love, mother, make my bed soon
I'm sick to the heart and fain would lie down."

"What got you for dinner Lord Randall my son?
What got you for dinner, my bonny young man?"
"Eels boiled in broo, mother, make my bed soon
I'm sick to the heart and fain would lie down."

"Where did she get them, Lord Randall my son?
Where did she get them, my handsome young man?"
"In hedges and ditches, mother, make my bed soon
For I'm sick to the heart and fain would lie down."
"Oh where are your bloodhounds, Lord Randall my son?
Oh where are your bloodhounds, my darling young man?"
"They swelled and they died mother, make my bed soon
For life is a burden that I must lay down."

Lord Randall then wills his lands and his castles, his horses and his falcons to various members of his family. In the last verse his mother asks:

"What will you leave your true love, Lord Randall my son?
What will you leave your true love, my beloved
young man?"
"A rope to hang her, mother, a rope to
hang her mother, make my bed soon
For I'm sick to the heart and fain would lie down."

I had to wonder why the mother asked the poor man so many questions instead of putting him straight to bed as she should have done; as my mother would have done. And why did the true love have to poison the poor bloodhounds too? This ancient ballad (of which there are many different versions) has haunted me, words and music, ever since.

Sometimes it was too wet to go outside. Violent summer storms would blind the windows with sheets of rain; flood water would pour under the ill-fitting back door and race across the stone flags of the kitchen. Then it was all hands to the broom, pushing the water back in waves towards the bursting storm drain. On these days Peter and I would draw or paint in watercolours, do jigsaw puzzles or play Monopoly. Some of the games went on for days, the board and its pieces being carried to a place of safety every night. Cherry, who was the apple of our grandmother's eye, would snuggle up to her in bed (grandmother used to rise at midday) and look at picture books. As a result of this intensive attention Cherry learned to read almost as she learned to speak, at the age of two.

On these housebound days my mother would sometimes sit me down and encourage me to learn passages of prose and poetry. I learned great chunks of the Bible in the Authorised Version from "The Bible to be read as Literature"; this for its style rather than its content. I assimilated passages from Wordsworth and from Milton. She showed me *L'Allegro* and *Il Penseroso*: I found *Paradise Lost* for myself. In times of stress or difficulty I can still call it up from the back of my mind.

"Thick as Autumnal leaves that strow the brooks
In Vallambrosa where th' Etrurian shades
High over -arch'd, imbower."

And escape from the pain of the present into Milton's *Etruria*. For this I am eternally grateful to her; what one learns at ten one retains forever: She taught me the technique of survival. What crassly indifferent parents allow their children to stuff their subconscious with nothing but the triviality of Disney cartoons; what criminals expose them to the images of cruelty and horror which may haunt them for the rest of their lives and which only death can expunge?

The last weeks of the holiday were overshadowed by the thought of going back to school. I was determined to avoid it if I could. I tried to get ill, but I was either too healthy or too poor an actress to achieve it. I tried to argue that I was needed to help in the household: I would scrub muddy vegetables; I would wash the dishes; I would clean the silver; I would take over the care of all the livestock. This didn't work either. I started to cry; I resolved never to stop crying; I cried for three days without success. My mother cried too, off and on but, like a stoic Roman matron, she refused to budge. In the end back I went.

In the soft autumn light Mandrake House did not look as threatening as I had remembered. Gillian was there, which was a comfort. I settled down to daydreaming about Odysseus and to drawing somewhat eccentric maps of the three-fingered Peloponnese. Things were different; things were better. I could handle this.

One day Dr Mandrake came into the classroom and said "You two are becoming sensible young women. I want each of you to come for a private interview in my study on Tuesday morning, Gillian at ten and Nemone at eleven." On Tuesday we duly went down together, Gillian went into the study; I sat outside. When at last she emerged her face was scarlet and she was on the verge of tears. I decided that she must have been very naughty and had been given a mighty blowing up. I wondered what crime I had committed. I went in trembling. Dr Mandrake was sitting in a swivel chair by his tall roll top desk. "Come here" he said. He gripped me between his thighs in a vice like grip. He smelled of constipation and bitter aloes. He started to finger my upper body. "Do you like that?" I was too frightened to say a word. At least he did not, then, stray below the waist. After an age he said "off you go. See you next Tuesday."

Upstairs Gillian and I compared notes. "What is he doing? Why does he do it?" we asked each other. We decided that he was testing our reactions. "He wants to find out how quickly you can close your ribs" said Gillian "before he gets to your heart."

The next Tuesday was the same and many thereafter. We called these dreaded sessions the P.I. *'a shortening of Dr Mandrake's 'private interviews'.* We told no one about them. Indeed, if we had broached the subject with anyone, we would not have known what we were complaining about. We had not yet tasted

Eve's apple and, in our innocence, did not understand what he was doing. We knew that we hated it; nothing more. I did not tell my mother: She thought the Mandrakes were wonderful, largely because they had taken in refugee children from Nazi Germany. It would never have occurred to her, innocent as she was herself, that such children were probably more vulnerable than many. It took me more than thirty years to tell anyone about what happened and that was after I had dealt professionally with any number of paedophiles.

One Tuesday morning Gillian emerged looking, not cowed and tearful, but furious and determined."I'm going to run away" she said. "Will you come with me?" I agonized, torn between a longing to escape this dreadful man, this horrible place, and a terror of upsetting my mother Finally, I told Gillian that I couldn't go with her; that I thought that she was awfully brave and that I would give her sixpence, all I had left of my pocket money, to help her on her way.

That night I went to bed almost too frightened to breathe. I developed a violent attack of asthma. In the middle of the night there was a hullabaloo downstairs, a furious pealing of the bell, a thunderous banging on the front door, followed by the sound of running feet. I ran out onto the landing and peered through the banisters. There was Gillian in the hall below, between two policemen, in floods of bitter tears. There was Mrs. Mandrake in her nightclothes, her hair hanging down her back in a long thin pigtail, expostulating. I had seen enough; I ran back to the dormitory and put my head under the bedclothes, gasping for breath, my heart thumping.

A short time afterwards Dr Mandrake arrived, snapping on the brutal electric light. He stood over my bed shaking with rage. "I know all about you" he shouted "I know all about that sixpence. You're rotten to the core. You're deceitful; convent girls always are. I can spot one from a hundred yards. Rotten, wicked, deceitful. Do you know why you've got asthma? It's because you feel guilty; you know you're guilty. You know what you are; rotten, wicked and deceitful." Gillian disappeared from Mandrake House. We never said goodbye; I never saw her again. Her name was not mentioned; it was as though she had never been born.

I remained at school for another two years. The Tuesday P.I.s continued with sickening regularity but now the pawing was sadistic rather than lecherous. I taught myself to a certain extent to distance myself from my tormentor, to squeeze my eyes shut and to pretend he was not there. Then, one marvellous day, I was not called down to the study. Dr Mandrake must have found another child. But the harm was done. My confidence, my self-esteem, had sunk to the bottom of my Wellington boots.

At about this time I began to suffer a new, recurring nightmare. I was standing outside a complex of low buildings, open at the sides, like cowsheds. There were no humans, no animals in sight but the sheds were knee high in excrement. I knew it to be human. It was only at the end of the war in Europe when the first photographs of the liberated concentration camps were published (these I saw in *Picture Post* despite my mother's efforts to hide them from me) that I understood what, prophetically, I had seen. This dream haunted me for the next ten years, then as suddenly as it had come, it vanished. I cannot explain it.

I cannot explain either, or understand, the Mandrake family. I have never decided whether Mrs. Mandrake was ignorant of her husband's behaviour, or whether she condoned it. For certain she adored him. Some of the pupils adored them both. One child, from a disturbed and unhappy background, arrived at the school with very few personal possessions. She was asked to write a wish list. She wrote:

> "I would like a hairbrush.
> I would like a fountain pen.
> I would like a doll's house.
> I would like to be adopted by Doctor and Mrs Mandrake."

They adopted her. Doctor Mandrake received an MBE in the New Year's Honours list: 'For services to childcare'.

This left me feeling more isolated than ever. I felt that I must be a disgusting little monster to be singled out for a punishment which I undoubtedly deserved. My own home seemed insubstantial; a million miles away. I tried to think of the wily

Odysseus. I tried to think of the leaf-strewn brooks of Vallambrosa. I tried to believe that one day I would go to another school; that one day I would be happy.

CHAPTER SEVEN
JIMMY

It would be unrealistic to imagine that a few sensible words from a kind old lag could, overnight, have transformed Jimmy from sinner to saint. He did, however, think about what Joe Kinsella had said from time to time when the flames of his cosmic anger were burning low and, when it became known that his mentor's release on parole was under consideration, he started to wonder whether he should apply them to his own life.

Jimmy had plenty to be angry about, over and above the fact of his conviction. Towards the end of his first year in Dartmoor he received a letter from a firm of solicitors in North London saying that they had been instructed by a Mr Jack Crawford to act on his behalf. He was puzzled by this: he did not know Jack Crawford personally but did know that he was reputed to be a receiver of stolen goods with extensive contacts in the underworld. It was possible that he knew the true identity of the murderer of George Ambridge. Shortly afterwards it was announced in the press that the Secretary of State had reopened Jimmy's case. He was visited by Detective Inspector Thorpe who interviewed him. His hopes rose, although as he wrote later, he had "a funny feeling about Jack Crawford".

In March 1943 he was again visited by DI Thorpe who told him, with smug satisfaction, that Jack Crawford had not paid the solicitor's bill and that the managing clerk of the firm had been sent to prison for fraud. The Home Office dropped the enquiry-. As could have been expected Jimmy, enraged, was back in the punishment cells.

There was more to come. Mary had not visited him since he left Wandsworth. Now she stopped writing. Jimmy's only correspondents were Annie and Miss Daley. Now, on the prison grapevine, he heard that Mary had found a new man and had moved in with him somewhere in Cricklewood, taking Little Jim with her. Jimmy, to whom the concept of marital fidelity was an alien one (at least as far as he was concerned) was nevertheless filled with a great tsunami of jealousy and rage. Yet again he made the long leap from the Governor's office to the punishment cells, back to bread and water, back once again to chokey.

Jimmy had written to Annie, asking in particular, for news of Little Jim. Annie, who was afraid to be the bearer of bad tidings, did not reply. He wrote again. She did not reply. He wrote again. She procrastinated. Finally, she wrote and asked him to send her a visiting order.

At the best of times the journey from Paddington to Princetown is not an easy one. This was the worst of times. The trains were slow, filthy and unheated, the stations unlit, filthy and cold. Annie had tried to make herself look smart so that Jimmy would be proud of her. She had also brought him something he'd always wanted and which she thought might give him some comfort: an enormous piano accordion. It seemed almost as large as she was and twice as heavy. Five hours in a third-class carriage from Paddington to Exeter St Davids; a couple of hours on the windswept platform waiting for the connecting train on the branch line which ran from Exeter to Plymouth, crossing the moor and stopping off at Princetown.[1]

When Jimmy entered the visitors' room and saw her waiting there with her absurd piece of luggage, when he saw how small and frail she looked in her thin coat and unsuitable high-heeled shoes, caked with mud from her trudge from station to gaol, when he realised how she must have earned enough money to pay for the wretched accordion on the cruel streets of London, he was moved with compassion for her more than with pity for himself. Tears streamed down her face as she blurted out the news of Mary's defection, or rather confirmed the reports which

Jimmy had already received.

As on many occasions in the past he said "Don't cry, mother. I'll make it up to you. I'll look after you, I swear."

"How are you going to do that, Jim?"

"I'll get out of this place. It'll be different. I swear it, on me son's life. I'll work me parole. However long it takes. I'll work me parole. I'll take you to Tangiers or the Souf of France."

Annie had missed her connection to the last train to London. She spent a cold and miserable night on Exeter station, sleeping on a bare wooden bench. Jimmy returned to his cell. This time he was determined to commence his education. With the help of Joe Kinsella, now prison librarian, this is exactly what he did.

Jimmy never learned to play the accordion. He had no ear for music and no one to teach him. But he did enjoy swaying and squeezing the instrument while bellowing:

> *"I wonder who's kissing her now,*
> *I wonder who's teaching her how.*
> *I wonder who's sleeping in my bed tonight,*
> *Holding her tight – night after night"*

to the ironic cat calls and applause of his fellow sufferers. And the rain beat down on Dartmoor.

NEMONE

I was twelve when I went to Tudor Hall. Originally, I had been put down for Sherborne, where my mother and her sisters had gone and where Cherry would go when the time came. My mother returned from interviewing the headmistress with a definitive no. "The woman's mad." She said, "She wore a gold lamé dress and her mind was elsewhere."

Tudor Hall had been evacuated, early in the war, to Burnt Norton, a manor house near Chipping Camden in Gloucestershire. The house, large enough to accommodate eighty girls and their teachers was still a family home, informal enough to have a friendly atmosphere. It stood at the crest of a low hill in the Cotswolds surrounded by well-managed woodland which in spring dazzled with sapphire bluebells and white garlic. I used to watch the foresters' tractor dragging out the timber thinnings and struggling in heavy mud. It seemed a crime to crush those fragile squashy flowers.

Miss Inglis was the headmistress, Miss Brampton her deputy. Both were tall women of statuesque figure with handsome bony English faces, their hair immaculately coiffed in the style still worn by the present Queen. They wore cashmere twin sets, triple rows of perfect pearls and Harris Tweed skirts which never showed a crease. Each was escorted by a giant poodle, not clipped in the silly French style but with curly coats cut short like proper British dogs. The poodles went everywhere, into lessons, into the dining room (where, unlike Mandrake House, staff and pupils sat together and ate the same food) into assembly; always silent, always perfectly behaved. It was said that Miss Inglis had refused several offers of marriage in order to pursue her vocation, that of educating girls. Certainly, there was a sense of dedication and energy about the place. It seemed that anything was possible, even for girls. Bridget Younger was going to be a concert pianist, Sarah Lutyens-Humphreys a sculptor; I was going to be the first Communist Prime Minister of Great Britain.

Miss Inglis taught religion which I did not care for. It was of course, incompatible with my politics. I was a militant atheist. I was the only girl in my year who refused to go forward for Confirmation in the Church of England. Miss Inglis also taught music with the help of two assistants, Miss Moloney, who failed to teach me to play the piano with any degree of competence but who taught us all to love the folksongs collected by Cecil Sharpe and happily to bellow the fine old Anglican hymns, and Miss Dyer who, so we believed, would become a famous composer. Miss Inglis herself was a fine musician who introduced me to Bach, whose music I had never heard before. (At home my parents loved Beethoven, Brahms and Sibelius but did not, as far as I can remember, have much interest in earlier music. Mozart was regarded as a charming lightweight: *Eine Kleine Nacht Musik* and that was it.) Under her tutelage Bach's music seemed to seep right through my skin into the very core of my being, so that, with poetry and the love of nature, it became the third element in my technique for survival: the voice of sanity; the transcendental voice.

Among the other characters in the continuing drama of school were Miss Ireland, who had a beautiful speaking voice; she always read the lesson at morning assembly and read it so well, always from the Authorised Version of the Bible, that even now, when I hear someone stumbling through the dreadful New Jerusalem translation, I can still hear her ghostly voice and remember how it ought to be done. There was Miss Linley, who taught me to love Keats but who was generally pitied because she dressed in baggy cardigans; there was Miss Gorst and Miss Bumpass whose friendship was so close that everyone remarked upon it but which none of us understood. Miss Gorst, who taught French, was a white Russian and, so it was believed, an émigré Princess. Miss Bumpass, who taught gym and games, was more proletarian but not to my taste; nor, I imagine was I to hers. I used to tease both with my politics and atheism: I had not yet learned how dangerous it is to make enemies of those with whom one is going to live and work.

Miss Bumpass, who was a muscular Christian and ran the Guides, was known by some as Prue Porker and by others as Bet Bouncer. At the first and only cookery class I have ever received (cooking carrots over a camp fire) I burnt the saucepan and failed to get my badge. The Guides, under her direction, had to perform some high-minded amateur dramatics with an evangelical message punctuated by awful songs which made Miss Inglis wince.

"Let's get together, let's get together and sing
In the spirit of unity although we cannot agree"

I told her that I wanted to resign from Guides. "Why?" said she. "No one ever resigns from Guides."

"It's because of the songs" I said. "They don't rhyme, they don't scan and they're full of clitches."

Miss Bumpas exploded "You may think you're a bookworm,

but you can't even pronounce the words you read. You're hopeless! You're conceited! Go away! I never want to see you again."

There was also poor Miss Loring who licked her lips like a grass snake and rolled her eyes when she failed, for the hundredth time, to get a simple mathematical proposition into my thick, innumerate skull.

Finally, there was Matron, a sharp little woman in whose room we used to have to queue up every morning to have our throats painted with some disgusting-tasting anti-septic substance to guard against infection. We also had to swallow a table spoonful of malt extract and cod-liver oil against deficiencies in the wartime diet. When we hit puberty with its concomitant nastiness we had to announce on the relevant day "Matron, I'm off games." She would then enter our names on the "to be excused" register.

I made a friend. Her name was Dione Phillips and we became inseparable. Together we would climb the ancient chestnut trees which lined the drive and whose dense hand shaped leaves would render us invisible to anyone below. Together we would explore the woods surrounding the school. These were strange enough, being intersected by water courses which bored their way through the limestone hillside with such ease that each stream flowed some hundreds of feet below the bosky escarpment. Slithering down those precipitous slopes we would come at last to the brook, the water ice cold and so loaded with minerals that every twig, every leaf it touched would be calcified, forever frozen into a ghostly grey skeleton of itself. Attempting to take the best of these back to school to show our friends we were inevitably frustrated: the tiny stalagmites were so brittle that they always fell to pieces in our hands.

We would race around the great neglected garden, untended since the outbreak of war. There were unmown lawns, beds of unpruned roses, avenues and squares of box and yew which had been spared the clippers. There was a drained pool, now standing forlorn and empty. A few years later when I came to read the *Four Quartets* everyone told me that it was a difficult work, impossible to understand, full of symbolism; I was struck with a great stab of recognition: I'd been there, seen that, got the T-

ferred to digging potatoes which was much less fun. Nevertheless we enjoyed our time as amateur land girls, got nicely tanned and felt virtuous into the bargain.

JIMMY

By-passing the dog-eared paperback westerns, Joe Kinsella led Jimmy to the dusty hardbacks towards the far end of the library shelves. They looked at the same time intimidating and neglected, as though no one had taken them out for years. He handed Jimmy a small volume, its damp red leather cover disfigured by a light patina of greenish mould. "Here, give this one a go" he said.

Jimmy ruffled through the thin India paper pages. "Boots, boots, boots" that's 'ighly intellectual" he said.

"Carry on" said Joe. "Try *Danny Deever*." For Jimmy it was another Damascus moment.

"WHAT are the bugles blowin' for?" said Files-on-Parade.
"To turn you out, to turn you out," the Colour-Sergeant said.
"What makes you look so white, so white?" said Files-on-Parade.
"I'm dreadin' what I've got to watch," the Colour-Sergeant said.
For they're hangin' Danny Deever, you can hear the Dead March play,
　The Regiment's in 'ollow square—they're hangin' him to-day;
　They've taken of his buttons off an' cut his stripes away,
　An' they're hangin' Danny Deever in the mornin'.

"What makes the rear-rank breathe so 'ard?" said Files-on-Parade.
"It's bitter cold, it's bitter cold," the Colour-Sergeant said.
'What makes that front-rank man fall down?" said Files-on-Parade.
"A touch o' sun, a touch o' sun," the Colour-Sergeant said.
　They are hangin' Danny Deever, they are marchin' of 'im round,
　They 'ave 'alted Danny Deever by 'is coffin on the ground;
　An' 'e'll swing in 'arf a minute for a sneakin' shootin' hound—

> O they're hangin' Danny Deever in the mornin'!'
>
> "'Is cot was right-'and cot to mine," said Files-on-Parade.
> "'E's sleepin' out an' far to-night," the Colour-Sergeant said.
> "I've drunk 'is beer a score o' times," said Files-on-Parade.
> "'E's drinkin' bitter beer alone," the Colour-Sergeant said.
>   They are hangin' Danny Deever, you must mark 'im to 'is place,
>   For 'e shot a comrade sleepin'—you must look 'im in the face;
>   Nine 'undred of 'is county an' the regiment's disgrace,
>   While they're hangin' Danny Deever in the mornin'.
>
> "What's that so black agin the sun?" said Files-on-Parade.
> "It's Danny fightin' 'ard for life," the Colour-Sergeant said.
> "What's that that whimpers over'ead?" said Files-on-Parade.
> "It's Danny's soul that's passin' now," the Colour-Sergeant said.
>   For they're done with Danny Deever, you can 'ear the quickstep play,
>   The Regiment's in column, an' they're marchin' us away;
>   Ho! the young recruits are shakin', an' they'll want their beer to-day,
>   After hangin' Danny Deever in the mornin'[4]

By the flickering gaslight of that subterranean room Jimmy saw a whole new world opening up before him. "Bloody 'ell Joe" he said "I can do that. I could be a fucking writer." Years later critic Nancy Banks-Smith was to describe him as perhaps the most important writer to come out of prison since Bunyan.

Jimmy fell on the books and read voraciously. In Kipling he found a world which made perfect sense to him, a world where men were bound together by ties of courage and loyalty, by the labour they did or the service they performed, where informers were detested, where women were remote and puzzling. In Dickens he found a universe inhabited by characters he recognised; the poor and dispossessed, the comic and bizarre, the chancers and survivors, and, somewhere on the periphery, women, who were either grotesque or angelic, unreal, essentially unobtainable. Later as his horizons widened, so did his reading. When I first met him, he was deep into the writing of Jean Genet.

In July 1943 the deputy governor, who had noticed his valiant efforts to educate himself, gave him a job in the library. The Governor, a cynical man, said that he would not last a week and soon would be back in Chokey where he belonged. Seeing him pushing a barrow load of books across the prison yard he remarked "The man thinks he's pushing a load of fruit and veg up the Edgware Road". In fact, Jimmy lasted in the job for two years, by the end of which the war was over.

It was at this time that the Home Office decided to transfer some two hundred lifers from Parkhurst to Dartmoor. The arrival of these characters, some repellent, some bizarre, some pitiful, gave him a rich vein of material to study. He talked to them, learned their stories and recognised their dramatic potential. The previous summer the Deputy Governor had arranged for Jimmy to enrol on a three-months correspondence course in drama with Ruskin College, Oxford. An unnamed tutor used to send him titles such as *The Sea*, *The Rehearsal* and instruct him to write a thirty-minute play on each. The tutor seemed pleased with his work: the Home Office gave him permission to extend the course through the Long Vacation. It seemed that Jimmy was turning from a trouble-maker into a model prisoner.

Then came a set-back. A supervisor from Ruskin intervened. He wrote to Jimmy saying that the plays were too violent to be performed.

Jimmy wrote back: "What about the Greek tragedies? What about Shakespeare? I live amid violence in a violent world. I write what I see."

The supervisor replied "No one will understand your vernacular. You will have to learn to write in proper English".

The correspondence continued. "I write what I hear and how I speak".

"If you continue with this arrogant vein and refuse to take advice, there is no hope for you. We are wasting each other's time. Find something else to do." So that was the end of that.

The blow to Jimmy's self-esteem was considerable. For several weeks he stopped reading and sank into a black depression.

Happily, Joe Kinsella came to the rescue."Remember what Bernard Shaw said" he advised "Those who can, do, those who can't, teach". The aching gloom in the pit of his stomach gave way to a healthy rage.

"The time's coming" he said, "when that whoreson is still writing stupid letters to old lags and I'll be driving a beautiful white Cadillac down Sunset Boulevard".

NEMONE

It was the last year of the war in Europe. My father came home briefly, told us that the Normandy landings were imminent and attacked the garden like a Soviet Stakhanovite. He made one brief appearance at Tudor Hall, a glorious creature in full uniform (which did my prestige no end of good) and then was off again. This time it was to Burma which had been occupied by the Japanese. There he was appointed Chief of Staff to Field Marshall Slim who commanded the 14th Army. He was to remain there until the final surrender of the Japanese and the end of what was called 'the forgotten war.'

Meanwhile my grandfather had died. My grandmother buried him, mourned him in her disciplined Roman way, filed his obituaries, wrote her thank-you letters and then quietly emerged from behind his austere shadow. She sold the house in Gilston Road where she had so many times entertained the leading Socialists of the day: Bernard Shaw, Beatrice and Sydney Webb, Ramsay Macdonald. She took a flat in Draycott Avenue near Sloane Square. The mahogany furniture which fitted so easily into the larger rooms at Gilston Road seemed heavy and oppressive in the flat. I do not think that she ever felt at home there. Certainly most of her time was spent at Black Dog, much to the delight of the Lethbridge children.

She was a handsome old lady. Her thick beautiful hair, which had never been impoverished by dye or chemicals, a striking mixture of dark brown and silver grey, was piled on top of her head and secured with two-pronged tortoise-shell pins. She preserved her fine aquiline profile by wearing a tight black velvet ribbon round her neck, or, on special occasions, a garnet choker. She had no trace of an American accent; my grandfather used to say she spoke the most perfect English he had ever heard. The Eppes family had had so little contact with the outside world that the language they spoke, the almost Shakespearean syntax they used, can have changed little in the centuries which had passed since they first arrived in America in the early 1600s.

Ensconced at Black Dog my grandmother subscribed to the *Manchester Guardian*, the *New Statesman and Nation* and Stephen King-Hall's *National News-Letter*. These she read from cover to cover every day. She corresponded widely, especially with the Fabians. She used to terrify the Rector of Berkley (a sporting parson of the old-fashioned variety) who was far less well read than she. She would summon him to Black Dog to tease him about the Thirty-Nine Articles which he had probably not read since he left theological college, if indeed he had ever read them at all. At one stage she caused him considerable distress by telling him that she was a card-carrying Zionist. The woman who had never been to school, the scion of a Virginian slave estate, who was ostracised on her arrival in India by the Mrs. Hawksbees of the Raj, had, at the end, become a lively and original thinker in her own right.

Meanwhile Buffy had taken herself to America, for reasons which were not clear at the time, but which became apparent later. Josephine, who was briefly married to a curator at the Victoria and Albert Museum, and who was now a civil servant in the Ministry of Agriculture, was posted to Liverpool with her department. Fair-haired Josephine had inherited her mothers' aquiline good looks. She was the youngest of the Maynard siblings. She thought herself a cut above the others as she was the only one to have been to university. Jack? An apple farmer in Kent. Buffy? An artistic dilettante. Nicky? An Army wife. She had, during her time at Somerville, absorbed some of the more negative aspects of the Oxford mindset: an over-critical approach to everything and a reluctance to expose her opinions and feelings on any subject, politics, literature, art or music. The Proms? (To which we listened every evening during July and August on the wireless) Populist and vulgar. Sir Adrian Boult? No good. Sir Malcom Sargeant? No good. Elgar? Out-dated and jingoistic. Benjamin Britten? Oh dear. And what a strange private life. Yet she was touchingly devoted to her siblings. She never learned that, in patronising them, she drove them mad. In all the years I knew her I never found out what she actually approved of or even liked.

Mrs Picket had died, succumbing at last to untreated diabetes. She was replaced by Mrs Axford, an alarming woman who suffered from alopecia and wore a bright red ill-fitting wig. She lived in the Standerwick cottages next door to her sister, another scary individual whom Peter and I disgracefully nicknamed Mrs Hoggernigger. Both women were filled with cosmic rage. Peter and I would stalk them behind the tall hawthorn hedge which separated their kitchen garden from the road. We found it hilarious when they would spot us and rush out with their hairy legs and huge feet thrust into their fluffy pink courtesan slippers to chase us with a broom, a garden rake or whatever weapon came to hand.

Of course all this had to stop when Mrs Axford came to work for the family; we soon learned to treat her with proper respect. She in her turn seemed quite fond of Peter and me; it may have been, of course, that she did not realize that we were the little fiends behind the hawthorn hedge. In the house she used to exorcise her demons by whacking the furniture; some of it carries to this day the furious scars she inflicted. 'Acky', as she was affectionately known, and my mother became firm friends. After Black Dog was sold and my parents moved to Devon, they would correspond. Acky wrote faultless copperplate script and used a formal turn of phrase. This she must have learned at the despised Berkley Village School my mother had rejected; certainly we did not learn anything so fine at the expensive boarding schools to which we were sent. Acky's husband was called Horace; she shortened this to Hor. Their sons were Gerald and Terence; inevitably they became Ger and Ter. My mother gave them mythic status in one of her childrens' stories.[3] She kept in touch with them all until at last the older generation departed for the great kitchen garden in the sky.

Suddenly our horizons rolled back in every direction. Peter and I had been given bicycles. This meant that we had the freedom of East Somerset and West Wiltshire. No restrictions were placed upon our explorations; just the gentle admonition "Be back in time for supper." Sometimes we would ride to Cley Hill, an outsize chalk tumulus (what they would call in the West Country, a 'tump') standing in isolation among the meadows and oddly cast adrift from its geological mother ship, Salisbury Plain. We would leave our bicycles at the foot of the hill and scramble to the top from where we could see our kingdom spread out below us, the long pale escarpment of Salisbury Plain rising from the emerald green meadows, the dark rectangular elm trees seeming to stride like giants across the countryside. Then sliding on our backsides to the bottom, we would reclaim our bicycles, enter Longleat through the main gates without let or hindrance and pedal up the drive between the blazing rhododendrons.

On occasion we decided that we wanted to swim and would turn off the drive across a stretch of countryside which could have been lifted from Dartmoor, with low scrub and heather growing alongside the track where we rode, making for Shearwater Lake. Once we were suddenly caught, in the open, by a freak hailstorm. Drenched, the icy pellets stinging our faces, we struggled on, determined not to be cheated of our swim. When we finally reached the lake we changed among the trees and then slithered down the steep muddy bank into the water which, cold as it was, still seemed warmer than the icy sleet-filled air.

On other occasions we would skirt the edge of Salisbury Plain and trace a circle round our home, going to Dilton Marsh, Upton Skudamore, Farleigh Hungerford and Norton St. Phillip then turn and make for Standerwick, going via Buckland Dinham and Mells. We would stop only to gaze through the gates of some manor house, secluded among its encircling chestnut trees, whose heart-stopping beauty forced us to pause long and look.

Every Wednesday, which was market day, we would ride into

Frome. This was our shopping centre and centre of the East Somerset universe. Frome is built up and down small steep hills, the grey terraced houses and innumerable small, grim chapels fronting straight onto the street. There was a cattle market in the centre of town and a department store called Fear Hills, which seemed to be the height of sophistication. When one bought something, the change was placed in a kind of tin an which, with a clang and a buzz, would whiz across the ceiling on a network of string running from counter to counter. We were sent to do the family errands, but our real purpose was to go to the market and gaze at the animals. Peter was already developing an eye for a promising calf which would stand him in good stead in later years when he became a farmer. I had set my mind on buying a beautiful rabbit which I would tame and make my own.

On high days and holidays, when the occasion merited it, Peter and I would be dispatched to buy a roasting chicken at a farm near the village of Rudge.

The Fowl Farm, as we punningly named it, lay in a hollow near the railway line which, even in the height of summer, was surrounded by mud so deep and so disgusting that it might have been on the Somme. The farmer, a wicked old hobgoblin who never spoke to us, was, so we were told, a widower. He lived with Leah, his only daughter, who would serve us. She would bring us the chicken uncleaned and unplucked, still warm and limp from its execution (Sadler would prepare it later for the oven) almost without speaking. She was a pitiful specimen of humanity, apparently simple-minded, with no front teeth. Her eyes were red, though whether from weeping or conjunctivitis it was impossible to tell. She had big, rough hands swollen with farm work, arthritis and laundry. Nevertheless, she always wore a fine gold wedding ring. It must have been her mother's, we decided. Peter and I hated going there and only went, under protest, because our mother asked us to. I believe firmly in the spirit of place. The spirit there was evil.

Eighty years ago, the Beveridge Report had not yet been published, the welfare state was in its infancy; there was no safety net for those in need. In the deep countryside there were extraordinary pockets of deprivation and hardship. There were derelict cottages, like Calfskin, whose occupants had simply disappeared; there were half derelict farms where the machinery was unguarded, the wells unfenced, the cesspits open. Generations of inbreeding and malnutrition had produced a race of Halflings, hump-backed, squint-eyed, many suffering from tuberculosis or rickets, wary and suspicious.

There was a cottage, not far from the Fowl Farm, which my mother used to visit. There lived a strange trinity, husband, wife and a handicapped son. My mother called them Faith, Hope and Charity. Faith was crippled and had never worked. Hope was simple-minded and could not work. Charity, the old lady, was a formidable character who, for years, had carried the whole weight of the family. She had been, so she told us, a warder "at 'olloway Castle. I done all the 'angings." At the word "angings" she would give a demonic chuckle and flash her toothless gums. My mother thought she was a rather splendid character. To me she was appalling. I could not erase from my mind the thought that she had broken some poor woman's neck with the same indifference as she would display when strangling the Christmas chicken.

The cottage, which was what Calfskin must once have been, had two rooms, one up and one down. It had no electricity or running water; there was a privy in the vegetable patch and water had to be drawn from a spring in the meadow nearby which also supplied the cattle drinking trough. Ivy had grown over the windows so that if anyone wanted to open them, they could not have done so. The air was thick and foul, a mixture of urine, sweat and rotting vegetables. Nevertheless, Charity presided over her household as though she were Queen of Holloway Castle, and always made us welcome when we called.

Peter and I decided to go camping. Both our mother and grandmother warned us that this would require some thought and preparation. I dismissed their advice airily "No – easy-peasy Japanezy." Peter, who liked a quiet life, followed my bossy lead. We found an old bivouac tent in the attic, two sleeping bags, a tin kettle, two tin mugs, a box of matches, a hunk of bread and a twist of tea in a piece of paper. Off we went on our bicycles, wobbling a bit because of all the luggage, to Salisbury Plain. We wanted to pitch our camp on the White Horse itself but when we arrived we found it alarmingly steep. The chalk lumps from which it was made were rough and slimy after a recent fall of rain: thoroughly inhospitable. We decided to move further up-. We carried the equipment up first, then went back for our bicycles. By the time we found a suitable spot to pitch our tent where the grass, although thin, was fragrant and soft we were exhausted and it was getting dark. We couldn't find any sticks for a fire or any water for the kettle. We had no margarine or jam for our bread and we had forgotten to bring a torch. We crept into our sleeping bags hungry and dispirited.

First light. We were too cold and miserable to get out of our sleeping bags. In the grey triangular aperture of the tent there suddenly appeared a dear face: our mother. In unison we said

"We're perfectly alright. We're having a wonderful time."

"Of course you are" she said "I just wanted to make sure that you hadn't strayed onto the firing range."

"Of course we haven't. We're not stupid."

"That's fine then. I'll be off to get my breakfast."

Within five minutes we had broken camp and started to manhandle our gear down the hill to my mother's car. Off she drove: we followed after her on our bicycle like tugs following an ocean liner. Peter and I were twelve and ten respectively. My mother was a very clever woman.

May 1945. The war in Europe came to a sudden end. The Russians had swept into Berlin, the Allies holding back politely so that the Red Army could take full credit for the victory after years of terrible suffering the Russian people had endured. Hitler was dead. The horror of what had happened in Europe was just starting to emerge.

There was a celebration party at Stanton Drew. Peter and I went on our bicycles. It was mid-May and the evening was long and light. There was a huge bonfire, baked potatoes with margarine and cups of tea. Everyone sang marching songs from the First World War. The Second, it was said, produced no songs, only sorrows. We all threw our identity cards into the flames and went home highly delighted. My mother and grandmother were too exhausted to come to the party or rejoice. The forgotten war in the East still raged and my father was far from home.

Peter anticipated the end of the war against Japan by making a patriotic vehicle. He took the carcass of an old chest of drawers and fixed it to a set of pram wheels. He covered it with Union Jacks and gave it the number "VJ 1945". We used it to collect dried bracken from the woods to use as animal bedding and to protect the tender plants in winter. Sometimes, as a special treat, Peter would use it to give Cherry a ride. She would sit there on top of the piled bracken, proud as Cleopatra on her golden barge.

The scullery was thick with steam, the stone floor awash with water, as Acky attacked the laundry with a hatred bordering on passion. The air was filled with groans and imprecations as she engaged her enemy in the big stone sink. First, she whacked it with the dolly, then she rubbed it all over with a great square bar of Sunlight soap, then she thumped it again with her second weapon of choice, the posser. Baskets of laundry awaiting her attack and completed tubs of washing, limp from her assault, made a barrier impossible to pass to anyone who wanted to use the back door. Next, with a curse, she dragged the mangle on its heavy cast iron stand from a corner and started to feed the dripping linen into the rollers. Finally, she hung it all out on a line which stretched the length of the garden, wiped her big red hands on her pinafore and grinned. "Blowing out nicely."

My mother gathered up slithers of soap and boiled them up in a saucepan to make shampoo. She called Cherry and me to have our hair washed. We hated this and called it "the tortures." The home-made shampoo stung our eyes; it seemed to take innumerable rinses to get rid of the slimy residue; the vinegar in the final rinse smelled vile. We were told to bury our faces in a bath towel and to pretend that we were going through a long, dark tunnel. It was a magical moment when it was over, and our mother told us to run out into the garden and dry our hair in the sunshine.

Although the war in Europe was over, the shortage of food, clothes and fungibles was worse than ever. Meat, sugar, cheese, eggs and butter were measured in ounces, week by week. My mother's housekeeping was made even more difficult by the fact that the schools would swipe from our ration books almost the entire allowance of these items for the year. This must have been hard indeed for those who lived in the city; for country dwellers it meant that our diet became virtually vegetarian. Porridge, made with coarse oatmeal and cooked overnight in a double boiler on the Aga, was our breakfast. Lunch, the main meal of the day, consisted of my mother's famous vegetable pie, or *dal baht* – which is orange lentils served on the same plate as Patna rice with a dollop of homemade chutney – or in summer, sweet corn, which we called by its Hindustani name '*bhootas*', or globe artichokes; both so sweet that they needed no butter. There was always pudding, baked apples spiked with cloves, pears from the Bishops Tongue tree which were as hard as wood until they were stewed with honey and spices; gooseberries or currants, wild blackberries in season, all eaten with the top of the milk carefully poured off from each bottle as it was opened and saved in a small china jug; in winter, bottled fruit from the still room. For supper we had brown bread, margarine and home-made jam.

When, after an absence of six years, the first oranges arrived in the shops, my mother made what she called "monkeys' marmalade" because not a scrap of fruit was wasted. Everything went into the saucepan; juice, pulp, peel, even pips. It was delicious, if not for the faint-hearted. I still find the shop-bought variety bland and pathetic.

Our Maran hens produced very few eggs. The corn which layers need was unobtainable and the chickens lived on a diet of vegetable peeling, unwashed, boiled up in a cauldron, mud and all, then mixed with bran. The poor things were so effete or so over-bred that the chicks could not break out of their shells; they had to be assisted with tweezers when the first gentle tapping announced that they were ready to hatch. Sadler and Acky thought my mother mad not to knock the lot of them on the head and have done with it.

The greatest problem of all was the shortage of clothes. My mother and grandmother pooled their clothing coupons with the childrens'. Tudor Hall demanded green serge tunics with beige blouses, knee length green woollen knickers worn with cotton linings, chill-proof vests with sleeves and green coats of fine tweed. Once these items had been bought and the obligatory uniform for Peter's prep school, there were no coupons left for anything else. Of course, as a child, one took these sacrifices for granted: it was part of a natural law that one would have what one needed while the adults went without. Twice a week the evening was devoted to mending, whether at home or at school. There were always fragile seams to be reinforced with bias binding, hems to turn up or let down and dozens of putty-coloured lisle stockings to darn with the help of a wooden mushroom or an egg.

It was back to Tudor Hall for the summer term but to Tudor Hall with a difference. The Pitt-Rivers family had reclaimed Burnt Norton and Miss Inglis had bought an enormous pile, in the best Stockbroker Georgian, near Banbury in Oxfordshire. There were dormitories big enough to accommodate twelve or fifteen girls as opposed to the cosy bedrooms at Burnt Norton. They had high metal radiators on which, in winter, we would dry our streaming handkerchiefs. There was a ballroom large enough to host the local hunt ball, with a sprung floor. Here Mrs. Constable taught us ballroom dancing "go round as though you are kicking up autumn leaves" she would say, as we attempted a slow fox-trot to the piano of Carol Gibbons, or the big band of Glenn Miller. There were numerous bathrooms all made of marble in different colours and in strikingly bad taste. Each opulent whale-sized bath was painted with a black plimsoll line exactly five inches from the bottom. "The King bathes in five inches of water" said Matron "so you must too." There was a swimming pool with chrome fittings and slimy green water; hard tennis courts and an indoor riding school which came with several horses, including an enormous chestnut gelding called

Golden Rod that moved like a rocking horse and scared me out of my wits. There was a resident riding master, Captain Anderton, a creature of superb elegance who wore boots of dazzling brightness and a green pork pie hat. He treated the girls with courteous disdain. We, in my year, were all madly in love with him, down to the last girl. We knew that none of us had a chance of catching his eye, five-foot Halflings in box-pleated skirts. We had seen the girls he approved of, drawling at each other in the stable yard; huge blonde girls with muscular thighs and a good seat on a horse, who hunted with the Quorn or Belvoir Vale and who sailed over enormous fences at the Kidlington point-to-point. He was like a Bronte hero.

We could, however, dream. Dione cut out an advertisement from a magazine. "BE TALLER" it shouted. The only problem was that one had to buy a bottle of snake oil or some such, £5 for a month's supply. Five pounds was to us riches beyond the dreams of avarice. Dione tried again. She wrote to a cousin in South Africa and asked her for some slinky dresses. Day after day we waited for the post, imagining ourselves transformed in the blinking of an eye into Phyllis Calvert or Margaret Lockwood, the pride of Gainsborough Studios.When the parcel finally arrived, we were broken hearted: inside lay a dreadful navy-blue garment made of some stiff canvas-like material, more suited to a footsore *voetganger* than an emergent English vamp. We gave up and decided to forget Captain Anderton and concentrate on our rabbits.

The best part of the new regime was the fact that we were allowed to bring our animals to school. The rich girls brought their ponies the poor girls various small mammals. When the news of this new dispensation reached Black Dog during the Easter holidays I was, at last, able to buy my longed-for rabbit. Her name was Cellophane; she was a cream-and-brown Siamese Sable; I chose her myself in the Frome market. I can remember to this day the feel of her silky-soft, loose skin, her chocolate ears covered in velveteen, but which were surprisingly muscular. I made her a harness out of tape and before long she was tame enough to come for walks, even swim in the pond. I corresponded with Dione; we plotted the coming term.

I put Cellophane into a basket and took her to school on the train; Westbury to Reading changing there and again at Didcot and Swindon, arriving at Banbury some three or four hours later. Dione, when she arrived, had done better than I: she had two rabbits, one black one white, Troilus and Cressida, although both were does. To hell with education! Dione and I were in our glory that summer, fussing obsessively over our rabbits and taking to task anyone who did not in our eyes, in the care of their pets, come up to our exacting standard of animal welfare.

The *ktima* was now in full production. The orchard was heavy with ripening apples; the espalier peaches and nectarines trained against the south-facing walls of the house, glowed orange and rose, even the strawberry grape, growing from an Appomatox cutting, was turning from green to a dusky pink. The soft fruit, in its big bird-proof cage, had already been harvested and filled the Kilner jars in the still room with good things for the winter. In the vegetable garden the early potatoes had already been dug and Sadler had started to build the earthen clamps, which looked like archaic burial mounds, to preserve the main crop of potatoes and other root vegetables for the winter. The asparagus beds had turned into a ferny jungle; the globe artichokes had shot up into blue eight-foot thistles.

In the flower garden the lawn was striped green velvet, and although the magnificence of June was long gone, the long herbaceous borders were glimmering with golden rod, Japanese anemones and the first blue Asters. The tall Michaelmas daisies at the back of the borders were just starting to show signs of the amethyst purples and dark crimsons to come. When Elise Eppes came to stay the following summer, she said it was worth crossing the Atlantic just to see the Black Dog garden.

The compost heaps and the business part of the garden, the cold frames, the stacks of cloches, the bundles of pea sticks, the nets and larger tools, had disappeared behind a neatly clipped beech hedge. Sadler stood guard over his kingdom as proud and proprietorial as though no-one else, particularly a woman, had ever pushed a wheelbarrow or wielded a garden fork.

On August 15th Japan surrendered at last. There was a V.J. celebration in Bath, with fireworks and people dancing in the street. We drove there in Ladybird, our little old Morris Minor. On arrival Peter said "We're not going to need these anymore" and snapped the hoods off the headlights of the car. (These had been obligatory since the beginning of the War as part of the blackout regulations.) We enjoyed the party then turned to drive home. Suddenly the heavens opened and within a moment the lights were extinguished by the downpour. We crept home, twelve miles along narrow country lanes, at five miles an hour. My poor mother was in a state of shock by the time we arrived back at Black Dog. But at least the war was over at last. In August my father came home. Japan had surrendered. He brought with him Major General Yamamoto's ceremonial sword as proof of surrender [4]. He seemed to glow with happiness: he had survived two world wars and untold horrors on the North-West Frontier; his house was still standing; all seemed set fair. Sadler and Acky, products of a deeply conservative and chauvinistic culture, were relieved to have a proper male governor at last. The only person who had reservations was Cherry, now four years old and suddenly dethroned from her position at the centre of everyone's attention, the apple of everyone's eye. When this strange man with a prickly face and smelling of cigarettes came to pick her up and kiss her, she burst into tears.

My father was anxious to make himself part of village life. He went down to the Bell, the local pub, introduced himself to Mr Bartle the globular landlord, and bought drinks for all the regulars. He wanted to integrate himself into the community but also to put down a marker as the governor of Black Dog. He also did everything he was able to, to put himself back at the heart of the family. He bought a lot of records for our wind-up gramophone. He himself adored Sibelius but he thought the children would rather listen to Gilbert and Sullivan. In fact we enjoyed both. He took us to the Theatre Royal in Bath to see the *Gondoliers*.

One summer morning when it was still dark in the nursery I heard my father's voice:

> "Awake! For morning in the bowl of night
> Has flung the stone which puts the stars to flight;
> And lo! The hunter of the East has caught
> The Sultan's turret in a noose of light.
>
> Dreaming while dawn's left hand was in the sky
> I heard a voice within the tavern cry
> "Awake my little ones and fill the cup
> Before life's liquor in the cup be dry.
>
> They say the Lion and the Lizard keep
> The Courts where Janshid gloried and drank deep
> And Bahram, that great Hunter – the wild Ass
> Stamps o'er his head and cannot break his sleep"

"Quick! Into the car" my mother said. "We'll stop for breakfast on the way."

"Where are we going?" I asked.

"Just wait and see."

We drove, not as we thought to Bath or to Weston-Super-Mare (Weston-Super-Mud, we used to call it) as we had anticipated, but the Lake District. After what seemed an eternity of boredom and car sickness we arrived at our farm-house destination. I was entranced by the ridge-backed fells, the black tarns between them, the hillsides golden with bracken, the blue shining surface of Ullswater.

"This is just like the Himalayas" I said.

"I'm afraid not" said my mother sadly. "Nothing can ever be like the Himalayas."

Back at Black Dog my father tried to teach me to shoot. There were always guns in the house, carefully stored in the stillroom well above child level. My father had a pair of beautiful eight bores; my mother had a light rifle which he had given her for a wedding present. There was also a quarter-size shot gun which he wanted me to use. He started by explaining the basic rules; always hold it tight to your shoulder when firing so that the kick does not spin you round; always break your gun when negotiating a stile or a hedge; always clean it and put it away safely after use. He taught me the old rhyme.

> *Never never let your gun*
> *Pointed be at anyone;*
> *If a sportsman you would be*
> *Listen carefully to me;*
> *Not all the pheasants ever bred*
> *Are worth the life of one man dead.*

One day he decided that I was ready for the real thing and took me out into the meadow at dusk. The rabbits were just coming out of their burrows for their evening meal of grass and dandelions. On his direction I stalked one, crawling on my stomach. I shot it. Never again! When I saw its small brown face streaked with blood I was sick with grief and remorse.

On hot summer afternoons, Peter and I would make up a heady mixture of beer and honey which we would then paint onto the trunks of the Lombardy poplars which ran in a long line between the orchard and the road. Once it was dark we would go out with a flashlight and see what our mixture had attracted. There would always be a number of tiny moths with transparent wings and the odd Daddy long legs; sometimes we would be lucky enough to catch a hawk moth, its pale velvet wings, marked with an eye, stretching the width of a small child's hand. This, in its drunken state, we would carefully remove from the tree and place in a glass jar at the bottom of which was a pad soaked in chloroform. Finally our trophy would be placed in a display case and added to the collection made by father when he was a boy at Uppingham, carefully labelled with its name, genus and the date. I feel rotten about this now, but, seventy years ago few people would have thought this a crime, or realised how rare or vulnerable these exquisite creatures were, or how finite their numbers.

It was all too good to last. At the end of September, just as Peter and I were preparing to go back to school, my father was posted to Germany.

CHAPTER EIGHT
<u>NEMONE</u>

It was the autumn of 1946. My father had sent for us: we were going to join him in Germany. He had requisitioned a house in Herford, a small garrison town on the river Weser in the province of North Rhine Westphalia. This is where, as Chief of Intelligence for the British Army of the Rhine, he had set up his headquarters.

"Young Bishop" he wrote to my mother (Michael Bishop was his A.D.C.) "has been doing his stuff and getting things ready for your arrival. The house is very warm, very comfortable but absolutely hideous. It is of the variety described by Hitler in his will as "Zur erhaltunt eines buergerlichen Lebens"– Being necessary to the maintenance of a petit-bourgeois standard of living. This certainly tickled my father's fancy. We were to expect furniture gleaming with chrome and pale veneer and with the bulbous contours that would remind us of Mrs. Stockbroker's choice at Norton Malreward. There was plenty for the children to do, he promised: there was a beautiful park and, as soon as the ice was strong enough to bear us, we would all learn to skate.

When Germany surrendered to the Allies on 7th May 1945, most of Central Europe had been reduced to rubble. A landscape of cinders; it could have been the dark side of the moon. Great cities had been razed to the ground; roads and railways reduced to long miles of craters; bridges bombed to smithereens; the great transcontinental rivers, the Rhine, the Elbe, the Oder, the Danube, the Vistula, made impossible to navigate by the presence of derelict ships and scuttled barges. No Government, no administration, no infrastructure. No industry; little agriculture. No mail, no telephone. No fuel, no light, little food, less hope. Across the Continent moved hundreds of thousands of dispossessed people fleeing from the Tartar hordes. The concentration camps had given up their dead; their half-dead joined the fugitives, the deserters, the refugees and the displaced, in a Westwards pilgrimage of uncertain destination.

In the third year of the War, when America joined Britain as an ally, it was foreseen by Churchill and Roosevelt that, at some time in the future the Allies would have to take over the administration of defeated Germany. Neither foresaw how poisoned the chalice would be from which they had to drink. With ringing optimism the Atlantic Charter (14th August 1941) declared:

"After the final destruction of the Nazi tyranny, they hoped to see established a peace which will afford to all Nations the means of dwelling in safety within their own boundaries, and which will afford assurance that all men in all lands may live out their lives in freedom from fear and want."

The principles of this anticipated urban administration were agreed between Churchill, Roosevelt and Stalin, when the end of the war was in sight, at a meeting that took place at Yalta in February 1945. Each of these great powers, Britain, the U.S.A and the U.S.S.R, were to occupy and administer a separate zone of Germany. The French were to have a zone of their own if they wanted it, provided that it was carved out of the British and American zones. The Soviets were yielding nothing.

They further agreed that their immediate programme for Germany would be as follows:

1. To destroy Nazism and militarism to ensure that Germany would never again disturb the peace of the world;

2. To disarm and disband Germany's armed forces and to break up the General Staff;

3. To remove or destroy all war equipment and to eliminate or control all industry having war potential.

4. To punish war criminals;

5. To exact reparations in kind for the destruction wrought by the Germans;

6. To wipe out the Nazi Party, laws and institutions and to remove Nazi and militaristic influences from public office and from cultural and economic life. (This last requirement was soon given the official but inelegant title 'De-Nazification.')

This was my father's brief when he arrived in Germany in September 1945. The British Army of the Rhine – and later its civilian arm the Control Commission – were already attempting the Herculean task of cleaning the Augean stables. The first priority was to find out what had become of Hitler and his immediate circle.[1] Goering had been captured by the Americans at Karinhall, his country estate in the Schorfheide; Himmler, disguised as a common soldier with a patch over his eye, had walked into a British Control Post, where, during the course of a body search he bit the cyanide capsule concealed in his mouth and after frantic efforts to resuscitate him, died within 30 minutes. It was known that Hitler, with Eva Braun, Martin Borman and the Goebbels family, had spent the last weeks of the war holed up in an underground bunker underneath the Chancellery in beleaguered Berlin, but, when the Russians finally overran the city, exactly what had become of them was unknown.

Those who had a vested interest in Hitler's survival encouraged rumours that he and his entourage had escaped from the besieged city; some said that they were in South America, others that they had found sanctuary with Franco in Spain. The British took the view that this investigation was not only historically important but politically vital. There was already in existence an embryonic resistance, the 'Werewolves', which had to be deprived of its focus. There were a few neo-Nordic romantics who believed that, when the stars were right, the Fuehrer would emerge from his *Götterdämerung* and, with the assistance of his astrologers, re-establish the Empire which would last for a thousand years.

There were those who believed that anything, but anything, was better than Communism. Most important of all was the need to outmanoeuvre the Soviets. It was obvious that the

U.S.S.R. had no intention of relinquishing what it had gained already in Eastern Europe: it seemed likely that it would, in time, push further west, whether by force or by subversion. What better excuse for this could there be than a living breathing Hitler biding his time to rally his forces and make a comeback? It is significant that the bunker beneath the Chancellery where Hitler was last seen was under Russian control, and, while the Soviets had access to eyewitnesses of those last days, they discouraged the British Intelligence Division's investigation and cast doubts upon its conclusions.

My mother received the summons with a mixture of delight and dismay. The happiness she felt at the thought of being reunited with my father was mixed with something akin to stage fright. The isolation of the years in Somerset had robbed her of her social confidence. Having thought that, once and for all, she was rid of gin and bridge parties she imagined that once again she was going to be thrown into a den of Mrs Hawksbees. She had overnight, to transform herself from country mouse into my father's suitable consort.

The most urgent problem was that she had no decent or suitable clothes. All the family clothing coupons had gone into our school uniforms; she had bought nothing for herself for over six years. However, as Scarlett O'Hara (heroine of *Gone with the Wind*) found when she pulled down the drawing room curtains at Tara to make a ball dress, necessity is the mother of invention. She found a length of lace which had been missed by the darzi (tailor) at Roorkee; this made a beautiful evening skirt. We raided the dressing up box for a diamante buckle to put at the waist. As far as underclothes were concerned, I had a sudden inspiration.

Early in the autumn term my school had been given a consignment of parachute silk, no longer needed by the Air Ministry. We had never seen anything as beautiful as those ethereal clouds of shining blue; we fell upon them like parched animals at a water hole, longing to assuage our suppressed femininity. But when push came to shove it was dauntingly difficult to sew: slippery, slithery, the sewing machine could scarcely engage with the glassy surface of the toughened silk. I tried again and with grim determination managed to make some camisoles and petticoats for my mother and myself. They were hardly Janet Reger, but they seemed from a different planet to the sturdy chill-proof vests and knickers in which I had spent my childhood.

A telephone call to Buffy in the United States did the rest. Soon dresses arrived for my mother and basic clothes for Peter and me. Cherry, being so small, had been the only member of the family fit to go into society: her little Viyella dresses lovingly smocked with cats, dogs and ducks by my mother and grandmother, could have taken her anywhere. I packed Cellophane into her basket and she went home with Dione to spend the Christmas holidays with Troilus and Cressida. The Black Dog livestock were entrusted to Acky while Sadler was put on fox watch.

The night before we sailed was spent in my grandmother's flat at Cadogan Court. As we stood in the entrance hall waiting for the lift to take us to the second floor, a little old man in a dark coat and bowler hat stepped out through the metal grille-like gates of the lift.

"That's Sir Geoffrey Lawrence" said the hall porter when he had gone. "E's the one that 'anged them all at Nuremberg." I didn't tell him that I was going to see all that sort of thing for myself, but I felt a sense of great solemnity.

The following day, as the boat train for Harwich puffed its ponderous way under the great cathedral arch of St. Pancras station, smoke from its engine mingling with the thick November fog, I felt my childhood slipping away. I knew that life would never be the same again.

We travelled from Harwich to Cuxhaven in a troop ship requisitioned by the War Office to take the army families to join their men folk in the British Zone. The voyage took the rest of the day and the whole of the following night. Our tiny cabin, like the inside of a tin can, smelled suffocatingly of diesel. What with that stench and the violent motion of the un-stabilized boat, we were all constantly and horribly seasick. To this day a whiff of diesel and I feel the ground move under my feet and my stomach heave.

Arriving at the mouth of the river Elbe in the freezing dawn Cherry sat up in her bunk and said "Look! There's an iceberg outside my window." And so there was, not a large one but an iceberg sure enough. The North Sea was trying to freeze. That winter was to be the coldest since records began. Regularly the temperature dropped to 30 degrees below zero and this was to continue until the following March. We disembarked ashen-faced and hardly able to stand. Then it was six hours in an ice-cold train which smelled of soot, old cigarettes and dirty lavatories. The box-like compartments were lined with plush, but plush which could not have been cleaned since before the war. There was a shiny stripe above each bench exactly where over the years innumerable greasy heads must have rested. We gazed out of the grimy windows over a snow-covered landscape, broken here and there by a group of osiers or a motionless windmill under a lowering, purple sky. As we travelled south and crossed the border from Lower Saxony into North Rhine Westphalia, we started to pass through war-ravaged towns flattened by bombs just as we had seen in Bristol, but where, in the fast-gathering dust not a light could be seen among the wreckage of what had once been homes.

Suddenly we had arrived at Herford. There was my father on the station platform, resplendent in his uniform, his aide-de-camp by his side. What a sorry, scruffy lot we must have appeared. Michael Bishop, the aide-de-camp, raised his supercilious eyebrows and examined his perfect oval-shaped fingernails but my father hugged us all tight. In a moment we were inside his black, elongated motor car, a Maybach, one of a pair so he told us, which had belonged to Himmler, and now requisitioned for his use. In ten minutes we were home. A great blast of warmth enveloped us as we went through the door, as though we had walked from mid-winter into summer. We were overwhelmed by the scent of hothouse flowers, azaleas and cyclamen, and then by the rich taste of hot chocolate. For the first time in my life I heard the pop of Champagne corks and the celebratory clink of glasses. Soon Cherry was asleep in my mother's arms and Peter and I were shown to our beds where we fell asleep under giant eiderdowns like soft white piles of cumulus.

The Yalta Agreement had laid down the principles by which Germany was to be governed. These principles were expanded into detailed edicts by a document agreed by the Joint Chiefs of Staff in April 1945 and referred to thereafter as 'J.C.S. 1067.' It was intended as a guide for the initial post-war period rather than an ultimate statement of policy. However, it remained in force for over two years.

It declared that: 'Germany is to be occupied as a defeated nation under a just, firm and aloof administration which will discourage any fraternisation.'

J.C.S. 1067 was classified as top secret and not published until many months later. General Lucius D. Clay, military governor of the American Zone, wrote "for some months we were carrying out a policy whose existence we could not even admit.".[2] It is ironic that, while fraternisation was forbidden, so many members of the occupied forces managed to marry German girls. The unreality of the policy was demonstrated when, at the Nuremburg trial, it proved impossible to find enough defence counsel who had not been Party members and the de-Nazification rule had to be waived.

I was awakened next morning by a strange white light playing on the ceiling of my bedroom. The blizzard which had threatened on our journey from Cuxhaven had exploded overnight and Herford was shrouded in snow. The daylight appeared to be coming from below rather than from the still lowering sky above. For a time I lay in bed enjoying the unfamiliar enveloping warmth. I could not remember ever awaking except in a freezing cold bedroom during the months of winter at home. One had to count up to five and then dare oneself to get out of bed. At Black Dog there was no heating above stairs so that the windowpanes would be obscured by an intricate tracery of frost ferns and one's breath would hang in the air like smoke before one's face. The only concession to comfort was the hot brick (kept during the day in the bottom oven of the Aga) wrapped in a piece of old blanket which one took, in lieu of a hot water bottle, to one's chilly bed. This German morning I jumped out of bed, dressed myself in my scraps of parachute silk and one of Buffy's American frocks and felt grown up; ready for anything. Great gusts of warm air floated upwards as I made my way down to breakfast.

What a strange breakfast it was: no porridge but great slices of dark red ham and thin pale cheese, dense black pumpernickel, pain au chocolat and a great basket of fruit so perfect that the apples could have been made of wax and the grapes of Venetian glass like those in the dining room at Gilston Road. We children thought this was splendid, but our mother was clearly uneasy. She found the heat suffocating and felt guilty to be the recipient of so much plenty in a world on the edge of famine. She told me later that she hated the hot-house flowers: "Look at those horrible cyclamen" she said, "those colours, shocking pink and magenta, don't exist in nature. Besides, a cyclamen should never be more than two inches high."

We decided to go to the park. "Remember not to fraternise" said my father, half laughing, as he left the house. There was no chance of that. When we arrived, there was already a crowd of German children playing on the swings and on the creaky iron roundabout. As soon as they spotted us they pelted us with snowballs of an extraordinary hardness. Peter pulled one in half; then another, then another. Each contained a stone. We did not stay to argue but beat a hasty retreat to the warm cocoon of our requisitioned house.

Next day we decided to go skating. The river Weser had frozen over. The sun had broken through the clouds and the ice was already covered with skaters of extraordinary skill and elegance. The three of us arrived with our borrowed boots. The houses, with their gables and steeply pitched roofs, the osiers along the riverbank, the happy skaters twisting and turning, their skates hissing on the shining and as yet unblemished ice, could have come from a Brueghel painting. Nervously we crept onto the ice. Immediately our legs flew from under us and we landed on our backsides. None of us could, for more than a moment, stay upright. This was made all the more humiliating by the fact that tiny children were arriving by the pram load, some looking even too young to walk but, once on the ice, skating off with Olympic speed and dexterity. It was when we saw a group of older children each with a snowball, skating towards us, that Peter and I grabbed Cherry, who was already crying with shock and pain, and made for home, back to the cocoon and our *buergerlichen Lebens*

I woke next morning with my face burning hot. I looked in the glass; my reflexion looked back at me, red as a radish. I was mortified. For days I had been wondering vaguely whether the A.D.C. would propose to me: I would turn him down, of course, as I had determined in my heart to remain faithful to Mr Rochester with whom I had fallen desperately in love with when I first read Jane Eyre. Nevertheless, it would have been nice to make that first notch on the barrel of my rifle, something to boast about when I got back to school. Although we had never spoken to each other, I still thought it might have been a shrewd move on his part to marry the boss's daughter. Now it was impossible: how would he even look at a stunted leper whose head hardly came up to his navel? I resolved to stay in my room until I died or at least we went back to England. I took the beloved volume of Jane Eyre down from its shelf and in a moment I was back at Thornfield, sitting by a blazing fire, talking about sewing with dear Mrs. Fairfax, waiting for the master to come home. A four-foot ten governess, poor and plain but with infinite expectations.

Peter meanwhile, practical as ever, took himself off to the barrack square. There he asked my father's driver to teach him to drive. He would have loved to have a go in one of the Maybachs, either the saloon which had collected us from the station or the coupé which Himmler had used for special occasions, but his feet would not have reached the pedals. So he learned in a little old Volkswagen Beetle. By the end of the Christmas holidays he was a proficient driver. Cherry was content to stay indoors with her storybooks, happy in our mother's company.

The days passed quietly. My face did not get better: it got worse. It was not simply red; it was revolting, covered with weeping sores. Finally my mother took me to an Army doctor. He took my chin in his hand and said "You poor little thing." had contracted impetigo. He prescribed me the appropriate medication. My mother said that it must have been that filthy train. I decided to become a nun: in an enclosed order.

After a few days when my face had started to heal, my father decided to take us all in hand. "You did not come here to read the Brontes" he said. We all were wasting our German adventure; we must get out and look around us. He coaxed us into the Maybach and we set out on a tour of the river Ruhr. If there was anything calculated to take one's mind off one's own small troubles and preoccupations, this was it. Düsseldorf, Dortmund, Duisburg, Gelsenkirchen, Essen, cities which had been the heart of the German steel and coal industry; home to Krupps, I.G. Farben, Mercedes Benz; which had provided the Third Reich with its military might; where a million slave labourers had toiled, starved and died, now lay silent, pulverised, flattened under a meagre covering of snow. Imagine Clydeside, Tyne Tees, Barrow-in-Furness and Jarrow drawn into one huge conurbation and the then smashed to pieces in a gargantuan pestle and mortar. Not a sound, not a light, not a sign of life, only a tangle of twisted metal and a mesh of collapsed power cables bore witness to what had once been the mighty Ruhr.

Near Düsseldorf we left the car and stood on the banks of the Rhine. We watched the steel grey water hurrying Northwards with a rush hour flotsam of grinding ice floes pushing one another, colliding, crashing, overtaking, grinding under an iron sky. It seemed that we were the only living things on an extinguished planet. It was as though Armageddon had been and gone and passed us by.

For weeks I had been screwing up my courage to ask the question "Did you see Belsen?"

"No" my father replied. "By the time I arrived it had gone. Flattened: Razed to the ground. There is nothing to show where once it stood. But I tell you a curious thing. One day, shortly before you arrived, I was driving across Luneberg Heath, when suddenly I was overcome by an overwhelming feeling of misery and fear. I told the driver to stop. 'This is the place' I said. I got out of the car. There was nothing there. But it was as though the earth, the sky, the wind were all weeping. Later I looked at the map. I had got the exact spot." We stood in silence. There was nothing to say.[3] Then my father announced "Tomorrow we go to Berlin. Let's see what you make of that."

Every four weeks he had to confer with his opposite numbers in the Allied armies of occupation. Berlin, as the historic Capital of the country was the obvious place for these meetings to be held. It also suited the Soviets. He enjoyed these meetings. He made a friendship which lasted for the rest of his life with the American General Francis Miller. The French he found somewhat prickly and aloof, but he was chuffed that, when the meetings concluded, he could drink his Russian counterpart under the table.

When the victorious Allies had, in April 1945, divided Germany into four zones, each with its own administration, the British had taken control of the North Western area from the Danish border down to Bonn in the south, taking in Hamburg, Bremen and the cities of the Ruhr. To the chagrin of the Americans, we had bagged what remained of Germany's heavy industry. The French, as Johnnies-come-lately to the agreement, had to be content with an hour-glass shaped chunk running from Coblenz in the north to the upper reaches of the Rhine and the Swiss border in the south. The Americans had the Zone 'with all the best views,' running from the Austrian border, taking in Munich and the whole of Bavaria, including Nuremburg and ending at Frankfurt am Main. The Soviets, when sweeping west through Eastern Europe, reducing Poland and the Balkans to satellite status, now occupied a huge wedge from the Baltic coast down to Dresden in the south from where they seemed to glower at Czechoslovakia. Berlin was bang in the middle.

Berlin itself was also divided into four sectors. Looking at the city as if it were a face of a clock, the French had 10 – 12, the Soviets 12 – 6, the Americans 6 – 8 and the British 8 – 10. The Western allies had the three airports, Tempelhof, Gatow and Tegal while the Soviets had a stranglehold on rail and road communications as all transport had to pass through their zone. In the heady days of April and May 1945 the Western Allies took the view that the Soviets were such decent and reasonable fellows that it would be unnecessary, if not downright insulting, to insist upon guaranteed access to the City. By 1948, after ever increasing tension, they came to regret their naiveté. The Soviets cut off all communication with the West and Berlin became an island marooned in the middle of the Russian zone. Hence the necessity for the Berlin Airlift.

It was bitterly cold the morning we set out for Berlin, so cold that children were skating on the glass-like surface of the autobahn. We were forced to drive two hundred kilometres with the near side wheels on the frost-crackling grass verge. In England at that time the first motorway was only a glint in the planners' eyes. Here the autobahn, Hitler's most positive contribution to civil engineering, bisected Germany from the Ruhr to Berlin. We had never seen anything like it: this huge main road on top of its embankment towering above the frozen meadows and bypassing the gabled villages with their copper roofed churches turned to verdigris. Away to the left a sign marked the turn off to Hameln, in English Hamelin.

Hamelin Town's in Brunswick,
Near famous Hanover city;
The river Weser, deep and wide,
Washes its wall on the southern side;
A pleasanter spot you never spied;

"It's not in Brunswick. It's in North Rhine Westphalia" I said to no one in particular, correcting Browning. I must have been feeling better. I was back to my usual know-it-all self. At this point Peter joined in:

Rats! They fought the dogs and killed the cats,
And bit the babies in the cradles,
And ate the cheeses out of the vats,
And licked the soup from the cooks' own ladles,
Split open the kegs of salted sprats,
Made nests inside men's Sunday hats,

And even spoiled the women's chats,
By drowning their speaking
With shrieking and squeaking
In fifty different sharps and flats.

The British Zone ended and the Russian began at Helmstedt, a bleak border post surrounded by razor wire and capped with search lights and a watch tower. Russian sentries wearing ankle-length great coats and armed to the teeth approached the car.

"This will take some time" said my father. My mother took us to the makeshift N.A.A.F.I. canteen while he and the driver remained in the car to deal with the formalities. There was only one type of hot drink on offer, a concoction so vile that none of us could decide whether it was tea, coffee or Bovril. It was so disgusting that it has passed into family legend. We were happy however to stretch our legs and stamp our frozen feet.

It was mid-afternoon when we entered the city of Berlin, but the desolate greyness of the place made it seem much later. The dark, threatening sky, pregnant with more snow to come, the dark ruined streets stretched before us in spectral monochrome. What had not been bombed or shelled into fragments had either been removed to Russia as agreed reparations or had been looted by the soldiers of the Red Army. Everything not actually nailed to the floor had been taken or smashed. Among the piles of rubble moved an army of female scarecrows, each wearing the headscarf knotted high on the forehead, which had become the hideous uniform of the age. Each carried a hammer with which she cleared the broken bricks of mortar, piling those which were worth saving into neat stacks.

My father said "They're the *trümmerfrauen,* the rubble women. They are the only people doing anything practical towards the reconstruction of their city. With luck they'll be finished in a thousand years."

When General Eisenhower halted his advance fifty miles from Berlin and allowed the Soviets to sweep into the city, it was seen by many in the West as a courteous gesture made in recognition of the terrible suffering of the Russian people under Nazi occupation.

"We'll meet in Dresden" Stalin had told him. Churchill alone recognised that this was a tactical disaster. Eisenhower, however, was not open to argument. He could not grasp the historic and strategic importance of Berlin. Decades earlier Lenin had said "He who has Berlin has Germany and he who has Germany has Europe."

At a time, when Stalin was affectionately known as 'Uncle Joe' and regarded as an affable old ruffian, few realised the madness of allowing him to establish himself in the German capital from which, at his leisure, he could plot his thrust into the heartlands of central Europe.

By ancient tradition a victorious army was permitted to sack any city which held out to the last. This is exactly what the Soviets did to Berlin. While the first wave of invaders were correct in every particular, almost as though they had been brought up on the Geneva Convention, the second waive was a rabble. When Milovan Djilas had, in 1944, taken Stalin to task over the atrocities committed by the Red Army troops in Yugoslavia (which was supposed to be the Soviets' ally) the old villain had said "If a soldier has marched thousands of kilometres through blood, earth and fire why can he not have some fun with a woman and take a few trifles?" The Soviet High Command had absorbed this philosophy and did nothing to curtail the excesses of a 'brutal and licentious soldiery.' They had arrived as liberators but within days had lost the hearts and minds of the Berliners. Rape, robbery and mindless destruction were the order of the day. From April 1945 to the fall of the Berlin wall the liberated were governed not by consensus but by the most brutal repression. There was little to choose between the old tyranny and the new.

"I like the Berliners" my father said "They're quite different from anyone else in Germany. They're strong-minded, independent and have a ripping sense of humour very much like the Cockneys, quite unlike the rest of these carnivorous sheep." We had drawn up outside a suburban house which somehow had survived the bombardment. It had been requisitioned for a British family and was the house in Herford all over again: outside, the desolation; inside, the familiar suffocating bourgeois comfort. That evening we went to the Opera. Our host, Colonel Wise, had got us tickets for *La Traviata*. "One good thing the Russians have done" said my father "is to kick start the musical life of the city. The Berlin Philharmonic is still going great guns under a lunatic called Celibidache. He looks as mad as a March hare with his hair standing on end, but he conducts Sibelius as you have never heard him conducted. Poor old Furtwängler is undergoing de-Nazification, which seems a bit unfair. Although he stayed on under Hitler, he saved a lot of Jewish musicians from the concentration camps."

The original Berlin opera house had been destroyed by bombs. The State Opera was now housed in the Admiralspalast, formerly a variety theatre. This had been restored by the Soviets (before a brick had been laid for civilian housing) in a lavish Second Empire style in order to give them credibility in the eyes of the world as upholders of culture and civilisation.

The Maybach glided through the Brandenburg gate into the Russian sector. The streets were dark and as desolate as ever, but decorated here and there with enormous posters of Stalin to remind us, if it were necessary, that he was the Fuehrer now. Inside the opera house the auditorium was resplendent with gold cherubs and sunbursts, with crystal chandeliers, red plush velvet seats and great swagged curtains. It was packed; as there was no heating everyone sat in their overcoats and a strong musty smell arose from the hundreds of closely-packed bodies. I sat next to a Russian soldier; I smiled at him and tried to engage his attention; he looked at me as though I was a worm.

Erna Berger sang Violetta. When she made her grand entrance in Act 1, down a long white marble staircase, she was wearing a red satin crinoline decorated with rubies and holding in her hand a glass of red wine which matched exactly the colour of that marvellous dress. I was transfixed. I had never in my life seen or heard anything so miraculous. For years afterwards Alfredo and Violetta haunted my dreams. Why couldn't they marry? Why was Monsieur Germont so beastly to them? Then why did he change his mind? It was for me the beginning of another life-long passion.

For the next couple of days my father was occupied with quadripartite matters of state. Given the choice between watching the *trummerfrauen* at their chilly labours or sitting in the warm cocoon of Colonel Wise's house day-dreaming of gold cherubs and wine-red satin and hearing again in my head that astonishing music, I chose the latter. No contest. I forgot Black Dog; I even forgot Thornfield and Mr. Rochester. I swanned through the salons of the Second Empire pondering the conundrums of class and chastity. <u>Class</u> was a matter which troubled us as a family very little: we were confident; we knew exactly where we came from and where we stood. It was boring having so little money but there are many things worse than that. The great estates acquired by the monastery robbers under Henry VIII, the fortunes amassed by the Victorian industrialists or twentieth-century arms dealers were all beyond the pale. When my cousin Eva Lethbridge said that a man was "in trade" she might just as well have said that he was a cannibal or a Sodomite. As far as <u>chastity</u> was concerned, for a girl in the 1940s the exhortation "not until you're married" was taken as read. But I had been reading about these poor girls whose fathers had died in the Napoleonic wars and who accordingly could never marry as they had no dowries. What were they to do? It seemed that they were accorded a place in Society and a certain respect; they were allowed their lovers, their jewels and extravagances, and, if pretty enough like Violetta, might just become the toast of Paris. The only thing a gentleman could not do was introduce one to his wife. Well – was that really such a loss? Really, what was Monsieur Germont fussing about? It was years before I read *La Dame aux Camellias* (of which *La Traviata* is the sanitised version) and realised what an embarrassment, what a handful, the heroine (there called Marguerite) was. For the first time I understood the extent of the problem.

My reverie was broken by my father. "Tomorrow is our last day in Berlin. We are not going to waste it. I am going to show you something which probably no other English children have seen. I am going to take you to the place where Hitler died". So it was back into the Maybach; back through the Romanesque pillars of the Brandenburg gate – amazingly still standing in the middle of the desolation – back through the mean streets of the Russian sector under the beady eye of Uncle Joe. I was thinking to myself that I had really had enough of bombed buildings but when we arrived at the Reich Chancellery I could see that this place was different. It was absolutely huge. Outside there was the usual tangle of razor wire and a sullen huddle of Red Army soldiers; inside one could see that, although the roof was gone and many of the walls, enough remained to enable one to see the ground plan. The Chancellery must have been the size of a small cathedral.

Albert Speers' monster was seven-hundred and twenty-five feet long. Hitler gave him twelve months to complete the project from start to finish. It was completed on 8th January 1939; two days short of the deadline. Hitler had told Speer that no expense was to be spared and the building was, accordingly, filled with marble, porphyry and mosaic, most of which ended up incorporated in a Soviet war memorial. "Hitler was particularly impressed by my gallery" wrote Speer in his memoir.[4] "because it was twice as long as the Hall of Mirrors at Versailles ... to be sure it was architecture that revelled in ostentation and aimed at startling effects. But that sort of thing existed in the baroque period too – it has always existed."

Hitler was delighted: "On the long walk from the entrance to the reception hall they'll get a taste of the power and grandeur of the German Reich!" he told his architect. On September 9th 1939 Hitler had addressed the construction workers of the site.

"Why always the biggest?" he said "I do this to restore to each German his self-respect. In a hundred areas I want to say to each individual "We are not inferior, on the contrary, we are the complete equal of every nation."

After the usual stupidities over leave to enter, we picked our way through the rubble and into the enormous study where Hitler used to hold court, sitting behind a marble desk the size of a billiard table. This had been smashed into a thousand brown- and tomato-coloured pieces. Souvenir hunters, we pocketed a chunk; Peter has it to this day at his farm in Devon. "I really would have liked his lavatory chain" said my father sadly "but someone had already bagged it when I arrived."

Everything of value was gone. The metal filing cabinets lay on the floor smashed open; their contents had either been destroyed before the Red Army arrived or subsequently removed to Russia. Of the two possibilities the former is more likely: of the vast mass of documents exhibited at the Nuremburg trial the bulk had been retrieved by the Western Allies as they advanced eastwards. The Soviets, horribly adept at obtaining confessions, did not comprehend the importance of documents as evidence. There were, they considered, easier ways of obtaining a conviction.

A gargantuan chandelier had crashed to the middle of the floor and lay there like some grotesque metallic octopus, its huge tentacles forever frozen in the rigor mortis of death. Moving closer, one could see that it had been made, not of ormolu and crystal, but of some base metal painted gold.

"It's symbolic of the whole Nazi regime isn't it?" said my father. "It must have looked quite impressive thirty feet up and sparkling with lights, but now you can see it for what it is: cheap, bogus and nasty."

We wondered why Hitler, who had the art treasures of Europe within his grasp (or at least in Goering's castle) put up with something so hideous.

"Maybe he liked it" said Peter.

A few yards from the perimeter of the Chancellery stood a low concrete structure, undamaged by bomb or shell. It looked like an enlarged coal bunker or boiler room. At one corner rose a twelve-foot pepper pot, cement grey and streaked with soot and dirt.

"This was added to prevent anyone pouring poison gas into the ventilator shaft" said my father. "There must have been plenty of people who were tempted to do just that." Opposite stood an iron door like the one that may be seen on an old fashioned safe, but twice the size. "This is our final port of call" he said "this is where the most loathsome regime the world has ever known came to its squalid and ignoble end." He rattled the door. "Damn" he said. "Bloody thing's locked. Bishop, be a good fellow and find somebody with a key."

We stood in the rubble, our breath drifting like smoke in front of us in the bitter air. I wished that I was anywhere else in the world; I shut my eyes and imagined myself in the kitchen at Black Dog, warming my back against the Aga and breathing in the spicy aroma of gingerbread gently baking in the bottom oven.

Then the keys arrived with a surly posse and were grudgingly handed to my father. Michael Bishop gave each one of us a torch. Slowly, the heavy doors swung open. There was an exhalation of foul air as though an ogre below had belched in his sleep. Ten years later that smell hit me with a stab of recognition as, for the first time, I watched an usher at the Old Bailey cut open a bag of blood-stained exhibits, polluting the air with the foetid aroma of sudden death. The colour drained from my mother's face. "Jack" she said "do you really think this is a suitable..."

"No I don't, not really. But I still think they shouldn't miss the chance of seeing a bit of history." "Well I'm going to wait in the car with Cherry."

Inside, the bunker was as black as pitch. Cautiously, with the aid of the torches, we made our way down a short flight of concrete steps, then sharp left into another corridor and down another flight of steps. On the left was a row of rooms which my father unlocked one by one; they seemed to have been kitchens or storerooms and everything of value or use had been looted or smashed. Then, passing through a bulkhead, we entered a wide passage with doors on each side. My father unlocked them too; they appeared to have been servants' quarters but, as we had come to expect, the contents of each had been smashed to pieces or removed. The last two doors were, as usual, locked; my father could not find keys to fit them on the bunch. "Maybe it's just as well" he said, "These must have been the rooms where Frau Goebbels and her children had their quarters."

"You mean there were *children* down here?" I asked.

"Yes. Six of them. The Goebbels killed them all."
"Their own children?"
"Yes indeed."
"Why did they have to do that?"
"Maybe they didn't want them to fall into the hands of the Russians."
"Did they think they'd go to heaven?"
"The Goebbels didn't believe in heaven" my father said. "They believed in historical necessity, whatever that is."

We came to a spiral staircase leading down. "Are you game?" asked my father.

"Of course," Peter and I replied trying hard to sound as though we meant it. There was no banister; we crept down, our hands on the outside wall. Now we could hear the drip-drip of water: We were so deep underground that the 30 degrees of frost had failed to penetrate the subsoil and foul water was liberated from its icy hibernation. Another row of locked doors, each opening to reveal the usual scene of destruction. The last to be opened contained nothing but a sofa, unvandalised and covered with pale patterned velveteen and defiled by a terrible brown stain. My father slammed the door and locked it firmly.

The passage was now awash with filthy water. I could feel it seeping through the soles of my boots. "Oh my God" I thought to myself "this is Bluebeard's castle. Please don't let him find any more keys." I saw that someone had dumped in the middle of the passage. "Can we go now?" I pleaded.

"Yes" said my father "I think we have seen enough." Back along the passage; up the spiral stairs, the sound of dripping water receding behind us. Along the labyrinthine passages, up two more flights of stairs and finally, our hearts pounding, we were out at last into the cold sweet afternoon air.

For twelve years Hitler had lived in a capsule of flattery and adulation. His charm was so great; his rages so terrifying, that no one dare tell him what he did not wish to hear. One example of this should suffice. In October 1941, after the initial success of the Russian campaign, Hitler announced that, for all practical purposes the war was over.

"The Russians no longer exist" he claimed. "The Russian Bear is dead."

When figures relating to Soviet tank production were shown to him, he flew into such a monumental rage that the figures were quietly buried. He went on to order the dissolution of forty divisions of the Army, the return of manpower to industry and the curtailment of armament production. No one had the courage, or the temerity, to advise him that these actions might be premature.

Hitler's psychiatric state was not assisted by the ministrations of his personal physician, an unscrupulous quack called Dr. Morell, who for the last two years had been treating him for stomachache with a patent medicine compounded of strychnine and belladonna. The patient swallowed it in enormous quantities. By the last year of the war, he was not only mentally unhinged but physically wrecked: a condition akin to Parkinson's disease made him tremble constantly and violently; one foot dragged behind him; his voice was hoarse and rasping; his hypnotic blue-grey eyes covered with a constant film of moisture. Yet he had lost none of his mesmeric power to charm, terrify and control those around him. They had adopted his bizarre view of reality and made it their own.

Goebbels, Hitler's Minister for Propaganda, was sure that the Reich would be saved at the eleventh hour by some miracle still being plotted in the stars. It was on the night of Friday 13th April 1945, when Berlin was held in an ever-tightening garrotte of armies approaching from every side and the centre of the city was ablaze from an R.A.F. bombing raid, that Goebbels heard the news of President Roosevelt's death. Immediately he telephoned Hitler in the bunker.

"My Fuehrer" he said "I congratulate you! Roosevelt is dead! It is written in the stars that the second half of April will be the turning point for us. This is it." His secretary, Frau Inge Haberzettel, who was present, says that Goebbels was "in an ecstasy".[5] The stars however did not move as predicted. Before the month was out the Third Reich lay in ruins, the puppet master and his puppets either disappeared or dead.

The 20th April 1945 was Hitler's birthday. The usual suspects, the old guard Nazis, Goebbels, Goering, Himmler, Ribbentrop and Borman gathered to wish the Fuehrer many happy returns of the day. They were joined by the Chief of the Army General Staff. These last screwed up their courage to tell Hitler that the situation was now so grave that he should leave Berlin at once and set up a new headquarters at Obersalzburg in the South where there was still a sizeable concentration of German troops. This suggestion Hitler received with blank incomprehension. He agreed, however, that Grand Admiral Doenitz should be despatched to the North to take command of the rump of the Army at Plön in Schleswig-Holstein. On his own future, however, he prevaricated. He could not believe that the proud capital of the Reich could fall to the Red Army which previously he had announced was finished. Others, however, made good their escape; Goering, characteristically, leaving with a motor caravan stuffed with looted works of art.

Of the inner circle only Goebbels with his wife, six young children and Martin Borman remained. They had been joined a few days before by Eva Braun, Hitler's mistress of twelve years. She saw more clearly than her lover the reality of the situation and came to share his end. Hitler, meantime, back in somnambulist mode, busied himself organising a counter-attack against the Soviets in the southern suburbs of Berlin. He put an S.S. General, Felix Steiner, in command and demanded hourly progress reports. The counter-attack never took place. Steiner commanded an army of ghosts.

When at last Hitler grasped the reality of this fact and Russian shells started to fall in the Chancellery garden, he went ballistic. "Everyone has deceived me! No one has told me the truth" he shrieked "the Armed Forces have lied to me!" Obergruppenfuehrer Gottlieb Berger, chief of the S.S. head office, was present at this outburst which he described in evidence at Nuremburg; "His face went bluish purple, I thought that he was going to have a stroke at any minute……. His hand was shaking, his leg was shaking and all he kept shouting was "Shoot them all! Shoot them all!"

Worse was to come. Not only had the majority of the old guard deserted him but now two key members were to stab him in the back. The first of these was Goering, who by a decree made earlier, had been named as Hitler's successor designate. From the relative safety of Obersalzburg he sent a telegram:

"My Fuehrer!
In view of your decision to remain in the fortress of Berlin, do you agree that I take over at once the total leadership of the Reich, with full freedom of action at home and abroad as your deputy, in accordance with your decree of June 29th 1941? If no reply is received by 10 o'clock tonight, I shall take it for granted that you have lost your freedom of action and shall consider the conditions of your decree as fulfilled....
Your loyal
Hermann Goering."

Hitler did indeed reply but not in the terms which Goering had expected. The telegram he sent informed Goering that he had committed high treason for which the penalty was death. However, because of his long service to the Nazi party and the State, his life would be spared if he immediately resigned all his offices. This was not enough for Borman, who had long detested Goering. Of his own notion and without reference to Hitler, he fired off a telegram to the S.S. headquarters at Berchtesgaden ordering the immediate arrest of Goering and his staff for high treason. It was only the arrival of the American forces that saved them all from summary execution.

Meanwhile Himmler had arrived at Lübeck on the Baltic coast. From the Swedish Consulate in this ancient Hanseatic port the Swedish diplomat Count Bernadotte had long been attempting to negotiate a cessation of hostilities. "The Fuehrer's great life is drawing to a close" Himmler announced. "You are to contact General Eisenhower and inform him of Germany's willingness to surrender." He then made the bizarre suggestion that the Western allies should join the Reich and make common cause against the Soviet Union.

These extraordinary negotiations could not long be kept under wraps. On 28th April Reuters dispatch from Stockholm broke the story. This to Hitler was the unkindest cut of all that "der treue Heinrich" – the faithful Himmler- should have deserted him was incomprehensible. He was the one member of the inner circle whose loyalty, whose robot-like consistency Hitler had never doubted. His face, an eye-witness said "became ashen white then rose to a heated red so that his face became virtually unrecognisable." He launched into the usual tirade of vituperation while those present cursed, wept and wailed obediently. Then he ordered that Hermann Fegelein, the S.S. General who had diplomatically married Eva Braun's sister and who was thought to be rather too close to Himmler, to be taken into the garden and shot. After that he seemed to feel rather better and withdrew with Goebbels and Borman into another room to confer.

Eva Braun made no effort to save her brother-in-law: "Poor, poor Adolf" she said "deserted by everyone, betrayed by all. Better that ten thousand die than he be lost to Germany."

This last betrayal forced Hitler into decisive mode. That night he married Eva Braun so that she could achieve in death what had so long eluded her in life: status, respectability and recognition. He also dictated two wills, one political and one personal. The political document began with the re-writing of history, continued with grandiose exhortations to the German people, the expulsion of Goering and Himmler from the Nazi party and concluded with the denunciation of "International Jewry." The personal will, a less predictable document, contained the following apologia:

> "Although during the years of struggle I believed that I could not undertake the responsibility of marriage, now, before the end of my life, I have decided to take as my wife the woman who, after many years of true friendship, came to this city already almost besieged, of her own free will in order to share my fate, she will go to her death with me at her own wish as my wife. This will compensate us both for what we lost through my

work in the service of my people."

His Executor, Martin Borman, was directed "to hand over to my relatives everything that is of value as a personal memento or is necessary for maintaining a petit-bourgeois standard of living."

Three copies of the will were signed and witnessed. They were sent out by messengers travelling as best they might through the Soviet lines, on foot. Two copies were destined for Admiral Doenitz at Plön, the third was addressed to Field Marshall Schoerner, still holding out near Obersalzburg. None of them reached their destination. One copy was burned in the forest by its bearer; the second was secreted in a locked trunk in Bavaria, the third was buried in a bottle in a garden at Iserlohn in Westphalia. It was this copy which was discovered by the British Intelligence Division and thence passed into the public domain.

On the afternoon of 29th April, Hitler received the news of the death of the Italian dictator Mussolini and his mistress Clara Petacci, executed by Italian partisans while trying to escape to Switzerland. The grisly details of their execution and the exhibiting of their bodies in Milan were not made public until after Hitler himself had died: nevertheless, the very fact that they had met their deaths at the hands of their enemies seemed to have stiffened resolution to take matters into his own hands. It seems that Franz Goebbels, Minister of Propaganda ('spin', as we would call it today) who choreographed the gruesome circus of Hitler's life was now called in to orchestrate the bizarre pantomime of his death.[6] On 30th April at 2.30 pm Erich Kempka, Hitler's chauffeur, was ordered to obtain and deliver to the Chancellery garden 200 litres of petrol in jerry cans. He had great difficulty in obtaining so much under the siege conditions which prevailed but eventually managed to obtain 180 litres. These were brought to the emergency exit of the bunker, in readiness for the Viking funeral. Meanwhile all but a skeleton staff were dismissed.

Inside the bunker Hitler and his bride said farewell to the inner circle of collaborators. Only Frau Goebbels did not attend and remained in her room. (Speer later described her as in a state of near collapse and suffering from a series of heart attacks at the imminent prospect of the death of her children. Earlier she had told Hanna Reitsch, the woman test pilot who had flown in a few days earlier at Hitler's request and who lived to sell her story to an English newspaper, "When the end comes you must help me if I become weak about the children. They belong to the Third Reich and to the Fuehrer and if these too cease to exist there can be no further place for them." The six children were aged from twelve to three years old.

Having said their goodbyes, Hitler and Eva Braun retired to their suite. Goebbels and Borman waited outside. A single shot was heard. After a few minutes they entered the room. Hitler's body was sprawled on the sofa, covered with blood.[7] His bride sat beside him her legs tucked up under her on the sofa, her head on his shoulder. She had swallowed poison.

The bodies, Hitler's wrapped in a blanket to conceal the damage to his head, were carried by S.S. personnel up to the garden. There they were laid side-by-side, drenched in petrol from the jerry cans and set alight. The mourners stood to attention, gave the Hitler salute, returned to the bunker and dispersed. The bodies burned for several hours, S.S. men from time to time pouring more petrol on to the pyre. Sometime that night what remained of the bodies were buried in a bomb crater in the garden.

Goebbels lived one more day. During that period Admiral Doenitz was informed by telegram of Hitler's death and his own appointment as successor. At 10.20 pm on 1st May, Doenitz announced over Radio Hamburg, accompanied by the slow movement of Bruckner's Seventh Symphony, "The Fuehrer fell this afternoon fighting at the head of his troops." This, the assertion that the Fuehrer had died a heroic soldier's death, was the last piece of spin to be produced by Goebbels, the master of mythology.

His mission complete nothing remained for him but to ensure that his unfortunate wife and children followed their master into oblivion. Sometime that night the children, Hela, 12; Hilda,

11; Helmut, 9; Holde, 7; Hedda, 5 and Heide, 3 were put to death. When the Russians arrived at the bunker they found the bodies of the children lying in bed. They were taken to Russia for post-mortem examination. It appeared that they had been sedated with morphine and then killed by cyanide poisoning. The face of Hela, the eldest child, was badly bruised. She must have resisted her executioner. In 1959, in court proceedings, Dr Helmut Kunz, an SS dentist who had been brought in to put down Blondie, Hitler's dog, described how he and Dr Ludwig Stumpfegger, an SS physician, had killed the children on the direct order of their mother.

The childrens' remains were later cremated and ashes thrown into the river Elbe.

Next, side by side, the Goebbels ascended the concrete stairway into the Chancellery garden. There they were shot in the head by an S.S. Orderly. Four jerry cans of petrol remained from Hitler's funeral; these were poured over the bodies and set alight. It was insufficient to do more than char the bodies which were left alone and unburied as the survivors in the bunkers made good their escape.

This was the story my father told us on the long drive back along the autobahn to Westphalia. As we entered Herford he said "You know I had grave doubts about publishing Hitler's will. Some of it had a kind of crazy nobility about it which I was afraid might appeal to the carnivorous sheep."

"What's wrong with these people?" I asked him.

"What's wrong with them is that they never had the benefit of the Roman occupation. When Augustus lost his legions pushing towards the Elbe in 8A.D. the German tribes went back into the trees and didn't re-emerge for over 1,000 years."

That night I went to bed at 8 o'clock. I was asleep the moment my head touched the pillow. I woke at midnight feeling as though something terrible had happened, the ammoniac stench of that hideous place still in my nostrils. I could not stop thinking about the Goebbels' children. I got out of bed and went to the top of the stairs. Downstairs I could hear the murmur of voices. My parents were talking about the plot of 20th July 1944:

the attempt by high-ranking army officers to murder Hitler and the dreadful consequences of its failure. My father was saying "They hanged him from a meat hook with piano wire and made a film of him dying." I had heard more than enough. I went to bed and put my head under the bed clothes my hands over my ears. "I don't want to live in this world anymore" I said "Unless I can be a child again."

> *Happy those early days! when I*
> *Shined in my angel infancy.*
> *Before I understood this place*
> *Appointed for my second race,*
> *… O, how I long to travel back,*
> *And tread again that ancient track!*
> *That I might once more reach that plain*
> *Where first I left my glorious train,*
> *From whence the enlightened spirit sees*
> *That Shady City of palm trees.*
> *… Some men a forward motion love;*
> *But I by backward steps would move,*
> *And when this dust falls to the urn,*
> *In that same state I came, return.*

CHAPTER NINE
NEMONE

For several weeks I wandered round in a daze, trying to make sense of what I had learned. Everything had a sense of unreality, as when after a long night by a hospital bed – in a nightclub even – one emerges suddenly out of the dark into the dazzling sunlight of early morning. The young nurses coming off the nightshift, the stragglers making their way to find a coffee shop after a night of debauchery, even a passing dustcart, take on a surreal quality halfway between hallucination and dream. Brought up, as I had been, in a gentle discipline based on reason, cause and effect, I could not comprehend a system where reason had been thrown out of the window and the antilogic of the lunatic asylum prevailed. I was conscious too, of a sense of evil so real that it was almost palpable. It was as though one was locked permanently in one of those terrible nightmares of early childhood, with a monster snuffling his way round the corners of a darkened room.

There was a Christmas party in the officers' mess at Herford for all the children of the service personnel; an ugly Christmas tree crudely dressed with coloured baubles and hung with tinsel like a barrow boy's stall. The fathers had learned and rehearsed a German nursery song (a kind of child's guide to the orchestra in which each instrument played a solo part):

Ich bin ein Musikante	Oh, I am a musician
Und komm' aus Schwabenland;	And come from Swabia.
Wir sind auch Musikanten	We also are musicians
Und komm'n aus Schwabenland.	And come from Swabia.

Ich kann auch blasen,	I too can blow
Wir könn'n auch blasen.	We too can blow
Die Trompete. Die Trompete.	The trumpet, the trumpet
Teng tentereng, teng tentereng,	Ta ratatata, ta ratatata
Teng tentereng, teng tentereng,	Ta ratatata, ta ratatata
Teng tentereng, teng tentereng,	Ta ratatata, ta ratatata
Teng tentereng, ten teng.	Ta ratatata, ta ta.

My father took the part of the *"Dudelsackpfeifer"* the bagpiper, which we found hilarious. All the children joined in the chorus. Then we sang *Silent Night* for which we had specially learned the German words. It sounded so beautiful and mysterious that I resolved to learn the German language as soon as I got back to school.

Stille Nacht, heilige Nacht,
Alles schläft; einsam wacht
Nur das traute hochheilige Paar.
Holder Knabe im lockigen Haar,
Schlaf in himmlischer Ruh!
Schlaf in himmlischer Ruh!

Suddenly it was time to home to England. My father decided to spare us the train: his driver was to take us to Cuxhaven to join the boat. The luggage was loaded into the Maybach and we went back into the house to thank the staff and say our goodbyes. When we came out ten minutes later we found that the boot had been jemmied open and everything was gone: all our Christmas presents including Cherry's longed for dolls' house, Buffy's beautiful American dresses, everything. My father was enraged, my mother philosophic: "These poor people have so much less than we do" she said. We children howled.

At Cuxhaven, as the ship drew away from the waterfront into the bitter, grinding ice flows of the North Sea, Hitler and his hobgoblin court; Goebbels the *spinmiester*, the malevolent dwarf; Goering the voluptuary, dressed in a Roman toga, his toenails painted scarlet, his head adorned with the antlers of St. Hubertus, crowned, not with a crucifix but with a swastika encrusted with diamonds; Himmler, the wall-eyed automaton; the slimy and manipulative Borman, at that time still unaccounted for, gradually receded to the back of my mind.[1] Slowly they were replaced by the comforting images of my darling grandmother, of Cellophane and Dione, Acky and Sadler.

Yet, as we approached the low coastline of East Anglia, I was filled, almost against my will, with a great regret. I wished that we did not, so soon, have to leave Germany. I saw again in my mind's eye those frosty landscapes, the frozen river fringed with osiers, the little churches with their copper roofs where I imagined Bach conducting his cantatas. I could hear, in my mind's ear, that music: so confident, rational and sane and yet transcendent, ineffable, so that, if anything in this world had the power to do so, I knew that it could heal the broken heart of Europe.

We never returned to Germany. My father was eager that we should go back in the Easter holidays, but my mother had so bad a conscience about living off the fat of the land whilst so many starved that she resolved never to return. She won the argument. She was not alone in her feelings of guilt. Lady Churchill and the Duchess of Athlone wrote a letter to *The Times*.

> "Sir,
> The undersigned wish to protest against the policy of allowing the wives of British officers and officials to join their husbands serving in Germany. This allows many to lead lives of luxury which are not only in crass contrast to what the occupied people have to bear, but also to the wartime of austerity of our lives in Britain ... We ask our Government to put a stop to this."

My mother's decision was hard for my father to bear but separation had become so woven into the fabric of their marriage that he accepted it with his usual stoicism.

That winter, the winter of 1946-7, was the toughest the British people had yet endured. Even at the height of the Battle of the Atlantic, when German submarines decimated the convoys bringing vital supplies across the ocean, the shortage of food and fuel was not as severe as when the war ended. The reason for this was the termination, on V.J. Day, of Lend-Lease.

President Roosevelt, a visionary internationalist, realised that at some stage America would have to enter the war. He had first, however, to convince his electorate, still licking its wounds after the recession and having no desire to re-engage with the ugly mess that was Europe. He understood also that Great Britain could not continue to go it alone: however indomitable the spirit of the people, they needed supplies, above all they needed armaments. Lend-Lease was devised and the necessary laws enacted during the winter of 1940-1 before the Japanese attack on Pearl Harbour put an end to all prevarication. "This was a great promise for the future: Great Britain would not fail for lack of dollars ..."[2]

The President explained to his electorate that the primary purpose of Lend-Lease was defence of the American (rather than the British) people. It was obviously in America's interest that the British should be supported in their struggle. Lend-Lease would not be used to maintain Great Britain as an industrial power: indeed after representations from American captains of industry, restrictions on British exports were put in place, "for fear of outcry from American competitors". Thanks to this, Great Britain virtually ceased to be an exporting country. She sacrificed her post-war future for the sake of the war.[3]

While the principal aim of the scheme was the manufacture of armaments, an ancillary, but immediate, result was the arrival of extra food in Great Britain. When President Truman, who lacked Roosevelt's international vision and who was, in many ways, an old-fashioned isolationist, terminated Lend Lease on V.J. Day, shortages really hit home. For the first time bread was rationed; coal was sold by the lump or weighed by the pound like potatoes. Petrol became almost unobtainable for private purposes. Rationing did not finally come to an end until 1952.

The position of civilians in Germany was infinitely worse. Over the winter of 1945-6 in Berlin alone more than

60,000 people–mostly the very old and the very young - died of starvation or cold, my father told me. A member of the Control Commission wrote home "The situation of the poor in Berlin is absolutely terrible. While the rich can buy anything – at a price – imagine spending the winter in a flat without heat, without carpets, with cardboard replacing glass in the windows, with nothing but potato soup for Christmas dinner".[4]

Meanwhile the Soviets took their revenge on their former occupiers by conspicuous guzzling, as did the French. General de Lattre de Tassigny, the French Military Governor, lived in his requisitioned chateau near Baden Baden like an Oriental nabob: "Distinguished visitors were greeted with ceremonial guards of Algerian cavalry bearing lighted torches and given banquets or operatic performances".[5] The British and Americans at least had the grace to import their rations from home but, nevertheless, the contrast between their lifestyle and that of the occupied Germans was grotesque.

Back at Tudor Hall I stood in front of the notice board in the hall. This displayed the seating plan in the dining room for the first two weeks of term. The idea behind this was that we were to learn dinner-party manners and to develop the ability to talk to our neighbours regardless of friendship or mutual interests. So, during the consumption of cereal, one turned to the right; when the bowls were cleared and the toast brought in, one turned to the left; when the tea was poured one turned again to the right. I was dismayed to see that on my right was seated Miss Inglis, on my left a horsey girl called Davina who was obsessed by ponies and gymkhanas.

"For what we are about to receive may the Lord make us truly grateful." The moment we sat down Miss Inglis turned to me and said "Now Nemone, I want you to tell me all about Germany." I was nonplussed: I had not yet come to terms with much of what I had seen and learned; I could not have articulated what I felt even if I had wanted to. I took the easy way out and told her about our visit to the opera. This was a successful ploy; Miss Inglis loved Verdi. I was just describing Violetta's marvellous crinoline when the cereal bowls were swept away. With some relief I turned to Davina "What pony have you got at the moment?" I asked.

"<u>Pony</u> is hardly the word for her" answered Davina "She's a thoroughbred Arab filly, grey, fifteen hands and with the makings of a champion."

"What's her name?"

"Amina, after the wife of the Prophet Mohammed."

"But I thought he had twelve wives. Were they all called Amina?"

"No, silly. Amina was the top wife." Tea was poured.

"Did you get to Berlin?" Miss Inglis asked "Did you meet any Russians?"

"Oh yes, I sat next to one at the opera. They are almost as bad as the Germans."

"Why do you say that?" "They are unfair. A Red Army soldier was marching some prisoners through the streets of Berlin and the wife of one of the prisoners was following after them crying and saying "Please let my husband go." And, do you know, the soldier was so sorry for her that he let the prisoner go free. Then, after a few minutes, he realised that he was one prisoner short, so he grabbed a man who was walking along the pavement, put handcuffs on him and marched him away with the rest of the prisoners."

"Is that so?" said Miss Inglis. "Oh yes: my father told me, so it must be true. And another Russian soldier stole a tap from a house he was looting and sent it home to his wife with a letter which said "Stick this on the wall and water will come out.""

"That sounds a bit of a fairy story to me" said Miss Inglis. I confess that I had some doubts about both stories myself, despite their provenance. However, I had recently read Lali Horstmann's memoir, which describes the arrival of the Red Army at the family estate in Brandenburg. She recounts both stories exactly as my father had told them to me. And she was there.[6]

"Did you see Hitler's bunker?" Miss Inglis asked.

"No" I lied. "The Russians would not let us in. They are going to blow it up soon anyway."

"What a pity. It would have been a wonderful chance to

learn a bit of history."

Davina's boasting had inspired me to announce "My father has got two Maybachs, a saloon and a coupé. Both of them used to belong to Himmler. The coupé has got a handle on the dashboard just opposite the front passenger seat. When there was a parade or something he used to stand up, grasp the handle with his left hand and with the right arm give the salute "Heil Hitler". Without thinking, I thrust my right arm up in a fair imitation of the Hitler salute, narrowly missing a milk jug nearby.

"Now you're getting silly" said Miss Inglis. "Just tell the story. You don't have to do the actions."

Mercifully at that moment Mrs. Brampton rose to her feet – everyone followed. "For what we have just received may the Lord make us truly thankful." Never was I so thankful, not to have received, but to leave the table.

In the freezing dusk of the late afternoon Dione and I met, as was our custom, in the animal house to feed our rabbits and clean out their hutches. The presence of dozens of small bodies took the chill off the air which was filled with a homely smell of clean sawdust and sweet hay. Dione made a more sympathetic audience than Miss Inglis. With her I did not feel the temptation to boast or to lie. In summary I told her the story of the last days of Hitler and his courtiers, although I could not yet speak of the Goebbels children. She listened in silence, giving the narrative grave attention. Then she said "Do you know, I think I know where Martin Borman is. Come with me. But shh! Don't make a sound."

We left the cosy warmth of the animal shed and made our way in the gathering darkness round the back of the school to the yard where the great dustbins were kept, where the staff parked their bicycles, and where the tradesmen went in by their designated entrance. This is where we used to go most afternoons to cadge cabbage leaves and carrot peelings from the cooks to feed our rabbits.[7] In a corner of the yard a concrete path, laid in a gentle gradient, led down to the boiler room. On either side sat two coal bunkers, one for coke and the other for anthracite. Both were three quarters empty. (Small wonder the school was so cold). Together Dione and I crept down the slope to see who was at home in the boiler room. In the dim red glow of the struggling furnace, a man was throwing chunks of wood, which looked like builders' off-cuts, into the fire in an attempt to supplement his depleted stock of hard fuel.

"That's him" whispered Dione "That's M.B." Stocky, shaved head, thick neck, it had to be him. "And look, he's got a funny little wireless – short wave – sending Morse code." I was awestruck.

"He must be in touch with the Werewolves." I said. The man turned round, caught sight of us and let out a roar. Off we scuttled like two little crabs disturbed in a rock pool.

"That's not English he's speaking" gasped Dione as we fled the yard. "It doesn't sound like German either" I said.

"It's old Bavarian dialect silly" said Dione. That was that. For three weeks we stalked the unfortunate boilerman. Usually, we crept into the cellar when his back was turned, freezing when he turned round as if we were playing grandmother's footsteps, and we were able to make good our escape without his seeing us. On several occasions he was too quick off the mark and drove us out with that alarming roar.

In school we used to say "M.B." to each other and collapse into helpless giggles. It was generally believed that one of us had an admirer with whom we corresponded in Bloxham School nearby. His name was Matthew Bannister or something of the sort. This seemed to us to be positively hilarious, we gained mystery and prestige.

Gradually however, our adventure became clouded by anxiety. Whatever were we to <u>do</u> with M.B. now that we had unmasked him? Should we call the police or tell Miss Inglis? The trouble was that either course of action would count as sneaking, a heinous crime in any schoolchild's eyes.

"Tell tale tit
Your tongue will be split
And all the little puppy dogs
Will get a little bit."

But was one allowed to sneak on a war criminal? Did his status make it permissible? Would it count as sneaking or something heroic? If we did turn him in, he would undoubtedly be hanged. For a moment I saw in flashback old Charity's sadistic toothless grin. Did we really want this horror on our consciences? Perhaps it would be best to confront him; tell him that the game was up; point out the error of his ways; give him a mighty blowing up and let him go. Day after day we chewed over our moral dilemma without coming to any conclusion.

Late one afternoon we paid our usual visit to the back yard. Peering carefully into the cellar we found it empty save for the little wireless which stood on a shelf near the furnace, quietly chattering away to itself. Holding our breath we crept down the ramp and nearer and nearer. At last we could hear the unmistakable voice of Tommy Handley on the BBC home service. "ITMA! It's That Man Again, It's That Man Again!" followed by the famous whine of Moana Lot. "It's being so miserable what keeps me 'appy."

Mortified, aghast, we turned to go. At that moment the bulky figure of M.B. appeared in the doorway almost completely blocking out the last grey light of day "Bloody ell, it's you two again" he said. In English, unmistakably. "I know what you're up to, don't I? You just want me to play you about, play you about, play you about." He approached. I could smell his onion breath. This time we did not scuttle, we sprinted out of the cellar, and pushing past him raced out of the yard, never to return again.

We had to make a new arrangement for our rabbit food. We took one of the kitchen staff, a young scullion, a country girl not much older than we were, into our confidence. We told her that we were frightened of the boiler man and didn't dare go into the yard anymore. She understood the problem: she mistrusted him herself. "'E's got a filffy mouff on 'im" she said. So every evening on her way home she would drop off a parcel of the precious vegetable parings at the animal house and place them by Cellophane's cage.

It soon flashed round the school that Matthew Bannister had jilted whichever one it was. We were regarded, no longer with wonder, envy and admiration but with pity and scorn.

That was a bitter winter. For three months the sky, hovering purple or black over the Midlands, would every now and again discharge a flurry of powdery snow. The ground was so hard that the horses were confined to the indoor riding school less they break their legs. Miss Bumpass however, had no such anxiety about the legs of her girls and three times a week we played lacrosse – "Lax" we called it – on fields of frozen mud, as hard and ridged as petrified lava. Our fingers, swollen with chilblains, burst and bled with every thwack of the lacrosse stick. Inside the school the temperature differed little from outside. Dione and I alone knew why the central heating didn't work but we would hardly have told anyone. Our streaming cotton handkerchiefs which we laid, out of habit, to dry on the iron radiators, froze stiff as boards.

Seven years later, when we shared a house in Bayswater together, Xanthe Wakefield told me that it was about this time that she and her family came home from India in the dying days of the Raj. She was sent straight to Wycombe Abbey, one brother to Eton, the other to Gordonstoun. On her first night at boarding school she must have looked so forlorn that the kindly matron sent her to bed with a hot water bottle. In the dark small hours, the thing burst and she awoke, not simply frozen but soaked as well. From that moment she resolved neither to understand nor to like, not even to attempt to tolerate the alien country which had been forced upon her. In her mind she still belonged to India, the earthly paradise she had lost. In this attitude she persisted, despite remarkable intellectual achievements, until the day of her death.

The worst of that winter was that the ice seemed to have entered Miss Inglis's veins. She had always been formidable but until now she had been attractive, charismatic with it. Now she appeared simply terrifying. With hindsight I can see that she was probably exhausted. It cannot have been easy at the outbreak of war to move school, staff and pupils from Chiselhurst (Tudor Hall's original home) to Chipping Camden; to negotiate for and to buy the mock Georgian pile at Banbury and to move again. I surmised that there were financial problems as well: overnight the school trebled in size and she began to charm, not the fathers who were service men but who were usually strapped for cash, but rather the hard-faced business men who had done well out of the war, one of whom might be persuaded to sponsor a new music room or science block. During the holidays I told my mother about what I had noticed. She was not surprised and quoted Kipling.

> *"'For it's Tommy this and Tommy that' and 'chuck him out, the brute!' But it's 'Saviour of his country' when the guns begin to shoot."*[8]

Like a beleaguered Prime Minister pushing a raft of unnecessary legislation through the House of Commons, in the hope of demonstrating to a hostile press and public that he is still in control of something or other, Miss Inglis started to make rules, silly rules, pointless rules. Rules pertaining to uniform; rules pertaining to silence; silence in the corridors, silence in the dormitories. All letters home were to be left unsealed so that she could read them. "I don't want you to be worrying your parents." We were outraged. The unwritten contract of trust between pupils and staff had been broken. The easy atmosphere of Burnt Norton was no more. We became sulky and resentful. Formerly we spoke of her between ourselves respectfully as "Miss Inglis" now we dared to use her Christian name, Nesta (but never in her hearing). Some years later when I returned to Tudor Hall to give a lecture on the Suffragettes, she told me, over a gin and tonic, that discipline had never been so difficult. I was still too much in awe of her to tell her why.

Our dissatisfaction took the form in the main of grumbling but on Sunday evenings we ran riot. Sunday supper was the only meal of the week where the staff was absent and we were supervised by unfortunate prefects. The meal was always the same: baked potatoes inadequately cleaned and still bearing the eyes and slug holes with which they had been harvested. Each girl was given one potato and a small pat of margarine. The potatoes were inedible: we went to bed hungry. The margarine, however, was fair game. Each piece was flicked up into the air until the ceiling became a constellation of small dim yellow stars. The wretched prefects, knowing that they were outnumbered, turned a blind eye to our hooligan behaviour.

Although we did not discuss it, the Martin Borman fiasco led to a kind of constraint between Dione and me. Moving as we were from childhood to adolescence, we had imagined ourselves to be more worldly wise and knowledgeable than in fact we were. Painfully we had now to acknowledge that we were just two silly kids. For a time, we hardly dared to look one another in the eye. Our conversations were confined to the welfare of the rabbits and Nesta's stupidities. For the first time I felt the weight on my shoulder of the black dog of depression, meaningless, endogenous depression, which has, from time to time, cursed my life ever since. Only the discipline of the environment forced me out of bed in the morning and through the activities of the day. On occasion I heard a low voice whispering inside my head "The fool hath said in his heart: there is no God".[9]

One morning I woke with a sharp stabbing pain in my back. At first, I wondered whether this, like the ghostly voice in my head, was simply a product of my imagination. Then it occurred to me that it might be real, physical in origin, in which case it would be a wonderful way of avoiding lacrosse that afternoon. I went to see matron. "I've got an awful pain in my back" I said "I think I must have slipped a disc." She slipped a glass thermometer under my tongue. Sharply she admonished me. "Don't ever try to diagnose yourself. Leave that to the professionals. A slipped disc does not give you a temperature. It's off to the San for you. Go and collect your things."

The school Sanatorium was lodged in a modest Victorian villa near the main gate. Too large to have been for a gardener or gamekeeper's cottage, it could have served as the dower house for the original manor which had been demolished to make way for the mock Georgian monster which was now the school. It had been intended to accommodate six sick girls: that winter it was housing three times that number. The bitter weather and our poor diet meant that the common cold often mutated into something worse. In those days one either had a 'chesty cough' in which case one had to endure the rigors of the main building or 'pneumonia' in which case one was transferred to the Sanatorium. Everyone wanted to get pneumonia: it was believed that the San was a place of unbelievable luxury: there was tea and hot buttered toast there, warm beds and blackcurrant jam. Nurse Withers who ran it, 'Witherby', as she was known, was an angel; one might almost be at home.

It had never occurred to me that Matron, usually so acerbic and brusque, was capable of an act of kindness. Having collected my nightdress, hairbrush and sponge bag as directed, I was bracing myself for the long trudge down the snow-covered drive, when all of a sudden there she was, outside the front entrance of the school in her black Morris Minor.

"Hop in" she said. On arrival at our destination we were met by a great gust of warm air, fragrant with the aroma of fresh toast and eucalyptus.

"Come on in sweetheart" said Nurse Withers. "We'll soon get you sorted, and a well-deserved cup of tea for Matron, I think."

Soon I was sitting up in bed my head bent over a steaming jug, inhaling the hot comforting infusion of fragrant herbs. Witherby covered my head with a soft red towel, better to capture the healing steam. "Only a red towel does the trick" she said "No other colour will do. It's magic you see." The whole house was filled with steam and red-towelled figures bowed over their jugs. Not one of us doubted the efficacy of Witherby's methods. Neither did the doctor, a big burly man in a Sherlock Holmes cape who visited every morning. He would make a brisk round of the beds, listen to our chests, praise Witherby's regime and disappear downstairs. There was no treatment he could offer us save words of encouragement: the only medicines available were Vick, eucalyptus and steam. The days of antibiotics and salbutomol had not yet arrived. Treatments had advanced but little since Charlotte Bronte's day when two or three of our little band of chest infections probably would have died. As it was, we all recovered, mainly as the result of Witherby's superb nursing and affectionate regime.

The house had not been modernised since its construction, probably in the 1880's. The only concession to the 20th Century was the electric light; that system in itself was a piece of industrial archaeology. Where they were exposed one could see that the electric wires had been encased in tubes of flexible grey lead. The building, including cellar, was four storeys high; every room had an open coal fire in a cast-iron grate. There was no other heating. Coal had to be carried up twice a day and ashes carried down. Every night the fires were bedded down with "slack pudding", a judicious mixture of coal dust and water. The fires would burn invisibly under this cover all night and in the morning be stirred into life with a rotating motion of a brass poker. Water was heated by a back boiler in the kitchen (which also provided a cosy open fire behind its brass fender); laundry was done in a coal-fired copper in the scullery; cooking on an antique iron range.

Nurse Withers ran her establishment with the help of two maids of all work, sisters, sixteen and seventeen respectively. Rosy and Ivy were large-bosomed country girls with thick curly brown hair, periwinkle blue eyes and complexions like Devonshire cream. The work they did must have been backbreaking, but they never complained; rather they seemed to delight in their physical strength. They had the sturdy willingness of pit ponies. Nurse Withers doted on them for their industry and good humour but also for their nubile beauty which did her no harm at all in the neighbourhood.

For the first week in the sanatorium, I was aware of little but the regular arrival of hot drinks, jugs of steaming eucalyptus and the benign presence of our nurse. Later, as I began to feel better, I began to notice things around me. First and most delightful was the presence, in a bookcase on one of the landings, of the complete works of Georgette Heyer. I could imagine nothing more delicious than lying in my soft warm bed and immersing myself in the world of *Regency Buck* and *Faro's Daughter*, the gamblers, rakes and tomboy heroines of Regency England. It would however, be a pleasure just tinged with guilt: nothing as lightweight had ever passed through the doors of Black Dog Cottage, where even the works of Enid Blyton were forbidden for being half-witted. I reckoned that I would have to remain ill for at least another eleven days in order to read them all.

I need not have worried. Witherby's system was working to my advantage. Every morning I would look out of the window and see the doctor's big brown Austin draw up at precisely five to ten. Within a moment or two I would hear him puffing up the stairs to make his rounds. It puzzled me at first that his car was still in place at a quarter to twelve. One of my fellow patients must be terribly sick, I thought, and he must be giving her intensive care. Then one day, padding down to the kitchen to cadge a cup of tea, I saw him: shoes off, feet in tartan patterned socks up on the fender, glass of whiskey at his right hand, basking in the best armchair. "Well, good for him" I thought "But I'm still going to keep a careful eye on things."

There was an abundance of food in Witherby's kingdom. Every morning a local farmer would bring to the back door an enamel pail of milk, fresh eggs and crusty loaves fresh baked that day. He took away with him, when he left, two big zinc buckets of fresh kitchen waste, as swill for his pigs. And occasionally a couple of bottles wrapped in brown paper or big cartons of Marlborough cigarettes or Lucky Strikes. I never saw money change hands but sometimes Rosy and Ivy would appear to give their father a quick kiss. There were also items unfamiliar to us from either home or school: long thin watery sausages, a pallid meat loaf from a tin called Spam, packets of dark chocolate cake to be reconstituted with water and baked in the oven. The cake boxes were decorated with a glossy looking woman whose name was Sara Lee. The provenance of this stuff became clear when one day I found the easy chair occupied by a fat man in a crumpled pale-grey uniform, the uniform of a sergeant in the United States Air Force. I was upset to see him stroking Witherby's hand. "She's *our* Witherby not *your* Witherby" I said under my breath.

"This is my friend Glen from Brize Norton" said nurse Withers.

"Hi sexy" said Glen "You'd make a bootiful child bride." This really annoyed me. Not only was he muscling in on

Witherby but he was also lying. I knew that I was a bootiful nothing, an ugly ducking in a towelling dressing gown. He obviously had his sights not only on Witherby but also on the luscious Rosy and Ivy.

Another day I was appalled to see the evil boiler man sitting in the easy chair. My heart thumped with terror and I crept back up the stairs without his having seen me. I should not have worried however: he was plainly so busy leering through the open scullery door that he would hardly have noticed the little frump in bedroom slippers. Rosy and Ivy, up to their armpits in opalescent bubbles, were tackling the laundry with dolly and posser and giggling the while.

Now I understood how it was that we were so warm so well fed and so well looked after. I had to tell someone. I asked Rosy to take a note up to the school on her afternoon off and soon Dione was knocking at the back door.

"I've found out that Witherby is *head of the Black Market*" I whispered "and M.B. is in on it too. Then there's a horrible American..." In spite of our earlier humiliation we were thrilled to have discovered another conspiracy.

"This could go right to the top" said Dione "Mind you monitor all Witherby's telephone calls."

This I did. Try as I might however, I found no evidence of large-scale criminal activity although some conversations were quite interesting. One day I heard her saying to Matron (evidently not as close to the Tudor Hall establishment as I had always imagined) "Any sign of a cheque yet? No? 'Ow does she think we bleedin' live? On bleedin' air?"

I felt proud of Witherby for speaking ill of Nesta. "No, I'm keeping them here" she continued. "None of my girls are going back to that bleedin' Stalag up the 'ill." That was good news. I needed another week to finish the final volumes of Georgette Heyer. Maybe I could spin out my pneumonia to the end of term. I began to work on the other girls, it was not difficult. We all agreed that we were still terribly, terribly ill. I correct myself. All except the horsy Davina who had arrived at the San the day after I had. She was missing her pony and determined to break ranks. The rest of us watched in disgust as her father came down from Birmingham, collected her in his Bentley and took her back to the main building. "All that for a bleeding 'orse" said Witherby. The rest of us found no difficulty in getting either the Doctor or Witherby on our side. I worried however that Davina might talk too freely at the school about our cosy little conspiracy, but there was nothing I could do.

Nurse Withers was a small, neat woman; her sharp features and crisp black hair suggesting Welsh descent. Her only fault, in the eyes of her young patients, was an embarrassingly loud laugh, but then one could have argued that it matched her bawdy sense of humour. She would have made a fine Doll Tearsheet.[10]

Going to her one day, diffidently, with a girl problem, she flung open a cupboard stacked with the necessary items cackling "'Elp yourself my darling. We can't have you dripping around like the dogs."

In every other respect I found her perfect and all her young patients adored her. I found her household immensely seductive. Even a whiff of corruption was exciting, although I had reservations about the involvement of the evil boiler man. Dione and I discussed this but came to the conclusion that as she was doing it for our benefit, not for her own, she must be forgiven. All my life I had lived under pressure; the pressure to achieve, to aspire, to behave, to excel. Here there was no such pressure. The ethos was of tolerance, of unconditional affection which extended even to those adopted into the charmed circle from outside, even to moody adolescent girls. The aim was to survive and to survive as comfortably as possible.

I wondered what had made Witherby what she was, what had formed her adorable character? One day, sitting by the kitchen fire under the friendly gaze of King George VI in his naval uniform and of Winston Churchill, who, although dethroned by the 1945 election, was still an icon in many a working-class kitchen, I asked her where she came from.

"Oxton" she said "Down the Nile. It was a real rough district when I was a girl. The coppers 'ad to go about in fours. Them was golden days" she continued. "Me dad 'ad a barrow down Oxton Market. I used to 'elp 'im out. 'E sold fruit and veg and I'd sell the flowers. Lovely tulips tuppence a bunch. They'd always buy from me 'cause I was so small. Then when we got 'ome I'd be wet and cold and 'ungry. Me Nan would put a great big towel round me shoulders and hug me tight. Then she'd give me a dirty great slice of bread and drippin'."

"And when you decided to do nursing, where did you train?" I asked "At the London 'Ospital. No, not with the elephant man darling, 'e was before my time. Whitechapel was near as rough as 'Oxton in them days."

Bow Bells. This explained everything. To Witherby the old East End, with its warmth, its tribal loyalties, the unconditional love given to one's own, had assumed the mythic status which India had for me. Memory and nostalgia had edited out every fault, every imperfection. To her those mean streets were bathed in a golden pre-lapsarian glow and trodden by Cockney angels.

I wanted to ask her more. Did she have a Christian name? I hoped it was not Olive or Ethel. Had she ever been in love? Or married? I was just trying to formulate my questions when there was a scrunching on the gravel outside. It was Glen from Brize Norton in his enormous putty-coloured Buick. I couldn't stand him. I fled. From the window on the staircase I could see him open the boot and start to unload his contraband.

"I hate you" I whispered "And your disgusting car. And why do you call that thing a <u>trunk</u>? Why can't you speak English?"

It was by now mid-March. The end of term was imminent. We had managed, all of Witherby's patients, to spin out our illness until this point. The doctor still visited every morning and we coughed a bit for him but we knew, and he knew that we knew, the principal purpose of his visit. One morning the unfamiliar sun rose and shone brightly over Oxfordshire, still covered in its shining blanket of snow but a blanket which was beginning to shrink and to fray at the edges. Shortly before the hour of the doctor's arrival, I heard a strange slithering sound on the roof as though someone, a burglar perhaps, had missed his footing and was sliding down the steeply pitched slates. This was followed by a thump as something hit the ground below. Running to the window I saw huge wedges of snow detach themselves from the roof and collapse in a heap on the still frozen gravel path underneath. At the same time, I heard the sound of running water as, for the first time in months, the frozen gutters began to overflow. Looking up the drive I could see that each tree was encircled by a dark ring where the natural heat and energy from its trunk had begun to melt the surrounding snow. Later walking out into the grounds, I could see that, wherever the snow had retreated, tiny yellow aconites with ruffled green collars and groups of white and green snowdrops had pushed themselves through the black sodden earth and were stretching themselves towards the light.

In the end-of-term excitement Rosy and Ivy were bouncing like rubber balls, happy on our behalf as we waited for the minibus to take us back to the main building. Our goodbyes were affectionate but perfunctory, so concentrated were we on the happy weeks to come. As we drove up the drive I turned to wave to Witherby, standing at the back door, a somewhat forlorn figure, outside what had been until now our safe haven, our adopted home.

Early in the summer term I went to pay Witherby a visit. She was sitting in her kitchen in the easy chair usually reserved for the gentlemen callers, wireless by her elbow, listening to the inanities of *ITMA*. The fire was out; the cast iron grate, unpolished, cold and grey. She gave me a hug and made the obligatory mug of tea.

"Where are Rosy and Ivy?" I asked.

"Gone" she replied. "The governor of Stalag up the ill said they weren't earning their wages down 'ere. So she moved them up to work in 'er bleedin' kitchen. And then she didn't like the way the Yanks from Brize Norton kept on calling round to court them, so she gave them both the sack."

"That's not fair"I interjected "It wasn't their fault that they were so pretty" "Bloody old witch" said Witherby. I hugged her. "Cheer up" I said "As soon as the hay fever season starts I'll see to it that we all get asthma. You'll get us all back and it will be just like old times."

"Ere's oping" said Witherby.

It rained in June and the hay fever season never happened. Rosy and Ivy were traced to their father's farm by two airmen from Brize Norton. They carried them off as G.I. brides. From time to time I have thought about them over the years. I hoped that they were well and happy: that their husbands were kind to them and that their children were as beautiful as they were. I prayed that they did not end up in some gruesome trailer park in Arkansas.

CHAPTER 10
JIMMY

It was July 1945. The Prison Commissioners had decided to reorganise the penal system. Dartmoor was to house Courts Martial cases and first-time offenders. The hard core of recidivists and those serving life sentences were to be distributed nationwide in a crazy game of bureaucratic pass-the-parcel. Several hundred lifers, including Jimmy, were to be transferred to Parkhurst on the Isle of Wight.

The lifers left Dartmoor wearing distinctive prison clothes. They were driven by coach to Portsmouth to catch the ferry to the island. They embarked in batches of two hundred, not only handcuffed, but also chained together like slaves in the cotton fields of old Mississippi. The quayside was crowded with curious spectators. Jimmy thought of the humiliation of Oscar Wilde, waiting on the platform of Clapham Junction for the arrival of the train to Reading Gaol. He bowed his head to avoid catching anyone's eye.

Once aboard the ferry Jimmy asked to see the captain.

"Are you the Guv'nor of this boat?"

"I am."

"Did you know that there are still mines in this here channel?"

"Very probably."

"Don't you realise that us lifers will drown like rats if we hit one?"

The captain ordered the prison staff to remove the handcuffs and chains. The screws demurred, citing Home Office regulations. The captain folded his arms and refused to sail. Telephone calls were made. After a stand-off lasting two hours the chains were removed, and the ship was on her way.

Jimmy was to write later that he could never forget his first sight of Parkhurst.[1] The warm red-brick buildings and the brilliant flower beds were in total contrast to the gothic gloom of Dartmoor. The Chief Prison Officer, Jack Hunt, actually smiled at the prisoners as they arrived at the gate after their short coach journey from Ryde. Jimmy's cell had a wooden plank floor, a bed with a proper spring mattress, electric light, a flushing lavatory and, wonder of wonders, a working steam radiator. At Dartmoor his cell had been something between a dungeon and a tomb, scooped out of granite rock, wringing with damp and lit by flickering gas. This, so he wrote, was like going from winter into spring. Outside on the landing, a radio was playing a jolly Eric Coates number, *Calling all Workers*.

Parkhurst was an enormous improvement on Dartmoor, but it was hardly Disneyland. Three gangs of professional criminals, the Scottish, the Northern and the London mobs vied with each other for control of the gaol. There was widespread corruption. The greater part of the prisoners' rations were seized by the gang leaders. There was a lively black market in stores nominally owned by the Ministry of Food but which were stolen and used as currency by the tobacco barons and dishonest screws.

Jimmy, who gave allegiance to none of the mobs, found a niche for himself within the prison as letter writer for the illiterate and barrack room lawyer for the aggrieved. He became adept at writing petitions to the Home Office. With practice he became ever more skilful and many of his efforts achieved good results for the petitioners. One common cause of complaint was that prisoners were not receiving the rations to which they were entitled. The Home Office dealt with this in a particularly inept manner. From now on, it was ordered, no food would be weighed or measured. (This, so it was argued, would make it impossible to prove that anyone had been short-changed.) The prisoners were outraged, the black marketeers (corrupt screws and prison-gangsters) delighted. Jimmy wrote a flurry of petitions. The Governor, a new man who had not been in charge of so tough a penal establishment before, was concerned. He did not want the authorities to conclude that he had lost control of his establishment.

He sent the principal officer to see Jimmy. The man came to him all smiles.

"Look, O'Connor" he said "the Governor's very disturbed about the contents of those petitions. Corrupt officers...well, oh dear me! What are you trying to do? What do you want?"

"I don't want nothing. Only an end to the corruption in this nick."

"Look here" said the chief, "I'll put a proposition to you. Tear up this nonsense and I'll go back to the governor and tell him you've had a change of heart. You then can have any job you want in this gaol."

"Any job?"

"Yes, any job you want."

"I'll think about it. Come and see me after lunch."

The officer duly came back after lunch, a rice pudding.

"Yes" said Jimmy. "I've made up me mind. I'll be the Governor's valet. I want complete freedom. I don't want to be a trusty, but I want all the privileges of a trusty."

This meant that he would not have to wear the red arm band which would have marked him out as having gone over to the enemy, as having given his word that he would not attempt to escape or abuse the trust placed in him. He would be able to abuse the system as much as he liked and with a clear conscience.

Jimmy got the job, much to the annoyance of the prison officers. It was, so he wrote later, unique in penal history.[2] He was entered on the payroll as an "administration cleaner" but cleaning formed no part of his job. At six in the morning he would light the coal fires in the Governor's office and in that of the Chief Officer. He would make tea for the administrative staff and fetch the morning newspapers from the gate. He had free run of the prison and access to confidential documents. He had his own office with a cozy coal fire and cooking facilities.

He wore a tailor-made suit and a white shirt which he changed twice a day. He had special soft suede shoes, hand-made and adapted, on prescription from the doctor, to accommodate his crippled arthritic toes. He felt like Jack the Lad.

On Saturday and Sunday afternoons the governor would leave his office unattended and go to watch football. The prison was manned by a skeleton staff. For a couple of weeks Jimmy kept a careful eye on what was going on. When he was satisfied that no one went near the Governor's office at that time he decided to act. It took him a full five minutes to find the keys. He took them and unlocked the Governor's roll top desk. Inside were the personal records of every prisoner in the gaol.

Weekend after weekend Jimmy trawled through the records. His feelings veered from amusement to anger to outrage. These documents, many of which were founded on the briefest of contacts between authors and subjects and the flimsiest of research, were intended to accompany each prisoner during his journey through the prison system and would be laid before the Parole Board when a decision on whether to grant or refuse parole was considered. Jimmy's own document, based on a five-minute interview with a deputy governor he never saw again, included the comment "This man is a scoundrel. His expressed intention of living a straight life will be short lived." He tore it up, an action which, in the end, did him more harm than good.

Many of the reports Jimmy read were wide of the mark, many absurd. "This man will die on the scaffold." "This man is a street corner boy who is likely to spend the rest of his life in prison." The man who was to die on the scaffold never re-offended and became the owner of a successful flower shop. The "street corner boy" became a monk and went to work as a missionary at a remote station up the Amazon. Reports on the valued prison informers gave him much amusement. "This man will do anything to curry favour with the authorities. He exaggerates the slightest incident and creates situations where none exist." Jimmy wished that the subject of this last report could have read it for himself. The man considered himself a very clever fellow.

There were, at this time, a number of members of the old Official IRA serving long sentences, twenty or thirty years apiece, in the system. Their records, which travelled with them from prison to prison every time they were moved, clearly identified them and their political allegiance. Each time they were moved they were subject to extra harsh treatment within the system and to many beatings. Jimmy decided to put an end to this. One Sunday afternoon he burned all their records. Naturally there was a Home Office enquiry. Jimmy was soon identified as the culprit, being the only other prisoner in Parkhurst whose records had mysteriously disappeared. He lost his cushy job and was placed in the maximum-security block. It was ruled that no prisoner in future should have access to administration buildings unless under the surveillance of a prison officer. This rule applied to every gaol in the country. Jimmy was made an honorary member of the Official IRA. This was however of little comfort to him. He had no interest in politics. All too soon, by order of the Prison Commissioners, he was back in Dartmoor, branded a recalcitrant thug who would not respond to decent treatment.

On their final release from prison, the IRA men went home to Ireland. They were mortified to find that, far from receiving the hero's welcome they had anticipated, they were ignored, ostracised even. They played no part in the formation of the Provisional IRA. They took no part in public life. Work was hard to find in Ireland for anyone at the time, for elderly men with no particular skills or education, virtually impossible. They disappeared from public view. Some even returned to England, merging into the old Irish communities of Birmingham and North London. One even became a Labour councillor in Hackney, a teetotaller, a moderate and respected citizen.

In the late 1990s, having suffered a series of strokes, Jimmy was a patient in St Anne's Home in Stoke Newington. I used to join him for Mass on Sunday morning in the convent chapel, then adjourn to his room to watch *Countryfile* and read the Sunday papers.

One such Sunday Sister Seraphim, who cared for him in

the men's infirmary, appeared at his door. "Two gentlemen to see you, James" she said. There they were, the two old boys. Lantern jawed, thick, curly grey hair, one missing an eye. There was a great deal of hugging and back-slapping. I felt that I was surplus to this merry reunion, I said my goodbyes and left. As I walked down the corridor I could hear the sound of laughter. I imagined that they were reliving their jolly japes at Parkhurst.

NEMONE

There are days when, as the sun climbs towards the meridian, the clear colours of morning, instead of becoming brilliant, diminish and dull. Vermillion fades to dusty rose, sapphire to exhausted mauve, emerald to grey lichen green. Technicolour pales to monochrome. On the five-mile journey from the railway station at Westbury to Standerwick, the end of term excitement, the anticipation of four weeks holiday bliss, was gradually overcome by a sense of inertia and depression. I saw the home I loved so much as no more than a long thin house, somewhat dilapidated, abandoned in the middle of a rain-soaked field in Somerset.

My mother greeted me with a mug of tea and a chunk of sticky dark ginger cake, still warm and fragrant from the bottom oven of the Aga. In spite of her gentle enquiries, I could not think of anything fit for her ears to tell her about the past term. The Martin Borman fiasco was too silly, too humiliating to repeat, the activities of Nurse Withers with her gentleman callers and black-market scams, would have shocked her to the core. I had nothing to tell her. Her silent disappointment made me hostile and resentful. I needed someone to talk to who would not judge me. Peter was not yet home from Uppingham, while my grandmother and Cherry, who enjoyed that wonderful closeness, that perfect understanding sometimes felt between the very old and the very young, seemed to be from another planet where there was little space for me.

I took Cellophane outside and released her into her large

wire enclosure. In a trice she was transformed from a sedate indoor animal into a wild spring rabbit, kicking up her long back legs and flinging herself onto the short green grass which thrust itself through the interstices of the wire mesh floor of her pen, gorging herself on its sweetness.

I pulled on my Wellington boots and set off down the meadow to the place where, the summer before, in a pollard willow, Peter and I had built ourselves a secret tree house. After that bitter winter spring had been delayed by several weeks. Although it was already mid-April, the flora suggested that the world was just about moving into early February. Patches of furry coltsfoot and metallic yellow celandines had only just appeared in the hedgerows, still leafless and dark, though touched here and there by a faint frosting of blackthorn blossom. No sign, as yet, of primroses or violets. Above the stream a few brown catkins hung, still tightly furled like tiny umbrellas. It would be at least another week, possibly two, before they opened up and stretched themselves out into the dangling golden lamb's tails which entice the first honey bees to their breakfast. The brook itself, glass clear in summer, was swollen, brown, muddy and opaque.

I climbed up into the big damp nest of twigs which Peter and I had constructed. I decided to stay there until dark – or even to remain there all night – wallowing in my teenage melancholia. I saw the future stretching out before me, a long vista of unremitting boredom interspersed by terrifying blocks of exams. No more Germany. No more adventures and conspiracies. No more Witherby. I would still have liked to be Prime Minister and save the world, but I knew that I had neither the energy nor the application to take even one step towards those ends. I knew that some of my peers were confident that, if they went to ballet class twice a week or riding school three times, they would, in time, evolve painlessly into Margot Fonteyn or Pat Smythe. Well, good luck to them, I thought. Hard work and dedication were not for me. Really there was little point in living.

Dusk fell. Under my backside the nest of twigs felt increasingly damp and cold. It was hunger, the thought of supper and the glow of warmth from the Aga, which finally brought me home. Nervously, I made my way back through the darkened meadows. I expected a serious scolding having stayed out so late and without explanation. I sidled into the soft yellow light of the kitchen hanging my head. The table had been cleared, the dishes washed and put away. Cherry and our grandmother had long since gone to bed. Cautiously I sought my mother's eye. Instead of telling me off as I had anticipated, she met me with a beaming smile.

"Buffy has just telephoned" she said. "She and her brand-new family are coming to stay tomorrow."

"How super!" I said.

"Yes. I'm going to make them a proper feast. I've ordered an enormous capon which we'll roast with root vegetables. We'll scratch together a salad with watercress and baby dandelions. There's plenty of bottled fruit in the still room, so we can have blackberry and apple crumble for pudding."

"Yummy" said I "and can we have baked apples too?"

"Of course."

"And junket?"

My misdemeanour forgotten, my mother told me to go down to the Fowl Farm first thing in the morning to collect the capon and a pint of double cream.

"I know it's not your favourite place but don't worry about it" she said. "The old boy died a couple of months ago and Leah has inherited the farm. She's a considerable heiress now. You won't recognise her. She's got a splendid set of false teeth and a frizzy perm. I suppose the old boy was a bit of a domestic tyrant."

"Oh yes, I'm sure of that."

As I reached the standing stone at the head of the muddy drive I could see Leah waiting at the kitchen door. If I had seen her in a different place, in a different context, I would not have recognised her. She looked quite different from the bedraggled creature of my recollection. She wore a floral pinafore, freshly starched, and pink satin slippers embroidered with pearls. Her large blue eyes, which I had never noticed before, her face having been so puffed and swollen with weeping, sparkled and her china-white teeth flashed like a lighthouse. I didn't know whether to shake her hand or hug her. So I did both. Glancing down I noticed that she no longer wore the wedding ring which had so excited my curiosity before.

Awkwardly I said, "I'm awfully sorry to hear about your father. He must have been a good age."

"Don't you worry about 'im, my darling." said Leah with a crocodile grin. "'E's nobody's loss, filffy old beast."

For a minute we stood in silence. She knew that I knew. We understood each other perfectly. Then we got on with the business of the capon. Leah drove a hard bargain.

By the time I got home carrying the capon in a string bag, Sadler had excavated the carrots and parsnips from their winter quarters in the clamp. He took the bird from me and, with a deft stroke of his knife, eviscerated it into a zinc bucket, throwing the streaming entrails into the ditch which ran behind the vegetable garden. "Fox'll like that lot" he said. Next, with the speed and dexterity born of long practice, he stripped it of its shining copper-coloured feathers. Finally, he lit a long wax taper and burned off every remaining bit of stubble, reducing the glorious cockerel into a limp pallid corpse.

I took myself into the scullery and began to scrub the muddy vegetables under the cold tap. Meanwhile my mother was warming the sweetened milk for the junket, testing it from time to time with her elbow, as she would a baby's bath. When it reached blood temperature, she added a dessert spoon of rennet, poured it into a shallow china dish and set it to cool on a slate shelf in the still room. Next, I went to work on the big green Bramley apples. Each one was cored, the cavity filled with raisins and dark brown sugar, the skin was studded with a perfect circle of cloves. It was placed in an enamel pie dish and pushed into the bottom oven of the Aga to cook for a couple of hours. Before long the kitchen was filled with the mellow autumnal fragrance of the apples as they baked, the scent of childhood, the scent of home.

When Buffy had left Nortorn Malreward for Washington DC she sought out an old flame she had known in London before the war, where he taught at the London School of Economics. His American wife had recently died, leaving him with two small children. Buff took Susannah and Richard to her heart and duly married their father. When the war in Europe came to an end, they decided to come home, travelling from New York to Southampton on the *Queen Mary*, recently decommissioned as a troop ship. They arrived late in 1946, just as we were leaving for Germany. They rented a house in Twickenham and Fred, Buffy's husband, returned to the London School of Economics where he became Reader in Statistics.

Buffy was keen to integrate her new family with her old. (Susannah was a year younger than I while Richard slotted neatly between Peter and Cherry.) She suggested that Susannah and I should correspond, so, for a year before the family left the States, we wrote to each other. I described Cellophane and her adventures while Susannah told me about a litter of six-toed kittens she had adopted. When we finally met in the flesh we were hardly strangers.

Nevertheless, I felt nervous about meeting my new cousin in the flesh. This thin shy brilliant girl had lost her mother, a tragedy I could hardly comprehend. As war children we were conditioned to the thought that we might well lose our fathers, who faced mortal danger every day. But to be deprived of one's <u>mother</u> seemed grossly unfair, something right outside the natural order of things. I was embarrassed at the thought of having to meet this poor child, just as people will sometimes cross the road to avoid having to speak to someone recently bereaved. I was also dismayed to learn that she was awesomely good at maths, a subject I could not comprehend.

However, as Buffy bounced off the train at Westbury, flanked by her tall thin excited children, her beautiful grey eyes sparkling, I felt my doubts and hesitations disappear.

"We won't get a moment's peace" she said "until Dickie has sung you his rude song." In a glass clear treble Richard began.

> *"Passengers will please refrain*
> *From urinating while the train*

Is standing at the station.
If you want to pass your water
Ring the bell and ask the porter;
He will tell you what to do."

We all laughed and set off to devour Leah's capon.
After lunch I asked Sue "Will you be going to Oxford?"
"No."
"Cambridge then?"
"No. I shall go to the LSE. Probably to teach."
"Why? <u>Whyever?</u>"
"LSE's serious. A serious institution."

There was no answer to that. I was dumbfounded. It had never occurred to me that there were more than two universities in the country. The only conflict was which one to choose. Nevertheless, even after this shaky start, Sue and I became good friends. Sue duly went to LSE where, like her father, she taught statistics. Our friendship has lasted a lifetime.

Dick and Cherry delighted in each other's company. Dick was, however, a somewhat subversive influence. Brought up in the city, he did not understand the rules which are second nature to country children: respect for crops and livestock, the mandatory closing of gates. Together they found a haystack in a meadow nearby and tore it apart to make a den. A couple of days later the infuriated farmer arrived at the back door demanding compensation. This my mother paid without argument, apologising profusely on the children's behalf. Poor Dick was appalled. He had not realised the enormity of his conduct. He begged my mother not to tell Buffy. After the misery of his early childhood, brought up by a series of unsuitable and sometime unkind house keepers, he was terrified of losing his adorable new stepmother. My mother promised to say nothing and kept her word.

More than sixty years later, long after Buffy herself had died, Dick and Sue visited my mother in the nursing home where she spent the last weeks of her life. Taking Dick's head between her hands she whispered "I never told Buff about the haystack." No one had more respect for children than she did and no one, by them, was more beloved.

We had other visitors that summer. This was the time when the British Raj was in its final stage of disintegration. Many families, friends of my own for three generations, having left India, were seeking to settle in what must have seemed an alien land. The post-war hardships and austerity, the strange new politics, the loss of a well-defined social hierarchy, the filthy weather, must have been deeply disorientating. I remember in particular the visit of the Tollington family. Exact contemporaries of my parents and grandparents they had stayed on in India for twenty years longer than we had. I remember the parents: charming, confused, touchingly anxious to adapt to this uncomfortable new life; the children, angry, hostile and, having been brought up under the gentle regime of Ayahs, spoilt, bossy and, so I thought, disrespectful to our own mother.

"Pick up my ball" I remember eight-year old Elizabeth ordering her. The Lethbridge children were shocked.

During the years we lived in Somerset there were many other visitors at Black Dog Cottage. Most came from overseas, American military and service families from the Commonwealth. We were never accepted by or made part of 'The County'. Until a general election was called. Then we were gratefully adopted by the old West Country Liberal establishment represented by the Hobhouse family and the great Quaker dynasties at Street, the shoe-making Clarks and Clothiers. My mother spent many evenings with Conradine Hobhouse, driving round the Wells constituency, lighting the oil lamps in drafty school halls for poorly attended political meetings as they struggled in the heart-breaking endeavour of trying to return a Liberal member to Parliament.

My parents had both voted Labour in the general election of 1945 which swept Churchill out into the wilderness and brought in the great reforming government of Clement Atlee. The Maynards had long been Socialists, despite Freda's Virginian background and my grandfather, after his Russian adventure had moderated his Marxist beliefs, and had contested several elections, unsuccessfully, on behalf of the Labour Party.

Corporal Jimmy O'Connor 10539.

France May 1940 – one month before the Lancastria disaster.

Jimmy (left) at Rouen - summer 1940 near NAAFI tent.

Jimmy driving army lorry en route to join HMS Lancastria. Within less than one year, Jimmy had been blown up on Lancastria, been tried for murder and spent 2 months in the condemned cell.

Major-General John Sydney Lethbridge

CB, CBE, MC 1945

John Sydney Lethbridge with Himmler's Maybach 1945-46.

John Sydney Lethbridge with Katharine Lethbridge and Cherry leaving Buckingham Palace after receipt of CB (Order of the Bath).

Young Jimmy training as pilot in the United States Air Force, Fairbanks Alaska USA.

CHAPTER ELEVEN

Jimmy

"I'm sorry to see you back here again" said the Chief Officer at reception. "Not half as sorry as I am to see you" Jimmy replied.

"You won't be needing none of this bollocks" continued the screw as he confiscated Jimmy's books and his accordion.

"What's this then? New Home Office regulations?"

"Nah. Just me absolute discretion."

"I'm appealing to the Prison Commissioners."

"You're walking on the fucking moon."

"You got to give me a receipt. In writing." The officer paused. Much as he would have liked to refuse this request, his bureaucratic caution overcame his desire to humiliate Jimmy further and he did as he had been asked.

Jimmy said no more. A couple of years before he would have thrown a tantrum and, no doubt, have been thrown into chokey with a hiding for good measure. He was, at last, learning to bite his tongue and be a little bit devious. Inwardly he raged. He had been deprived of the only things that made life even half tolerable by this idiot, who, in all probability, had never himself read a book or listened to a bar of music.

In his imagination Jimmy saw himself as Samson in Gaza, pulling down the temple on himself and his tormentors. He resolved to make himself immensely strong like his hero. Then, when the time came, he would commit some act of terrible violence and bring everything crashing down around him. He applied for, and was given, the job of stoker.

"More suited to your intellect," smirked the Chief Tormentor, "than being a poncy librarian."

Some things never change. While the world outside hurtled on in perpetual motion, whether for good or evil, inside the prison the system seemed hardly to change at all. Cruelty, stupidity and ignorance, flogging, mailbags, the quarry and porridge were central to daily life, just as they had been in 1917 when Eamon de Valera broke stones and dreamed of freedom for Ireland.[1]

The big old boiler, dating from the early days of the industrial revolution, was housed in a deep underground cavern. Here, in the warm, throbbing darkness, Jimmy made himself at home. He had his tin kettle, a single gas ring and a toasting fork made from a piece of bent wire. He took pride in polishing the boiler front with carborundum until it shone like a mirror. He enjoyed the feeling of immense physical strength as he shovelled tons of dusty slack to fuel his domestic monster. "Samson in Gaza, Samson in Gaza" he muttered.

Coal for the boiler and for a separate incinerator, where rubbish was burned and which was housed elsewhere, was brought to the prison in lorries driven by a private contractor. Once unloaded, the coal had to be shifted to its destination in wheelbarrows. These were large heavy things made of iron and clumsy to handle. Jimmy needed fourteen tons of coal a day to heat the prison and to supply hot water. To make the task easier he designed a light wooden barrow which would hold more coal than the old ones and which would save him several back-breaking journeys each day. A couple of friendly carpenters made it up for him in the prison workshop. An additional bonus was the false bottom which made an ideal receptacle for contraband. Letters could be smuggled out and tobacco smuggled in. It was, as they say, for Jimmy, "a nice little earner."[2]

A big marmalade cat made its home in the boiler house followed by a jackdaw which would perch, sometimes on

Jimmy's shoulder and sometimes on the cat's back. The bird became so tame that it would take a piece of bread from between Jimmy's lips. Gradually a number of feral cats joined them, preferring the warm cosy darkness to the never-ending rain outside. They formed a circle round the boiler, luxuriating in the warmth of the stone floor, their golden eyes shining like jewels set in the blackness. After every meal Jimmy bustled round the prison, collecting scraps to feed his growing menagerie.

All went well until the Chief Officer retired. Reggie Read OBE had spent thirty years in the prison service. He was, so far as the system allowed it, a kindly and humane man. He understood exactly what a life sentence meant and the importance of not depriving the lifers of all hope. He made small concessions, such as removing the bars from cell windows after the men had served four years and turned a blind eye to extra cups of tea and packets of tobacco.

All this changed when the Chief Tormentor was promoted to the top job. Back went the bars on the windows, tea and tobacco were at a premium. Bursting into the boiler room one evening and observing the circle of yellow eyes round the boiler, he ordered that all the cats in the prison should be drowned. Jimmy had become canny enough not to confront him.

"Quite right, sir," he said "they're only vermin. Leave it to me. I'll go and fetch a bucket." The cats, who are intelligent creatures and almost psychic in their understanding of human nature, started to creep, and then to race, out of the boiler room.

"Off you go, you lot. Fuck off out of it" Jimmy shouted to speed them on their way.

He stopped the daily collection of food scraps and told his like-minded mates to shoo any cats they saw out of the prison. Within a couple of weeks the place was crawling with rats. Enormous rats which had, over the years, developed an immunity to the poison which was laid out for them. Jimmy said nothing but watched with wry amusement the Chief Tormentor's growing frustration. After a couple of months, he decided to conduct a controlled experiment. He fetched his favourite marmalade tom from the place of safety where he had hidden him and set him to work. The rats had become lazy and over-confident. They were easy prey. It was not long before Marmalade happened to cross the Chief Tormentor's path, carrying in his mouth a large dead rat. Nothing was said, but, before long, Jimmy had restarted his collection of scrap food. Cautiously the cats crept back from the rain-swept moor. Before long the boiler was once again encircled by glowing yellow eyes and the prison was rid of vermin.

I do not know whether it was an old wives' tale or whether it was true but, during the time that capital punishment was part of the penal system, the Home Office used to receive two or three letters every day from people volunteering to perform the office of hangman. Certainly, there is a degree of sadism deeply embedded in the human psyche which renders this a distinct possibility. There is no more fertile soil in which cruelty and the enjoyment of cruelty will flourish than that which is to be found within a closed institution. In Dartmoor prison, on the days when corporal punishment was to be administered, there were more volunteers to administer – or to watch it – than they system could accommodate. Floggings were given either by the birch or the cat o' nine tails. Those who suffered them said that there was little to choose between them. Both left physical scars which lasted for life and psychological wounds which affected both victim and perpetrator.

On the day a flogging was to take place the atmosphere in the prison was so volatile that the prisoners were brought in from their working parties and locked in their cells ten minutes before the punishment took place. There they remained until half an hour after it was over. During this time an eerie silence hung over the cells. The whole prison was listening. Then there were footsteps as the condemned man was marched by an escort of six or eight screws through the prison and down the stone steps to the laundry where the punishment was to take place. There he was tied to a frame and the twelve old fashioned washing machines started up so that their rattle and whirr could drown his agonised screams. After it was all over the prisoners were released from their cells. Even then they spoke only in whispers. The screws walked on eggshells: they knew that the slightest thing could spark an explosion. It was twenty-four hours before the atmosphere returned to anything approaching normality.

On one occasion the victim was to be Timmy, a lad from Paddington, Jimmy's own manor. He had been sentenced to twelve strokes of the birch for assaulting a prison officer. Jimmy was, as usual, at work in the boiler house when the officer who had been assaulted and who was, by custom, expected to witness the punishment, came in and sat down near the boiler, smoking and grinning. He offered Jimmy a cigarette, which was refused. Maybe he wanted to show that he was a jolly good fellow; perhaps he wanted to get Jimmy to say something seditious for which he himself could be punished. Happily nothing was said. A minute later the punishment party passed by the open door: the prison Governor, the doctor, the Chief Tormentor, Timmy himself between four escorting warders. The screw who had been sitting in the boiler house got up, put out his cigarette and followed the party towards the laundry. When he heard the washing machines start up, Jimmy was physically sick.

Half an hour later the Chief Tormentor appeared. He was carrying the cane wrapped in cloth which was heavily stained with blood. He threw it on to the floor at Jimmy's feet.

"Burn that" he ordered.

"Not me, mate" Jimmy replied. "You used the fucking thing. You can burn it. And let me remind you, Sir, that there's a Home Office regulation which says that you can't use <u>my</u> furnace for burning rubbish. It has to be kept as clean as possible and receive only clean fuel. Take that fucking thing to the incinerator."

Jimmy knew the prison regulations like the back of his hand. He looked at his adversary with a triumphant smirk. The Chief Tormentor paused for a moment. Then he flung open the door of the boiler and flung in the cane. The sudden violent inward draught caught the jackdaw and swept it into the furnace. It was the screw's turn to grin. Without another word he stalked out into the rain, his thumbs stuck into the armholes of his waistcoat.

Jimmy slammed shut the door of the boiler and wept for

his jackdaw.

NEMONE

Even before we joined my father in Germany, I had begun to feel a certain disconnect from Tudor Hall. The noble chestnut trees where Dione and I hid high up among the branches and shared our childish secrets, the empty pool with its ghostly lotus, the garlic and sapphires of Burnt Norton, seemed part of the memory of halcyon days already fading fast. Here, at Banbury, in this huge pretentious, ugly house I felt that I was being rushed towards a destination which I did not want or understand.

On 20th November 1947 we were given the whole day off to celebrate the wedding of Princess Elizabeth and Lieutenant Philip Mountbatten RN. We crowded round the wireless in the assembly hall to listen to the broadcast from Westminster Abbey. Most held their breath when the Princess said, in her little thin, high-pitched voice, "I do". There was an audible intake of breath. Some girls hugged each other and, I dare say, shed tears. The broadcast was repeated several times during the course of the afternoon and rapt attention given it. I felt annoyed and frustrated: this really was too silly. From that moment I knew that there was no place for me in this world and that I must make my own way somewhere else.

During the winter holidays in Germany I discussed matters with my mother. "I'm never going to get married. I don't want any children." I announced.

"That would be an awful pity" she replied; "you'd be missing the most important thing in your life."

"I won't have the time" I said "I'm going to go into politics".

"Well at least get your education first."

"What's the point of education if you're just going to get married?"

"It'll make you a more interesting person for your hus-

tory." And, as I was to learn later, in the evaluation of evidence.

I was disappointed when Miss Blackburn told us that we were to study the Renaissance and Reformation. I had hoped that we would concentrate on something closer to our own day, something which would help to advance my coming brilliant career in politics.

"But no" she said firmly, "if you don't understand the Renaissance and Reformation you can't possibly understand the world we live in now." As usual, she was right.

Mrs Blackburn was, by conviction, a Quaker. Not an old-fashioned Quaker like the great Liberal families of Somerset who still, in my childhood, addressed one another in the archaic manner "thee and thou" in the vocative, but devout nevertheless. She had that disconcerting habit typical of her community of never telling even a white lie to ease the difficulties of social intercourse. I remember my mother asking Violet Clothier, a Quaker guest, whether she was cold (sitting in a raging draught in our cold and uncomfortable house). "Yes. I am" our guest replied. Firmly. Without embarrassment. In my family, where a little Irish blarney combined with a touch of English diplomacy made the courteous white lie acceptable, this seemed odd. While the Lethbridges would have said that we were fine, she said she was cold. Some found this directness alarming. Mary Berry, who was at Bath at the same time, though junior, to me, said in a recent television interview that she found Miss Blackburn unhelpful and intimidating.[5] This disconcerting honesty did, however, give her great strength as a teacher. She assessed one's work on its merit alone while another teacher might mark it up to boost one's confidence of mark it down if one seemed to be getting big-headed.

Under Miss Blackburn's Quaker regime every lesson would begin, not with the banging of desk lids and angry exhortations to settle down, but with a brief period of silence and meditation: water in the desert. Under her leadership the School became one of the most academically successful girls' schools in the country.

Every weekday morning for the next two years I would ride my bicycle up to the village of Beckington. There, in a folly built from great spiky lumps of flint under an Ilex tree, I would hide the bike and take the country bus to Bath. I would not read during the journey as looking down made me travel sick, but I had a good hour in which to think.

When I was a small child my mother had made me learn passages from the New Testament by heart. She did this because she loved the language of the King James Bible. The content interested her less. I was entranced by both. It never occurred to me that the Gospels were anything but true. After fifty years in the law I still read them, not as allegory or myth, but, with all their differences and discrepancies, as witness statements which have about them the ring of perfect truth.

As I trudged the pale golden streets of Bath, stopping sometimes to gaze into the steaming waters of the Roman baths where gigantic goldfish lurked in the jade green depths, sometimes entering the Abbey where marble statues of fat plutocrats supersede the pious relics of medieval devotion, in my mind I chewed over what I was reading at the time. It was the Renaissance and Reformation as promised by Miss Blackburn, Tawney's *Religion and the Rise of Capitalism*. I wanted to align myself with the Christian faith: the problem was it took so many forms. While I was drawn to the gentle goodness of the Quakers, the politics of the Levellers, I could not understand how any doctrine which came into being centuries after the death of its Founder could be valid. The Apostolic Succession seemed to make more sense. As for the Church of England: how could anything, so I argued to myself, founded by the mass murderer Henry VIII be taken seriously?

I remember Christmases past. The preparation, the anticipation, the childish excitement. The tree, decked ethereally with silver cobwebs and glass icicles, the log fire blazing in the grate, the sweet spicy scent of the plum pudding. Then suddenly the overwhelming sense of anticlimax. Whatever was all this for? Even as a young child I longed for someone at least to acknowledge whose birthday it was that we were celebrating. I must have been about ten when, on Christmas night, I took my hot brick wrapped in an old piece of blanket to bed with me, as usual.

I also took my copy of Milton's poetry. I snuggled underneath the eiderdown with the brick for comfort and read *Hymn On the Morning of Christ's Nativity*:

I
It was the Winter wild,
While the Heaven-born child,
All meanly wrapt in the rude manger lies;
Nature in awe to him
Had doffed her gaudy trim,
With her great Master so to sympathize:
It was no season then for her
To wanton with the Sun her lusty Paramour.

VI
The Stars with deep amaze
Stand fixed in steadfast gaze,
Bending one way their precious influence
And will not take their flight,
For all the morning light,
Or Lucifer that often warn'd them thence;
But in their glimmering Orbs did glow,
Until their Lord himself bespake, and bid them go.

VIII
The shepherds on the Lawn,
Or ere the point of dawn,
Sat simply chatting in a rustic row;
Full little thought they then,
That the mighty Pan
Was kindly come to live with them below:
Perhaps their loves, or else their sheep,
Was all that did their silly thoughts so busy keep.

X111
Ring out, ye crystal spheres!
Once bless our human ears,
If ye have power to touch our senses so

And let your silver chime
Move in melodious time;
And let the bass of Heaven's deep organ blow
And with your ninefold harmony
Make up full consort to th' angelic symphony.

This became my annual ritual until I left home and could go to midnight mass.

CHAPTER TWELVE

JIMMY

He had not seen Mary for nine years. She had long ago stopped writing to him. His son was a stranger. Annie was finding the long and expensive journey to Princetown increasingly burdensome. Because of the length of time he had served, in accordance with Home Office regulations, Jimmy was given permission to spend twenty-eight days in a London gaol in an attempt to repair his domestic relationships. So late in 1949 he arrived at Wandsworth.

The South London prison was hardly an improvement on Dartmoor. It rained less than in sunny Devon but, as the prisoners were locked in their cells for nineteen hours a day (twenty-two at the weekend), they derived little benefit from the more clement weather. The place was filthy, crawling with vermin. But at least faithful Annie visited every day, James Senior, gaunt and ghostly pale in the terminal phase of tuberculosis, once a week. Mary did not come at all. No one thought to bring little Jim.

After a week Jimmy was given a job in the Miscellaneous Stores which at least took him out of the cell, which he shared with two others, for a few hours each day. It was there that he saw for the first time the row of shiny black japanned boxes sitting on a shelf in a neat row. He asked one of his fellow storemen what they were.

"Them's the hanging kits" the fellow replied. Wandsworth prison was the distribution centre for the hangman's grisly paraphernalia, eleven feet of rope for a white man, thirteen for a black. One contained two ropes for a double hanging. When an execution was ordered, a box would be dispatched to the prison where it was to take place. This could be anywhere in the United Kingdom, the British Zone in Germany or in the Colonies. After the execution had taken place the kit was returned to a little shop in the Old Kent Road where it was reconditioned. No one seemed to know how many times the kit was re-used or exactly how it was re-conditioned.

Harry, the storeman, pointed out box number six. "That's the lucky box, Jim" he said. "When we send that one out we always lay bets that it won't be used. Nine time out of ten the geezer gets reprieved". Jimmy wondered whether number six had been sent up to Pentonville for him.

At the end of the month Jimmy was returned to Dartmoor. The prison medical officer, Dr McKay, called him in for a check-up. "Bloody hell, Jim, you look terrible." (Jimmy had lost a stone in weight). "What happened? Did she come to see you?"

"Nah. She never."

"Look laddie" said the kindly Scotsman "I'll give you a couple of days in hospital. I'll give you some glucose and Eastern Syrup to put a bit of meat back on you."

"Thanks, but no thanks" replied Jimmy "I'd sooner be in the boiler house with me cats".

Two days later he was called in to the Governor's office and told that his father had died. As he had just spent a month in London he would not be permitted to return there for the funeral. James was laid to rest in a pauper's grave at Kensal Green close to Kitty and Timmy. Annie was the only mourner. After the funeral she drank a solitary pint of stout in the Warrington and, chin on hand, looked back on her seemingly pointless life. One of useless sacrifice.

At his last sentence review, Jimmy had asked whether he could have any indication as to when he might be released – in three years, five years – whenever. He was told that no such information could be given.

"Look guv" he said "I've been here longer than any man. Can't you give me a date to look forward to, a bit of hope?"

"Sorry O'Connor, there's nothing much I can do for you."

"Well, can't you transfer me to one of them open prisons, the new ones?"

"They're not designed for men in your category. The answer is no."

Jimmy sank into depression. In all the years he'd been in gaol he had never felt so low. All the fight seemed to drain out of him. All the little schemes and rackets – mostly concerned with the trading of tobacco which had kept him energised – seemed to lose their value. Against all the evidence he had clung to the hope that he and Mary might achieve some kind of reconciliation, that he might see his son grown to manhood. He remembered the day he had taken little Jim on the number 9 bus down to Hamley's to buy his first train set. That little boy who held his hand as they walked through the mean streets of Kilburn was no more. What was he now? Cunning and streetwise or a dreamer? Respectable citizen like his pious great uncles, altar servers at Homer Row, or a scallywag like his grandfather? He wondered whether he would ever see him gain. He wished that he had swung into oblivion at the end of Pierrepoint's rope.

A few weeks later Jimmy's fortunes took a turn for the better. In all probability the kindly Dr McKay had put in a word for him. He was told that he was to be transferred back to Parkhurst. His journey to the Isle of Wight was markedly different from the occasion he had travelled there before, chained to a couple of hundred other prisoners, like slaves in old Mississippi. He wore civilian clothes and a warder travelling with him removed the handcuffs and gave him a plug of tobacco for his pipe. As he watched the morning sun sparkling on the Solent he felt his spirits lift.

Parkhurst had changed since his last sojourn there. It now accommodated dozens of old lags designated incorrigible rogues and sentenced to Preventive Detention under a Criminal Justice Act long ago repealed. Jimmy wrote in his memoir[1]

"Looking into the cells of these veterans was like visiting a respectable alms-house; white-headed old boys sitting happily beside their radios, sucking their old pipes, carpet slippers placed neatly under the bed. On the wall might be a picture of the King or Queen, or souvenirs of service in World War 1. There would be bright curtains at the window and a carpet on the floor. A cat might be purring on the bed. A chew of tobacco and then I'd sit there and listen. "This ain't a prison. It's a blooming convalescent home. In my day, boy, you used to have the old ball and chain round your leg. "Face the wall" when you come out of your cell. "No talking." They call this bird today. It's a lark." "Old Jack was the oldest burglar in England. He had no time for the modern cosh merchant. Like all old timers he despised young tearaways. "They haven't got the guts to stand up and have a clean fight. It was different in my day. We had to learn to work proper. None of this here bashing old women on the head for a few bob. We used to get the old stick out, the jemmy, and work all night. We took pride in it."

Jimmy described how Old Jack was ninety years old when he was finally released but a month later, he was back inside charged with being on enclosed premises in possession of housebreaking implements. "He didn't want to steal anything. he wanted to get back into Parkhurst. He missed his frying pan and all his old pals. He had no home to go to outside. They said he looked the picture of happiness when they put him back in the dock. His only worry was whether he would get back to his own cell."

The governor of Parkhurst, affectionately known as 'Black Jack', ran an enlightened regime. He achieved a sensible balance between carrot and stick. Looking back on this, his second sojourn at the prison, Jimmy could not recall any incidents of suicide and few of self-harm. There were remarkably few occasions of violence between prisoners and staff. While Black Jack was less than delighted to see his former valet back from Dartmoor, he appeared to bear him no malice for the destruction of the IRA records years before and gave him a coveted job in the Miscellaneous Stores alongside two other lifers. This kept all three out of mischief.

Saturday football was an important item in the prison regime. Playing the game and attending the matches was a coveted privilege and exclusion an effective punishment. Of course the system was abused from time to time, matches were rigged and betting scams operated, but its existence led to a much happier atmosphere than that hanging over the sullen misery of Dartmoor. The high point of the season was the Cup Final played between A and B wings. Although he was never a football fanatic, Jimmy really enjoyed this and placed several successful bets on the outcome. (In the outside world he had supported Everton, having made friends with several Everton players when he was serving in France at the beginning of the war.)

For the first time in years the Governor gave permission for a concert. Jimmy wrote to the manager of a repertory company playing a summer season at Ryde and asked him to bring his show, the comedy 'Love in the Mist' into the prison one weekend. On a beautiful, bright Sunday afternoon Jimmy met the company at the gate. Dressed in a crisp white shirt and trousers and wearing dark glasses, he forgot that he was a prisoner and imagined that he was Val Parnell putting on a command performance at the Palladium.

After the success of the play the prisoners started putting on shows of their own. At Christmas 1950 it was a pantomime, 'Little Red Riding Hood'. Father Bear was played by Scarface Nick, so-called because of the seven-inch gash across his face, Mother Bear by Jim the Penman, reputed to be the best forger in England. Little Red Riding Hood was played by Robbie Valentine, then in his fifteenth year of a life sentence for murdering his wife and her lover. The pantomime was a roaring success and was the inspiration for Jimmy's own play 'Her Majesty's Pleasure' which was later produced by Granada Television. With Bob Hoskins in a leading role the play received critical acclaim.

All was not sweetness and light, however. The great reforming Labour government which swept to power in 1945 was faltering. The prison population feared that a return to Conservative rule would mean an end to the enlightened regime which obtained in Parkhurst at the time: maybe an end to football, summer shows, Christmas pantomimes; back to the bad old days of mailbags, silence and bread-and-water. In the General Election of 23 February 1950 the Labour party had scraped back with a majority of five. It seemed that Clement Atlee's days as Prime Minister were numbered. It was obvious that another General Election would have to take place shortly.

The Home Secretary, Mr Chuter Ede, was to visit the prison. As when Empress Catherine the Great visited the Russian villages, there was panic. Painting and polishing, scrubbing and scraping, clean new seats on the lavatories. The cooks produced a special menu which the Governor tasted in advance of the Minister's arrival "smacking his lips as though he had just had some caviar from the Mirabelle" as Jimmy wrote later.

There were four men working in the Miscellaneous Stores that day, Jimmy, Robbie, Little Red Valentine, and another lifer. In came the Minister, escorted by the Governor and Chief Prison Officer. Although it was strictly forbidden to do so, Jimmy decided to take a chance and approach the great man.

"Excuse me, Sir" he said "Can I have a word with you?"

"Yes laddie. What can I do for you?"

"Sir, you've the reputation of being a very fair man" said Jimmy. "I've got a little request to make. They're a bit right wing in this nick, I come out of the back streets and my parents always voted Labour." (In fact neither James nor Annie ever voted at all.)

"They won't let us have the *Daily Herald* in here. Only the *Daily Telegraph* and *The Times*. We'd like to read the other side, the *Daily Herald*, the voice of the Labour Party, the voice of the workers."

"Is this correct, Governor?" asked the Home Secretary.

"Well, er yes, Minister. Commissioners' orders."

"Well, you'll have the *Daily Herald* in future laddie." And so it was.

"One other thing, sir, if you could help me. If you'd just get your little book out and put my name down. I'm doing a life sentence, sir. I've been here a number of years. I've got a little bit of form, but if you was to dig into it you'd see that I was no big time criminal. I'm not likely to be a danger to society. I've got a wife and kid sir. I want to settle down, go to work, build up a little haulage business. I hate to say it, sir, but there's an election coming up, not too far away in the future. There's always the chance that you can lose the election and if them Tories get in I've got no chance of getting out."

The Minister laughed. "What did you say your name was?"

"I didn't sir. O'Connor Sir. O, apostrophe, C O double N O R. James O'Connor, d.o.b. 20.05.1918."

Mr Chuter Ede took a notebook from his pocket and wrote it down.

"I'll look into it" he said "I'll look into your case."

Weeks and then months passed. Jimmy heard nothing. He began to sink back into depression. Then one day he received a letter from, of all places, Ethiopia. Bishop Matthew, who had confirmed him in the condemned cell and was now an Archbishop in charge of a vast African diocese, said that he was sitting on the terrace of his palace in Addis Ababa with Father McMenomy, who had been the priest on the *Lancastria*. He sent Jimmy a copy of his latest book and asked him in the friendliest terms about his plans for the future. Jimmy started thinking about the *Lancastria* and, in particular, about another survivor of the disaster, Harry Grattridge. A petty officer at that time, his career had prospered. He was now a commander in the merchant marine. Jimmy wrote to him, apologised for the address from which he wrote, reminded him of the circumstances under which they had last met. He told him of his wish to get young Jim out of the back streets of Kilburn. Harry Grattridge replied and eventually arranged a place for young Jim at the Mercantile Marine Training College. This transformed the young man's life.

*   *   *

October 25th 1951, the date of the general election. Jimmy felt increasingly despondent as the results came in. It was obviously going to be a close-run thing. In the event, although Labour got the larger popular vote, the Conservatives won by twenty-six seats. Attlee was out, Churchill was back in. Jimmy's heart sank.

The following morning he was called into the Governor's office. His heart was in his mouth. Maybe as a last gesture –

maybe, just maybe...

"I have to inform you, O'Connor said the Governor, "The Secretary of State has ordered that you be released on March 15 1952."

Jimmy walked out of the room in a daze. Five months to wait – it seemed unreal. Most lifers got three or four weeks notice, no more. He was afraid that something would go wrong and block his release. Those sixteen weeks seemed full of pitfalls. Back in his cell he began to worry. He worried about Robbie who had served fifteen years and who was bound to resent his being released after ten years and ten months. He worried about money. He wondered how he would manage on the five shillings and a letter to the Prisoners' Aftercare Association at Ecclestone Square he would receive on his release. He worried about who would be there at the gate to meet him. What about little Jim?

He lay down on his bed and fell asleep. A couple of hours later he was awakened by the sound of heavy footsteps and the jangle of keys. The door burst open and the cell was full of people, prisoners and screws who had heard the news of his impending release.

"Congratulations! Heard the good news."
"Good luck, Ginger."
"You're a lucky devil!"

Jimmy reached out for a cigarette and matches on top of his locker. He could not move. "Listen" he said "I can't bloody move. Someone light a cigarette for me."

"Leave off, Ginge. Don't take the piss."

Realising that he was serious, someone lit him a cigarette and someone else sent for a stretcher. He was carried to the hospital, unable to move anything but his head. His wrists and knees swelled up like balloons. He was given aspirin, belladonna and gold injections. A rheumatologist came down from London to examine him. Bee-sting injections were prescribed. Unfortunately, the orderly who gave them misread the prescription and, instead of giving him ten thousand units, gave him a hundred thousand. Jimmy woke at half past three in the morning to find a priest standing by his bed.

"What are you doing here, father?"

"I'm here to give you the last rites son. They said it was touch and go, son, touch and go."

After he had been anointed, Jimmy rallied. The following day he had a relapse and the priest returned. This time the improvement was maintained, and he slowly got better. By Christmas he was able to walk a few steps.

In February 1952 he was transferred from Parkhust to Wormwood Scrubs so that he could be treated at the Hammersmith Hospital, which is next to the gaol. He enjoyed the short trips to the hospital thinking that in a few weeks he would be walking the streets a free man. By this time he was almost fully restored to health. On the morning of 15 March 1952 he was able to walk down to the Chief Prison Officer's office to sign for his licence. This document stated that the Secretary of State could recall him to prison at any time he saw fit. This licence was to extend for the whole of his natural life. At the same time, he was assured that he would only be recalled if he committed a crime of violence. In his own mind he was certain that he would never again commit a crime of any kind. He was true to his resolution.

Faithful Annie was waiting at the gate to take him home.

NEMONE

The Flying Dutchman roared into my young life like a tsunami, wreaked havoc and, sixty years later, drifted gently out again like an exhausted Autumn breeze. As a last act of homage, I spent a week at Aldbourne where he had bought a cottage, helping Gina, his widow, sorting and shredding the mountains of love letters from his many lovers he had received and preserved over the years. For a moment we must rewind to the early months of 1950 and the dying days of the Attlee government.

My father had known Anthony Marecco in Germany, where, as junior counsel to Hartley Shawcross, he was one of the prosecuting team at the Nuremburg trials. My father, as Chief of Intelligence, was investigating and supplying the material upon which the prosecution was based. Now the Flying Dutchman was back in England and had been selected as Liberal candidate for the Wells Division of Somerset in the forthcoming general election. My mother backed him in this (my father, as a public servant, had to maintain the appearance of political neutrality) and with the Hobhouse, Clark and Clothier families, threw herself into his election campaign.

The first time I saw this tall, terrifying figure with its Hispanic good looks standing in front of our fireplace like an incarnation of Mr Rochester, I was lost. I was back at Tudor Hall, gazing at the resplendent figure of Captain Anderton, a four-foot halfling in a box-pleated skirt.

When, after a long, alarming silence, he suddenly spoke to me and asked me what I did, I was struck dumb. How could I tell this gorgeous creature I was still at school, still at bloody school?

I made myself his slave. By day stuffing envelopes with elections addresses, walking the muddy Somerset lanes to knock on cottage doors, by night, by the yellow light of oil lamps lit in draughty village halls and schools, I absorbed the noble Liberal message; the Whig view of history, Henry George's theory of land tax, the Enlightenment, Churchill's (always a liberal at heart) magnificent vision of a United States of Europe. When the Liberal Party was slaughtered in the polls (though, in the Wells Division, we came a respectable second to the Tories) I wept bitter tears. In all my life I have never wavered in my political allegiance; I have never cast a winning vote.

Anthony came to the house after the election to pay his respects to my mother and to thank her for her help. As we walked to his car he said to me "Next time you come to visit your grandmother in London give me a ring. I'll cook you lunch in my flat." He passed me an envelope on which was written "GRO 1409". I have it to this day.

CHAPTER THIRTEEN

Jimmy

Back at Bristol Gardens Annie had saved up and bought a bottle of whiskey to celebrate Jimmy's return home. A group of friends and neighbours were already sitting around the tiny living room, eyeing the bottle thirstily, when mother and son arrived. Among the guests was a fat little man in a shiny blue suit, the lapels of which were liberally drenched with cigarette ash: Tom Tullett of the Sunday Express.

"You've got a great story here, Jim" he said. "Give it to me exclusive and my paper will see you alright."

Without even reading it, Jimmy signed the proffered agreement. The reporter finished the last of Annie's whiskey and left to continue the drinking session in his favourite pub in Fleet Street.

Tullet got what he had come for, a front page exclusive. Jimmy didn't get a penny. Others, however, were more generous, as the poor so often are. Within hours he had been showered with gifts of money and clothes from people who knew what it is to have nothing.

After a couple of hours in Annie's flat, Jimmy announced that he was going to see his son. He made his way north into the familiar streets of Kilburn. Although it was ten years since the Blitz, the area was still half derelict. Many houses were boarded up and interspersed with piles of rubble overgrown with purple buddleia and willow herb. The little shops were half empty (food rationing was not to end for another year). Only the pubs gave signs that the once vibrant Anglo-Irish community was still alive.

Jimmy knocked on the door of what had once been his home. Although it was early afternoon the curtains were still drawn. After a pause, he knocked again. There was the rattle of chains being unhooked and bolts drawn back.

"Bloody hell" he said to himself "sounds like the fucking nick." Then, shouting, "Open up! I ain't going to bloody eat you." The door opened a crack and Mary's nervous face appeared. Jimmy pushed the door open with his shoulder. "I've come to see me boy" he said.

In the front room twelve or fifteen men were sitting around dragging on their cigarettes. The air was thick with smoke. Jimmy formed the impression that they had been there all night, waiting for him. "I want to see me boy" he repeated. "Where's Jim?"

"He's been working" said Mary in a shaky voice. "He's fast asleep in bed". "Well fucking get him out of bed. Tell him his Dad's here."

Mary disappeared into the passage, sobbing gently. None of the men said a word. "Well, you *do* look a load of half-wide mugs. You should look in the mirror at your fucking faces. Did you think I was going to kill you?"

One of them piped up "Don't be like that, Jim. We don't mean no harm."

"Oh so you're the geezer are you? Are you the one what's nicked me wife? Tell me!" "Not me, mate" answered the fellow, trembling.

Another man, white as a sheet, was shaking like a leaf. Mary reappeared from the corridor and put her arm round the man's shoulder. Jimmy turned on her "Tell me, d'you love this fellow?" She didn't answer but continued to sob. "Well, he wants to know, even if I don't."

"I don't know" she stammered.

"Well make up your fucking mind. Anyway, where's me son?"

At that moment young Jim appeared wearing vest and pants, rubbing his eyes.

"You know who I am, don't you?"

"Yes, you're me dad."

"And who's this geezer?"

"It's me Uncle Arthur."

"Tell me, son, who do you want to be with? Me or him?"

"Uncle Arthur. Can I go back to bed?"

"Go back to bed. Go to fucking sleep. Good luck to you. You won't see me no more."

For the next hour Jimmy stamped round the gloomy streets of Kilburn, barging into pub after pub, looking for someone to whom he could pour out his frustration and rage. Finally, in the dear old Chippenham, he found Billie the Orphan, sitting at the bar tenderly nursing a pint of bitter. Jimmy told him his story.

"The fuck-pig's nicked me wife, me son and me home. I'm fucking well going to kill him."

"Bloody hell, Jim" said sensible Billie. "You've just done a life: d'you want to do another?"

"What then?" asked Jimmy.

"Find yourself another bird, make a couple more kids, get a nice little council flat. There's still plenty of villainy we can do together. Have a pint?"

When time was called Jimmy made his way back to Bristol Gardens. Annie was still up, sitting with one of the guests who had been there earlier.

"The Old Bill's been round, Jim" she said. "Told you to keep away from Mary. Didn't say why."

"Why?" roared Jimmy. "Why? Because she wants me back in the nick so that she can keep her fucking pension. That's why."

Annie's remaining guest looked embarrassed. "I'd best make a move" he said. "I'll take me bits and pieces and have it away." Annie handed him his modest toiletries in a paper carrier bag. "And here's a nice piece of bread pudding for the morning." Then, addressing Jimmy, she added, half apologetically, "He's on the dust. He has to start early, half past four o'clock."

At a glance Jimmy took in the man's situation: his pathetic luggage, his shabby clothes, his big simple harmless face. He felt a stab of compassion. "Don't leave on my account, mate. Stay here" he said. "It's okay by me."

"I've got a bed at Rowton House" the chap answered, "I'll be fine". Jimmy turned to his mother. "If you've found yourself a boyfriend, Mum, then good luck to you. You're over twenty-one. Make us all a cup of tea."

This Annie did. The three sat up late, reminiscing about their strange respective lives. Ted Rogers and Annie had met in the Warwick Castle pub a few weeks after James senior's death. He had moved in with her shortly afterwards. He had been a miner in the Rhonda Valley before the war but had left his home and walked to London at the height of the depression. He had been there ever since. "He's a good man, Ted" said Annie, "he's not clever like your Dad but he don't never hit me and he sings lovely, in Welsh. [1]

Sunday morning. Young Jim was working as a page boy at the Savoy. Having graduated from the Mercantile Marine Training College, he was waiting for a ship to join as a member of the crew. It was half past seven in the morning when he walked into the hotel through the service entrance, smart and chipper, the *Sunday Express* tucked neatly under his arm. With his lantern jaw and thick auburn hair it was obvious that he and the man in the front page photograph were from the same gene pool. "On your toes, Ginger" said one of the kitchen porters. "Guvnor wants to see you in his office."

In the hotel manager's room, open on the desk for all to see, lay the Sunday Express.

"This fellow here – anything to do with you?"

"Yes, sir. It's me Dad."

"Sorry son, but you're out. Ruin the reputation of the hotel. Pick up your gear and get on your bike."

Young Jim felt a great stab of indignation at the injustice of the manager's conduct. He was, however, too inarticulate to do anything but mumble "Alright then" and collect his possessions.[2]

After a few days he began to feel uneasy as well as hard done by. His conduct towards his father had been pretty shabby. He decided that he must make amends without upsetting his mother or insulting Uncle Arthur. He was able to make contact with Jimmy with the help of Billie the Orphan and the Kilburn bush telegraph. Before long father and son were sharing a friendly pint in the Chippenham. Their ensuing friendship was to last for the rest of Jimmy's life.

Another interested reader of the *Sunday Express* was Mrs Van der Elst, philanthropist and dedicated campaigner against the death penalty. She had been for many years compiling a dossier of capital cases where the guilt of the person accused was seriously in doubt. Jimmy's case seemed to be exactly such a one. She instructed a solicitor and a private investigator to act on Jimmy's behalf. They traced and interviewed George Sewell, an important witness for the prosecution at Jimmy's trial. Sewell now admitted that he had purchased the gold watch and chain, significant exhibits in the case, from Jimmy, as part of the proceeds of a burglary in Bath several weeks before the date of the murder.

When Jimmy heard this, in his own words he "went ballistic". He stormed down to Scotland Yard and confronted Chief Inspector Thorp. He demanded to see the watch and chain, accusing Thorp of framing him. Thorp was oddly conciliatory. He told Jimmy that the items had been returned to the jeweller in Bath. He sent for the stolen property book and showed him the signature of the jeweller, a Mr Littuar, who confirmed that he had received the watch and chain from Scotland Yard in the summer of 1942.

Mrs Van der Elst set up a conference attended by counsel, solicitor and enquiry agent. They discussed the next steps to be taken in Jimmy's case. Did they now have enough to mount an appeal against conviction? When the enquiry agent was instructed to travel to Bath and interview Mr Littuar, Jimmy felt a sense of impatience and frustration. After all, he had himself seen the jeweller's signature in the stolen property book. Why did everything have to take so long? Why was his team so cautious?

Tom Tullet's piece in the *Sunday Express* had aroused considerable interest in Fleet Street, not all of it sympathetic. At the time, the early fifties, the police were largely held in respect and the idea that a jury could come to a wrong decision in a capital case was regarded as highly unlikely if not bizarre. This was a time, pre 10 Rillington Place, pre Hillsborough, before the notorious comment by Lord Denning "the idea that a jury of twelve good men and true, the Court of Criminal Appeal and the House of Lords could all be wrong is absolutely preposterous".[3] In the public imagination, the kindly village bobby, the Dixon of Dock Green, the Fabian of the Yard, was closer to the truth than the sometimes sinister and manipulative figure of today's perception. Imagine the headlines in the tabloid press *"Nat Thorp framed Jimmy O'Connor, An insult to a brave man, to a whole body of brave and honest officers."*

Mrs Van der Elst, a sincere and idealistic campaigner, did her cause few favours by her eccentric behaviour. For years she would turn up outside the prison where an execution was to be carried out in a chauffeur-driven Daimler wearing a garden party hat, waving a handmade placard and wailing. To the public she became a figure of fun. It took three serious left wing political activists, Victor Gollancz, Canon John Collins and Arthur Koestler, who together mounted a ten-year campaign, to sway public opinion against the obscenity of the death penalty. Although the Metropolitan Police were, in general, a popular and respected force, the occasional criticism arising from Jimmy's case must have been deeply disconcerting to Chief Inspector Thorp. As he was to say later, the unfamiliar and sometimes hostile attention of the press "got under his skin".

One of the newspapers which took a sympathetic view of Jimmy's case was *The People*, a Sunday tabloid. The editor commissioned Duncan Webb, the paper's chief crime reporter, to travel to Bath with Jimmy to interview Mr Littuar, the jeweller whose shop had been burgled. Driving overnight the two men found Mr Littuar "a nice old gentleman with a Van Dyck beard wearing a silk dressing gown" opening up his shop. He gave the two drinks while he ate his breakfast. They discussed the case. Mr Littuar was polite and helpful. He told them he had never signed the stolen property book; had never received the gold watch and chain, had never met – or even heard of – Chief

Inspector Thorp. If there was a signature in the stolen property book, it must have been a forgery.

The People declined to run the story. Maybe it was too critical of the police to accord with editorial policy. Duncan Webb and Jimmy – even more so – were frustrated and angry but nothing could be done.

During the course of the investigation Jimmy had met a journalist called Jack Fishman, then news editor of *The Empire News*, a Sunday tabloid in the Kemsley group, now defunct. More courageous than the editor of *The People*, Fishman decided to publish early in May the story of Jimmy's expedition to Bath and his interview with Mr Littuar. The following day Jimmy was contacted by Billie the Orphan "The Old Bill's been round, going off alarming. They don't like the story in the Sunday paper. They said you're to contact them."

Jimmy was nervous. He feared for his licence. He decided to consult Jack Fishman who advised him to telephone Thorp from his office. This he did, while Fishman listened on an extension. Fishman later made a witness statement, under oath, which was supplied to the Home Office when Jimmy and the family endeavoured to re-open his appeal. The statement ended with the following exchange:

"O'Connor suddenly said "You know I'm innocent and I'm going to keep on till I prove I didn't do it". Thorp's reply was "I'm warning you, Ginger, drop it. Or I'll put in on you again like I did last time. Next time it will be for the rest of your life". Thorp then hung up." [3]

A couple of days later Mrs Van der Elst organised another conference in the Temple. It was attended by counsel, solicitor, enquiry agent and Jimmy himself. He felt profoundly depressed. He knew that he could not ignore Thorp's threats: if he carried on with his campaign, continued with his allegations against the police, the likelihood was that his licence would be revoked and he would, in his own words, "be back in sunny Devon for the rest of my life". He felt bitterly ashamed that he had let down these good people whose time and money he had wasted. He could only cling to the knowledge that one day Thorp would retire, and that gradually public opinion would become more liberal. It might even accept the possibility that the criminal justice system is less than perfect, that, on occasion, it might even get things horribly wrong.[4]

NEMONE

All the drudgery, all the hard work, finally paid off. I was offered places at both Somerville College Oxford and at Newnham College Cambridge. It was an afternoon of thick fog and I was walking Lob, our Old English Sheepdog, through the water meadows at the back of the field we called Czechoslovakia, when I heard my mother squelching through the sodden grass carrying not one but two telegrams. We hugged each other half laughing, half crying. "Which is it to be?" In spite of my loyalty to my father, a Cambridge man, I chose to go to Oxford where both my maternal grandfather and my aunt Josephine had been so happy.

My grandmother invited me to stay with her in London as a reward for my success. Buffy would take me out and improve my cultural education. This was not difficult as her brother-in-law (Josephine's husband) was a curator at the Victoria and Albert Museum.

There was however a problem. I had no decent clothes. All our clothes coupons had been spent on dreadful pleated skirts and chill proof underwear. My mother had no interest in fashion. How would I ever transform myself into the international vamp which I fully intended to be? Women's clothes in the forties and the beginning of the fifties must have been about as ugly as it was possible to be. Not only the box pleats but the thick lisle stockings, the masculine shoes and the horrible headscarves knotted at the front were an abomination. Even the Princesses Elizabeth and Margaret, who were remarkably pretty girls, looked hideous in their ATS uniforms.

I knew that there was another world out there. I remember an issue of *Picture Post* with photographs of a Christian Dior model wearing a pale green silk dress overprinted with cobwebs. It had a long full skirt and a nipped-in waist. 'This is the New

Look for 1947' read the caption. Oh, how I wanted to be the goddess who wore it!

GRO 1409. I do not know to this day how I screwed up enough courage to ring the number on the envelope but ring it I did. A few days later I found myself walking along Piccadilly, half dazed, half dreaming. Having joined the train at Sloane Square I stood the whole way to Green Park, although the train was half empty, to avoid creasing the green New Look coat which I had so carefully stitched from a paper pattern the week before. Up the steps, out of the Underground, turn right towards Hyde Park Corner, pass the In and Out Club, turn into White Horse Street, pass a shop selling suitcases and into the hustle and bustle of Shepherd Market. Press the intercom, up five flights of stairs, arrive breathless at the tiny flat perched among the rooftops of Mayfair. There he was, Mr Darcy, Mr Rochester, tall, Hispanic and terrifying. "Come in" he said at the top of the stairs. "I shall call you Susan. Nemone is such a silly name."

The walls were covered with books from floor to ceiling. On every flat surface were photographs of a beautiful woman, usually shot in profile, her chin resting on her long, elegant, exquisitely manicured hands. "This is Louise, Louise de Vilmorin. We live together in France near Strasbourg. She doesn't like to come to London very much.

"She's so beautiful" I ventured.

"Oh, she's beautiful alright but we make each other very unhappy. Her latest book has just been turned down for the Prix Femina which adds to our misery. Do you like kippers?"

"I like everything" I replied obediently.

"That's just as well. They're the only thing I know how to cook."

We moved into the kitchen. The books had been replaced by wine racks. Every cup, every piece of china was inscribed with the name Louise. My host cooked the kippers in a jug of boiling water. We ate the kippers and drank red wine from huge glasses, inevitably engraved with the name Louise.

We talked gravely about Germany and my father, then a few minutes after half past three, the Flying Dutchman said "well, young lady, it's been lovely talking to you, but I have work to do. Can you find your way home?"

"Of course. I'll be fine" I said. I wondered whether he would kiss me. But no. No kisses.

"Remember me to Lady Maynard. I'm very fond of her." Three steps to the top of the stairs and I was gone. I wondered whatever he wanted of me.

JIMMY

Jack Fishman did his best for Jimmy, helping him to publish his material in Fleet Street. Jimmy did not have the education necessary to work for the quality papers; he was restricted to working for the tabloids. Nevertheless, for the first couple of years he did well, having contacts and access to material which others did not. However, he met with jealousy and opposition from the Fleet Street professionals and was denied membership of the National Union of Journalists. This meant that he was forever limited to working as an informant or stringer rather than an accredited card-carrying journalist. Fortunately, he was able to supplement his income with the assistance of the Irish construction industry.

1952 saw catastrophic floods in the Thames Estuary and East Anglia. Over a thousand people died and many more lost their homes. As was always when there is a sudden need for a large labour force skilled or willing to work in construction, the Irish community benefitted. Billboards with good old Irish names like Murphy and Kelly sprang up everywhere. Construction companies recruited labourers every day from Kilburn and Cricklewood. Jimmy was among their number. For several weeks he worked near Benfleet in coastal Essex, building the sea wall. *Picture Post*, then published by Hulton now sadly defunct, ran the story.

Meanwhile Jimmy divorced Mary and moved in with a kindly widow in Paddington. Annie and Ted continued to live together in unsanctified bliss. "He gave me twenty golden years" as

Annie said after Ted's death in 1970.

Young Jim finally got his boat and spent several years on *The Queen Mary*. He had always wanted to fly and, when an opportunity arose, he joined the United States Air Force stationed at Fairbanks Alaska. He then took advantage of the fast-track route open for veterans of the US Armed Forces and became an American citizen. He married his commanding officer's daughter and, after his retirement from the US Air Force, moved to Oakland California where he made a modest fortune in container shipping. The manager of the Savoy, by his foolish snobbish action in dismissing him from his job, had in fact, done young Jim the greatest of favours.

NEMONE

After a couple more days in London I arrived home to find a small brown paper parcel waiting for me. It was addressed in the strong characteristic handwriting I was to come to know so well over the years. I have never been able to throw away a scrap of it, however insignificant the message it conveyed. It was designated firmly to Miss Susan Lethbridge and contained two books, volumes one and two of twelve, in translation by Scott Moncrieff, of *À la recherche de temps perdu* by Marcel Proust. "This book will change your life forever" wrote the Flying Dutchman. *"The world will never seem the same again. Let me know when you're ready for the next two volumes. I'm off to France for two or three months. I'll telephone you when I get back. Would you like to go to the opera? Two or three months"*. Two or three years it would seem.

I had time to spend before I went up to Oxford. One morning, scanning the small classified advertisements which appeared on the front page of *The Times* (Kennel, Farm and Aviary being my favourite destination) I came across an entry which seemed to have been inserted especially for me. "Female student wanted to teach English conversation to French children. Alsace province. No other duties. Reply in confidence to Box No..." I looked at the map of France. The small town of Dettwiller, from whence the advertiser had written, was only some twenty miles from the place where the Flying Dutchman and his lover lived. It looked as if the hand of fate had moved to help me.

My hosts, the family Duval, owned a shoe factory located in the wine growing area of central Alsace. Low rolling hills covered with blue green vines stretched as far as the eye could see in every direction. There was a handsome church which, something I have never encountered since, was shared by the Catholic and Protestant congregations. On Sunday mornings the bells rang a soft contralto carillon, quite different in character from the sparkling treble chimes of the English tradition.

On entering the Duvals' house for the first time, I felt a strange frisson, half guilt half delight. It was so obviously a Catholic house. The stoop for holy water at the door, the crucifix in every room, the picture of the Sacred Heart or the Assumption – I knew my mother would have been appalled had she seen the house. She would have thought it crude, tasteless. I was being corrupted, brainwashed and I was delighted. At the same time, I wanted to hug her and tell her that I was sorry. I didn't want to hurt or insult her. I was exercising my own free will.

My young pupils, all girls, were a delight, friendly and eager to learn. Their father was an affable sexual predator who took my rejection of his persistent advances with unruffled good humour. Their mother, who was, when I arrived, in the second trimester of pregnancy, seemed withdrawn, depressed even. Her husband's lechery (which he made no effort to conceal) seemed to have exhausted and defeated her. The little girls, bright and observant, were in no way fazed by their father's behaviour or by my obvious embarrassment. They used to dissolve into fits of giggles every time they observed their father's wandering hands starting on their shameless journey.

On Sunday Monsieur Duval would drive the family to mass in an antiquated Hispano Suiza, and, having dropped us off at the church, would continue up the hill to the factory to do, so he insisted, some urgent business there. Madame Duval wore a black lace mantilla, and I was delighted when she gave me one of my own. The little girls looked enchanting in their long white socks and short lace gloves, clutching their mother-of-pearl rosaries.

And what of the Flying Dutchman? I found the local telephone directory but could discover no entry under his name or that of Louise de Vilmorin. I was too embarrassed to intrude on Madame Duval's unhappiness and too cautious to encourage Monsieur's lechery to ask for the help of either in tracing the object of my desire. Nevertheless, I have fond memories of those weeks in Alsace. There were trips to Strasbourg to visit Madam Duval's parents, or to go shopping. The narrow medieval streets had been extensively damaged (but lovingly restored after each conflict) in the Franco-Prussian war and then again in two world wars "always by the same barbarians" said Madame's father bitterly. There was, however, a moment of magic when, turning a corner in one of those twisted streets, the dark red cathedral suddenly "rose like an exaltation" before one's astonished eyes.

There were those three-hour Sunday lunches in the orchard when, having returned from mid-morning mass (celebrated in Latin according to the Tridentine rite) we would find the long table already set up for luncheon under the ancient gnarled apple trees. The pâté de foie gras and the chicken liver mousse, marbled with green pistachio nuts and black truffles surrounded by fine sparkling jelly were already awaiting our attention on a big flat white dish in the centre of the table. This cold hors d'oeuvre would be followed by soup, either an emerald green puree of fresh peas or a delicate lettuce soup mysteriously named after its inventor, a Capuchin monk called Père Tranquille. The soup would be followed perhaps by a cassoulet incorporating goose and haricot beans, or the traditional Alsatian choucroute garni, or on high days and holidays several simply cooked chickens garnished with a sauce made of pink crayfish described by Elizabeth David, as "the palest of rose pink sauces of the most perfect creamy texture and subtle flavour...the most lyrical of dishes".[5] After this the children would be allowed to leave the table and play, just as Peter, Cherry and I had been at Christmas dinners past. The adults would indulge themselves further with glasses of the locally brewed Mirabelle liqueur, until the pudding arrived.

*   *   *

Summer was drawing to a close. Soon I would be going up to Oxford. One morning Madame Duval said to me "I can't allow you to leave without seeing the most important picture in France. We're going to Colmar."

Madame Duval drove us – that is, the little girls and myself – some thirty miles through the vineyards to the small town of Colmar where the renowned Isenheim altarpiece was displayed in a small museum. Free standing, it was the only objet d'art in the room. Brought up, as we are, on the sublime, somehow sanitised crucifixions of the Renaissance or the grave formality of the Byzantine rite, Grünewald's altarpiece is truly shocking. Painted at the time of the Thirty Years War, when a gibbet stood at every crossroad, war crimes and atrocities must have been commonplace, the altarpiece shows it as it must have been. The dreadful grey-green face of a man who had died under torture can only have been painted by someone who had seen such a thing for himself. The little girls stood at the end of the room, huddled together. I felt that their mother should not have confronted them with such a nightmare.

Madame Duval stood in front of the crucifixion, her rosary in her hand. Tears were streaming down her face. Then she turned to me and took my hand. "Come" she said. We walked round to the back of the altarpiece. Jesus was depicted in scarlet and gold. Crude but dazzling. Triumph. Resurrection. We hugged each other, a little sheepishly perhaps. I'd never seen Madame happy before.

Then we went to a nearby patisserie and ate some ice cream before taking the darkening road home.

                    *   *   *

At Christmas Marie Laure, the eldest of the children, wrote to me. After the usual salutations, she wrote Maman desires to be remembered to you. She regrets that she was not so nice with you but she was not very well at that time. After you departed

He was taken on by Peter Rawley, a professional agent, who saw the potential of this man who wrote from experience and in the vernacular. A series of short stories was published in *Today*, a magazine published by Eddie Shah and now sadly defunct. He even wrote a treatment – or synopsis – for a film which he sold in a pub to someone from Ealing Studios for £100. It became, after development, the classic comedy 'The Lady Killers'. This nearly broke Peter Rawley's heart.

NEMONE

I arrived home from France to find my father enjoying a short period of leave from Germany. My parents, obviously, asked me about my time with the family Duval. I found it difficult to give a true account of my experience: I did not mention Mr Duval's behaviour as I knew that it would shock them and would make it difficult to get permission for any further trips abroad. I did not mention the Flying Dutchman or my feelings for him. The whole thing seemed silly and humiliating. I could not however conceal my great new passion: it all came tumbling out: a visit to Colmar, the Isenheim altar piece, the Damascene moment.

"I'm going to be a Catholic. Next week. Now. Immediately."

There was a horrified silence. Then my father said "I hope you're not serious."

"I am"

"That damn French family must have got at you."

"They haven't. I made up my own mind."

"You're only seventeen" my mother interjected. "You're far too emotional. All over the place. It was Shakespeare who talked about the 'boiled brains of seventeen to twenty-three'."

"Show me the reference" I said. Insufferably. "I've never come across the passage."

"Don't be rude to your mother" my father shouted. "Apologize."

"Sorry Mummy."

"Well, you've got to admit this isn't a rational decision. It's retrograde."

"How can you possibly say it's retrograde? The Church is the glory of Europe and has civilised half the rest of the world."

"While I admit that there's something to be said for the Roman church worldwide – I have to admit that I admire the medical missionaries in India – the Church in Ireland is VILE. It undermines the Empire. "

"So what?" I muttered.

"Your Irish Protestant grandmother must be turning in her grave."

The argument rolled on for a couple of days. In the end I agreed, reluctantly, not to do anything irrevocable, until I came down from Oxford. There, for the time being, the matter rested.

It was a relief when the letter arrived. The large, strong familiar handwriting.

Dear Susan,
I'm going to be in London for a couple of weeks. Benjamin Britten's new opera Billy Budd is opening at Covent Garden. Would you like to see it? I'm sure that your grandmother would put you up. Let me know what you think.
Love
A.

It must have been a relief to my mother to see me suddenly transfer my affection to things worldly from things celestial. It was good to find ourselves as one again as we made arrangement for my trip to London and discussed the all-important question of what to wear. I had one evening dress: bought for my first dance, held at Uppingham, the year before. It was a copy of Princess Margaret's bridesmaid frock worn at her sister's wedding. White georgette printed with tiny flowers with a demure shawl collar. We agreed it was too girly for a grand metropolitan evening.

My mother said "That'll solve the problem; I'll give you your Christmas present in advance." She unwrapped the dress from its tissue paper covering. I tried it on. It was perfect. Dark green silk with a gold thread running through the fabric. To me it seemed the acme of sophistication. Christian Dior's New Look.

The gardenia. A thing of immaculate beauty. At the base of one of the waxy white concave petals, a single raindrop. A few glossy green leaves, then a frill of cellophane bearing the legend Moyses Stevens. Finally, a handwritten note 'Wear this flower for me in your hair this evening'. My grandmother pinned the gardenia to the top of my ponytail. Off I went to the opera. In my glory.

There is no sound in the world more thrilling than that of an orchestra tuning up before a performance. My head was spinning, and I dared not look at the Flying Dutchman as we took our seats in the stalls. The house lights went down and the curtain went up. The stage had become the deck of a man o' war late in the eighteenth century, at the time of the Munity on the Nore. Sailors swung to and fro in the rigging. The loathsome Claggart bullied the young midshipmen. The saintly Billy was obviously doomed to tragedy.

The interval. The Flying Dutchman said that we should get a glass of champagne. Then, "I'm vaguely looking for some friends of mine". A tall, alarming woman swept down the wide marble staircase followed by a posse of acolytes. My heart thumped with fear.

"Oh my God. It's Miss Inglis."

A wave of terror and guilt swept over me. I had never explained to her why I had left Tudor Hall or apologised for it, then I realised I was mistaken. It wasn't Miss Inglis at all. The Dutchman presented me to the Duchess of Westminster. She gave me a chilly nod and turned her attention to my escort.

One of the acolytes, perhaps sensing my discomfort, asked me kindly "How are you enjoying the opera? Do you like the music? Do you find it a bit modern?"

"The story's so awful, so unfair; I can't even *hear* the music."

After poor Billy had sung his farewell to Starry Vere and duly swung from the yardarm, we joined the Duchess's party and made our way to the 400 Club in Leicester Square. As we took our places at a table in the darkened room, the Dutchman said "I've already got a bottle of whisky here. It's been waiting for me since 1939. A waiter brought the bottle, half full and inscribed with his name. 'Mr Anthony Marreco.'

"Charming tradition" said the Duchess. "That's why I like this place."

Bobby Harvey was at the piano. He sang:

"Sempi Lou, when she was two,
Was pure as the driven snow.
At seventeen, her slate was clean
Pure as the driven snow.
Ho! Ho! Pure as the driven snow."

The Flying Dutchman and the Duchess danced. After five minutes or so they were cheek to cheek. I sat sadly watching the room. All eyes were drawn to a statuesque woman in a column of white lace and white satin pumps. Expressionless, exquisite, an ice princess. Barbara Goalen, pictured in every issue of *Vogue* that year. In my flouncy green dress and childish gold sandals I felt utterly diminished. When finally I got to dance with the Flying Dutchman he was stiff and I was awkward. Cheek to check was out of the question. After all, my cheek only reached halfway up his chest.

Back at the table the conversation turned to Germany. Everyone pressed the Dutchman on the subject of the Nuremberg trials and his role in the prosecuting team. "Tell us about Goering's suicide" commanded the Duchess. "How did he get away with it?"

"Oh, he took a cyanide capsule into the loo and bit into it. He was dead within thirty seconds."

"Is it right that the Americans made a total balls-up of the executions?" interjected one of the acolytes. "Pulled their heads right off? Why didn't we give the job to Pierrepoint He's supposed to be the expert."

"Ssh!" said the Duchess "Bendor!" not in front of the child."

On the way home in the taxi the Flying Dutchman put his arm

round my shoulders.

"There's something I've got to tell you" out I blurted "I'm going to be a Catholic."

He pulled his arm away. "Don't be pathetic Susan" he said "<u>Nobody's</u> a Catholic."

Despite that inauspicious first date, the Flying Dutchman continued to ask me out, sometimes to the theatre or the opera, sometimes to another lunch of kettle-boiled kippers at Shepherd Market. From time to time more volumes of Proust arrived by post at Black Dog Cottage and I assimilated the great themes of jealousy, snobbery and class. As he had said before, the world never seemed quite the same again. Anthony seemed to slot so easily into that convoluted universe, one so different from the simpler, more straightforward one into which I had been born. In private he never touched me. We talked gravely about politics, about Germany, about genocide, about my father. In public he liked to present me, a flower in my hair, to his friends, all of his generation. Once this had been done, he ignored me.

At Christmas there was a family conference at Black Dog.

"What are we to make of Nemone's demon lover?" asked Buffy.

"It's quite obvious" answered Josephine, "he's using her as a stalking horse".

"Who is he stalking?"

"I've no idea – well, one of his elderly ladies I suppose. He should be ashamed of himself, chasing a little schoolgirl."

Buffy then confessed "I looked him up in Debrett. Seems that he was married to a daughter of the Duke of Rutland during the war. Divorced after two years."

"He does love a Duchess alright. There's a picture of him dancing with the Duchess of Argyll at the 400 in this week's Tatler."

"Naughty Marg of Arg!"

"Most unfortunate" said my grandmother. "Her reputation…"

"But he's <u>such</u> a dish" said Buffy with a sigh.

"I'm so worried. Just so worried" said my poor mother.

I closed my eyes and said nothing. I wished they'd all shut up and go away. Was I living in the middle of a silly Victorian novel or what? But at least Mr Rochester's mad wife in the attic came to a sticky end so everyone could live happily ever after. Anyway, soon I'd be going up to Oxford.

Jude's 'Christminster', just over the horizon, glowing against the night sky.[2] Christ Church and Trinity, Magdalen and Merton, Balliol and BNC. Oriel and Exeter, All Souls and St John's. Remote and mysterious Campion Hall. Soft golden Cotswold Stone, wide quadrangles and hammerbeam halls. Then the brave new women's colleges, austere in aspect but bold in aspiration, the three saints St Anne's, St Hilda's, St Hugh's, snobby Anglican LMH, non-denominational scholarly Somerville. The slow flowing rivers Cherwell and Isis, Christ Church Meadow, Bagley Wood and Boar's Hill, its pleasant hostelries: The Mitre and The Trout, The Bear at Woodstock and The Rose Revived. Oxford had been my childhood dream, now it would become my alma mater.

Somerville, an unassuming brick-built edifice, stands on the Woodstock Road next to the Radcliffe Infirmary. It has a pleasant green quadrangle where, one summer evening in 1914, Vera Brittain put on a full evening dress and fur-lined cloak to introduce herself to the formidable Principal. When I went up in 1952, I wore a little tweed suit and lace-up walking shoes to meet Dame Janet Vaughan, a distinguished scientist but a modest woman, without airs or graces. No dressing up for her.

Vera Brittain, coming, as she did, from a family of midland industrialists and brought up in the high-bourgeois comfort of an affluent Edwardian household, found Somerville spartan and dispiriting. The dreadful food, brown Windsor Soup and rhubarb and custard, the dirty dishes piled up in the serving hatches; above all, the cold. At home every room had been heated by a fire of shining coal nuggets laid and tended by a housemaid in a starched uniform. At Somerville she struggled unsuccessfully to light a pile of coal dust and pieces of slate to warm her icy bedroom.

To me, however, after the wartime austerity of Tudor Hall and Black Dog Cottage, the place seemed the pinnacle of luxury. My room, with its comforting radiator, its soft cosy bed which, so legend relates, in previous generations had to be pushed out into the corridor when a gentleman caller came to tea, I decorated with Fra Angelico pictures which I had cut from old Phaidon books and framed. Along the top of the wardrobe, I arranged a row of rosy apples which I had brought from the Black Dog orchard. Dulce Domum.

Every morning, at exactly seven thirty, breakfast was laid out in the dining hall. Clean white tablecloths, clean white china bowls in which were propped up somewhat limp slices of toast in the precise ration of two thirds white to one of brown. One collected one's toast, added margarine and marmalade (in minute quantities: butter was a rare luxury and rationing not finally abolished until later that year), then found somewhere to sit. I chose a place at the bottom right-hand corner of the hall. There I was joined by other girls and there we remained, save for the period in the second year when we were moved out into digs in North Oxford, for the remainder of our time at Somerville.

We became friends, in some cases, for life. Dear girls! How I remember your eager faces, our remarkable talents, your eccentricities! Xanthe Wakefield, survivor of the Quetta earthquake, whose parents and grandparents had been friends of my own family in India; Xanthe, with her pixie haircut and her tame rat snuggled in her bosom; Anjali Chanda, beautiful as a tropical flower; Lindsey Miller and tiny mathematician Eva Deutsch; Evelyn Wardrop and Karen Lund, gravely Scandinavian but, surprisingly, to marry bon viveur Reggie Bosanquet[4]. There was Montserrat Trueta who wore diamond earrings and whose Spanish grandee father withdrew her from Somerville after a year because he found our ways too emancipated (or louche) for his approval; there was Elizabeth Heritage, there was Wendy Woodstock who liked to dress as a cowboy and Jennifer Weston who wore exquisite couturier clothes but who gradually became distanced from the rest of us on account of her great wealth; there was dear sweet unselfish Audrey Briscoe who sat on our bedroom floors and listened to our woes. In later years, when I tried to explain to Jimmy the importance of those friendships and their innocence, he would shake his head and say "Sounds like a load of fucking lesbians to me" Far from it! We all suffered, frequently and painfully, from heterosexual heartbreak.

In the 1950s we felt a sense of elation and achievement at having reached Somerville at all. We were aware of the struggles our grandmothers had endured to achieve an education. We were conscious of the sufferings of the suffragettes and, not only physical cruelties inflicted upon them but also the humiliation and scorn they endured. Even at this time there were intelligent women of my mother's generation who spoke disparagingly of them.

"Women were granted the vote" it was said, "as a reward for the hard work they put into the war effort. Strident harpies like the Pankhursts, attention seekers like Emily Davidson, did more harm than good".

I thought about my aunt Josephine Maynard who, within the family, was regarded with something approaching awe for her achievement in gaining a place at Somerville. Here, among the Somervillian high achievers, no one had beard of her. I thought of Vera Brittain who had to overcome every kind of obstacle to gain even a basic education, let alone a place at Somerville, only to discover, in 1919, on her return to Oxford after a period of outstanding and heart-breaking war service, that her achievements in that wider world were regarded as nought by the Somervillians who had remained at home. Funny old world, I thought.

We all admired Vera Brittain. Even more strongly we worshipped her daughter Shirley Williams, who had gone down in the late 1940s. She cast a long and brilliant shadow over Somerville, just as Jeremy Thorpe did over the University as a whole. We all believed firmly that she would be – must be – Prime Minister. Never once did I hear the name 'Margaret Roberts'.

Audrey Briscoe and I were the only undergraduates who had chosen to read Law. Somerville had no resident law tutor so on Friday afternoons, Hazel Stuart (later Lady-Fox, who was to marry Sir Michael Fox, later a Lord Justice of Appeal) a barrister practicing at Fountain Court in the Temple, would come up and give us a tutorial. Hazel Stuart was Lord Denning's step-daughter and, in those days, when women were largely persona non grata at the Bar, jealous contemporaries would claim that she had been given a tenancy in Chambers only because people wanted to know what the old boy was up to. Denning was, at the time, regarded as a dangerous revolutionary. Later, of course, he was regarded as an arch conservative.

For the rest of the week Audrey and I were farmed out to Keble College where an academic called Davidge taught law. No one seemed to know his Christian name. He was known by everyone as 'Davidge's Father' because his son was a famous rowing blue. He had not wanted to take us on. At first he sulked, later he took us as a bad joke. Because we became adept at covering up for each other's failures and mistakes he named us 'Strophe and Antistrophe'. It was said that he dined out on Audrey's answer to the question:

Q. "What is the remedy for breach of contract to marry?"
A. "Specific performance"

Finally, in exasperation, he announced "Neither of you is clever. The idea of your going to the Bar is laughable. But it hardly matters, as you will both commit matrimony."

I found the Honours School of Jurisprudence both boring and frustrating. Miss Blackburn had wanted me to read History. This I foolishly refused to do without researching the alternative. I had long wanted to go to the bar as the obvious route into politics for which I had a passion. I was shocked to find that the first year would be spent studying Roman law in Latin, the Institutes of Gaius and Justinian; the second, in medieval land law, mostly in Norman French. Therefore, at the conclusion of two years, I knew how to manumit a slave and understood (just about) the influence of the dominant over the servient tenement. It was not until the third year, when we attended the blind professor Rupert Cross's hilarious lectures on criminal evidence, that we were exposed to anything having relevance to the world in which we lived.

Had it not been for the fact that I knew that a law degree would exempt me from part of the Bar final examinations, I would probably have transferred to a different subject. However, my father had already arranged for me to join Gray's Inn, one of the four Inns of Court, the others being Inner and Middle Temple and Lincoln's Inn). Those ancient and venerable institutions, dating back to the days of the Knights Templar, are responsible for the education, care and discipline of law students. One has to attend thirty-six dinners in hall, spread over a period of three years, before one can be called to the Bar. This is in order to absorb the forensic atmosphere and to meet future colleagues. Simply passing the exams does not exclude one from this requirement. Three times a term for the next three years I travelled down to London to dine in hall, drink wine (something I'd never done before) and engage in the most pleasant networking.

Women were not, at that time, admitted to the Oxford Union. One could, however, make a direct approach to the political societies. I joined the Liberals and within a short time achieved a minor role within the association. I wanted to invite Jeremy Thorpe to come and address us; he frequently came back to Oxford and spoke at the Union. I obtained his home telephone number and, shaking with nervous anticipation, rang it. A grim-sounding woman answered me, Jeremy's mother, Lady Thorpe. "I do not permit calls to my son from GELS" she barked and hung up.

I wrote some poetry which was published in the *Oxford Liberal*. The critic from Isis described it as "sadly banal in tone". Oh dear, my political career seemed to be getting off to a bad start. It was obvious that I wouldn't get into Parliament at this rate. Farewell Shirley Williams!

Two gorgeous young men in tight cavalry twill trousers and Chelsea boots bounced into my room. "Hello. I'm Anthony Champion de Crespigny. I'm your cousin" said one.

"I'm Julian David" said the other. I'm going to marry Caroline Cavendish. I'm your cousin too." Then in unison. "We're taking you to a party. Ten o'clock. At the House. Caroline's having a hissy fit so we're taking you instead."

I was perplexed. I didn't know these charmers. I didn't know anyone at "the House" as Christ Church was sometimes known. Besides, Somervillians were not allowed out after seven thirty without special permission granted for special occasions, such as dining at one of the Inns of Court in London.

"This can't be right" I said "I don't know anybody in the House"

"You soon will" said charmer number one. "The tiny Baron. Michael de Stempel. It should be quite amusing: The Queer Peer will be there and Jeremy Sandford from Folly Bridge, and maybe the wicked Guinness boys – Desmond's eyes a startling blue and Jonathan's a striking aquamarine – with their little half-brother Max Mosley."

"But why invite _me_?" I asked.

"We've been told that you're quite decorative." Then, kindly, "and so you are."

"We'll show you how to escape from Somerville" said charmer number two. "Jinny Waldegrave does it every night."

I was persuaded. I climbed out of a second-floor bathroom window, then, my heart in my mouth, traversed the narrow gap between Somerville and the Radcliffe Infirmary, entering the hospital through the open window of a sluice. Then, creeping past the darkening wards, I found the stairs leading to Accident and Emergency and finally made my way out into the street. There my two charmers were waiting.

"A word to the wise" said Julian, "when we arrive be very careful what you say. It's no good just being a pretty face. You've got to be acceptable too."

"What he means" interjected Anthony "on no account tell them that daddy's a curry colonel or that you like Ealing comedies".

Furiously I said "My father's _not_ a curry colonel and I _love_ Ealing comedies. I've changed my mind. I'm not going to your silly party."

"Sorry darling" said the first charmer, You'll never be able to climb back into your college. We'll just have to ring them and say we found you in a distressed state – drunk probably wandering the streets. You'll be sent down rusticated at the least."

"Very well. I'll come. Just don't insult me."

Christ Church, 10 pm. No question of climbing in there. Straight in through the porter's lodge and across the huge quadrangle. At the top of a wide oak staircase double doors stood open. Above them was painted the legend: 'The Baron Michael de Stempel'.

"Deary, deary me" laughed one of my escorts, "didn't we throw a tantrum when the college failed to give us our handle. It was only when someone pointed out that Granny had married into a South African hedge fund that they relented and acknowledged our title."

The huge, dark room lit by branches of long, thin candles and hung with Byzantine icons seemed more Ruritania than Oxford. Attendants, college staff or caterers? I wondered, offered champagne and miniscule game pies. Someone, college staff or actor? announced us. Our tiny host, dressed in white tie and tails and gleaming with orders and decorations, dismissed poor Julian with an airy wave, although it was generally known that he was going to marry Caroline Cavendish. Anthony's name pleased him. "Champion de Crespigny! So delightfully feudal! Your ancestors must have served the Norman monarch. I, of course, can quarter my arms with England, Spain, France and Imperial Russia."

While Anthony and our tiny host were comparing ancestors, my eyes were drawn to a corner of the room where a languid young man with golden hair sprawled (like the picture of the dying Chatterton) on a chaise longue chatting in German with a beautiful girl who sat on the floor by his side.

"Prince Rupert zu Lowenstein" warned Julian. "Don't even try to speak to him. He won't answer you. You're not nearly grand enough. As for the girlfriend, Princess Marie Gabriela von Urach generally known as Mariga, don't ever go on one of her picnics. Her Mercedes is full of crumbs – and rats."

At that moment a slight commotion drew our attention back to our host. A tall, dark vulpine young man swathed in black had just arrived and had been announced.

"His Serene Highness Constantine Nicoloudis! Prince of Greece!"

He bowed from the waist and waved his swordstick like a mythical sorcerer's wand.

The Baron did not reciprocate. Instead, he flew into one of his famous tantrums.

"Remove that man at once! He is fraudulent! I do not recognise the title! There are no princes in Greece."

His Serene Highness having been chucked into outer darkness, the party resumed its civilised flow. Some hours later, with dawn breaking over Oxford's dreaming spires, my charmers and I made our way, via a couple of coffee stalls, back to the gates of Somerville.

"What a topping party!" said one of them "Absolutely spiffing. Next time we'll take you to breakfast with Desmond Guinness."

The porter's lodge was already open. I slipped through unnoticed and made my way up to my modest room, with its Fra Angelico prints and homely rows of apples picked from the Black Dog Orchard.

Not all the invitations I received were as Ruritanian as the one just described. A few days later I found myself on the bus to Boar's Hill. I had been invited to tea by Professor Gilbert Murray, the classicist who, some sixty years before, had been my grandfather's neighbour on Buttery Staircase at St John's College. Their friendship had endured.

I was late. The invitation had been for four o'clock; it was already ten past when I was ushered into the dining room where an Edwardian style tea had been laid on the long mahogany table. To my huge embarrassment the collation had already started. I mumbled my excuses which were ignored. I took my place at table. Conversation continued between Professor Murray and his four or five other guests as though I was not there. He sat at one end of the table, his wife, Lady Mary, who was in an advanced stage of dementia and did not speak at all, at the other[6]. I could not have taken part in the conversation even if I had felt confident enough to open my mouth: it was entirely academic gossip about appointments and reviews. However, the food was perfect for a hungry adolescent: scones and honey, a great deal of bread and butter with different kinds of home-made jam which was offered in cut glass dishes. Tea was poured by a uniformed maid. At the end of the session, having said goodbye to his other guests, Professor Murray spoke to me for the first time.

"I remember your grandfather with the greatest affection. A fine academic mind. It is to be regretted that he did not remain at St John's where he would have been an ornament, but chose to pursue other avenues. I am told that I met his daughter – your Aunt Josephine – who was up during the thirties I believe – but I confess I cannot recall...."

Meanwhile Lady Mary had risen from her chair and was toddling round the table, licking the jam spoons.

I was not invited back.

Trinity term came to an end with a sequence of commemoration balls and hangovers. I was totally, utterly besotted with Oxford. The prospect of over two months at home filled me with dismay. How on earth would I spend the time? I compared notes with Susan Banwell;[7] an undergraduate at St Anne's and my friend and contemporary, whose family lived just over the border in Wiltshire. We decided to break free and go to Europe.

Susan's friend Jeremy Isaacs[8] had bought an old army lorry and, with a couple of lads from Oriel College, had decided to drive to Greece. For the price of a contribution to the cost of the petrol Susan and I joined the party travelling as far as Venice. There we dropped off and stayed in a convent located on one of the lesser canals. For a couple of weeks we gloried in the pictures and palaces, swanned round the lagoon taking in Murano, Burano and Torcello, then set off hitchhiking westwards past views of the distant Dolomites, the medieval towers of San Gimignano, the moss-green mosaics of Ravenna. By the time we reached Milan we were penniless and bedraggled but had the good fortune to be taken in by a kindly old gentleman who fed us, allowed us to stay in his flat and told us (privately and separately) that we reminded him of his late dear mother and would like to marry us. This seemed a little odd: Susan was a tall slender blonde while I was small, dark, and, if truth be told, somewhat tubby. Nevertheless, we were both touched by the compliment and enjoyed listening to 'The Four Seasons' on the old gentleman's gramophone. Vivaldi was not yet fashionable and neither Susan nor I had heard the recording before.

Lethbridge Family – Black Dog Cottage Somerset.

Nemone as a law student 1954.

Nemone Call Photo 1956

Gray's Inn girls on occasion of Queen's visit 1956.
Front row Monique Viner (later Judge) Noreen Collins
(later Judge Nina Lowry), Nemone.

Nemone with Paddy Pakenham – Managing Clerk of Lincoln & Lincoln Solicitors, outside Arbour Square Magistrates Court 1957.

Nemone and Kray Brothers

Jennifer Weston launching Dorthe Maersk
at Odense Denmark 1953.

Susan and Asa Briggs wedding Wiltshire 1957

Nemone at the Briggs' wedding.

Nemone visiting the Lethbridge family tomb 1610 & John Sydney's Lethbridge memorial. Exeter Cathedral.

Wedding photo Dublin 15th August 1959.
Anne Curnow, Jimmy, Jack Fishman and Nemone.

Cherry in her Wedding dress

Exeter Cathedral

Cherry, Jimmy and Nemone

Cherry's wedding day.

Nemone and Jimmy at Cherry's wedding.
News of their marriage was
reported from this wedding.

Daily Mail reporting Nemone and Jimmy's marriage.

Jimmy on set for his play

(Coming Out Party) 1967.

Jimmy at the BBC.
Filming of one of his plays.

Le Figar0 28th April 1966. Jimmy and Nemone's
story made headlines around the world.

Jimmy O'Connor – photo Karil Evans Giles

Mykonos, Vrisi - Nemone and Jimmy and Pirelli (cat)

My son, Milo O'Connor, meeting Barbara Windsor June 2013 at William Pattern School Summer Fair. Barbara had attended the Stoke Newington primary school when she was a little girl. On meeting they discussed the times Nemone defended her then husband, Ronnie Knight. Photograph Clare Bradley Myers

CHAPTER FIFTEEN

JIMMY

Anthony Eden was Prime Minister; Billy Hill was the self-proclaimed boss of Britain's underworld. Gambling was illegal, so was the practice of homosexuality. The Metropolitan Police were institutionally racist; the Flying Squad corrupt. The Costa del Sol was a twinkle in a property developer's eye: successful criminals spent their money in Tangier or the south of France. Men were still hanged by the neck until dead.

Now, in the early 1950s, the social scene had begun to change. The Rich List was overtaking the *Almanac de Gotha* as the class divide moved from the horizontal to the vertical. Pedigree was dethroned by money. Stately homes were handed over by the cash-strapped owners to the National Trust. Spivs and racketeers made it on to the Honours List. Princess Margaret ditched her deb's delight and consorted with actors and photographers. Diffidence declined. William Stormont and some Bullingdon chums stole the Stone of Scone from Westminster Abbey and repatriated it to Scotland. For me the symbolic tipping point came when Rupert zu Loewenstein waived his princely principles and became financial advisor to the proletarian Rolling Stones.

The symbolic epicentre of these changes was to be found, tucked between the great white mansions of Belgravia, in a small, apparently unpretentious pub, The Star Tavern, Belgrave Mews. Run by a shouty, foul-mouthed Irishman named Paddy Kennedy and his severe, well-organised wife, it became epicentre of the extraordinary social revolution which began in the early 1950s and which rumbles on today. The Star became Jimmy's home from home.

On the ground floor there was little to distinguish it, or its clientele, from the average hostelry in wealthy south west one. Here Mrs Kennedy pampered the customers, maintained order, kept the books and made certain that nothing took place which might upset the Inland Revenue or the brewers. Upstairs (to which Paddy regulated access), two worlds, cafe society and the underworld, collided; not in hostility but in the most affable and tolerant way. Actors and aristocrats, gangsters and politicians drank happily together until Paddy decided to shut up shop for the day and take his favourite punters to the races.

NEMONE

Back to Oxford, Michaelmas term. This marked the beginning of a lifelong friendship with Ned Sherrin. He was a delight. Audrey discovered him when she auditioned for (and won) a part in *The Candlelight Review* which he produced. He was, at the time, a second year undergraduate at Exeter College and leading Oxford impresario. She came back from the audition singing

> *"Topping term and happy hols*
> *To all the chaps in all the colls,*
> *To all the bods*
> *In all the quads*
> *Young greek gods*
> *And odds and sods..."*

She brought him into hall at lunchtime and introduced him to everyone at the Bottom Table. With his short blond hair, rugby player's physique and bouncy eagerness of a Labrador puppy, he became a kind of collective boyfriend to us all. He was, however, careful not to single out any one of us for special attention – whether to avoid jealousy or to give any one of us ideas above our station – I was not sure. However, I did feel a certain proprietary affection for him because he came from Somerset and knew the woods and fields of home. Xanthe and I were his preferred dancing partners; Xanthe he took to the Exeter Commem. He took me to the Merton.

Everyone in my year had read *Brideshead Revisited*. The first half of the book, with its air of romantic nostalgia and its mysterious adrogeny, suited our mood exactly. At the time the love that dares not speak its name hung like a wraith, a faint whisper of musk, over the University. Few men were openly gay and those who were, and wore their sexuality on their sleeve, relied on their status or on the classical tolerance of the place for protection. Once they went down, of course, the cold wind of reality chilled them to the bone. Formerly admired and petted, regarded as some kind of classical favourite, once he stepped outside the charmed circle, the Queer Peer became a common criminal and was sent to prison. The preferred relationship under the dreaming spires was a romantic friendship, probably platonic and certainly tinged with pain.

I had never given thought to the sexual preferences of my two charmers, regarding them as hilarious dandies, but when the three of us dropped off at Black Dog on our way to a dance at Hadspen House in South Somerset, my father (briefly home on leave from Germany) took one look at them and condemned them as "disgusting homosexuals" with whom I was to sever contact.

During my time at Somerville I never knowingly encountered a gay woman, with the exception of one poor girl who changed her name to Dennis Compton in homage to the test cricketer and then disappeared from sight.

As for Ned Sherrin, it was not until years later, when we were working together in Manchester on a current affairs programme for the BBC,[1] that I realised where his true interests lay. Late one night, hurrying down Platform 1 at Manchester Piccadilly to catch the sleeper to London, Ned said, laughing, "Look carefully into each carriage, when you see someone you fancy, just pounce!"

It struck me that Xanthe and I had been his alibi girls.

My two charmers didn't care for Ned. He was too middlebrow for them. As for Ned himself, he hardly noticed them. Underneath that puppy dog exterior there lay a core of steel. He had no interest in anyone he did not believe to be destined for the A list. The ghostly European aristocrats, the English dandy charmers, did not in any way impress him. His solid Somerset sense kept him grounded. In the meritocracy.

Caroline Cavendish must have been having another hissy fit. The charmers had invited me to go with them to breakfast with Desmond Guinness. Across another enormous quad, up another wide oak staircase, through double doors flung wide open and into the Guinness quarters, already heaving with guests when we arrived. The usual suspects, Rupert zu Loewenstein, Mariga von Urach (later to marry Desmond Guinness and to become famous in Ireland for her rat-infested picnics) big brother Jonathan of the green luminous eyes, tiny Michael de Stempel, Jeremy Sandford, hung-over from the previous night's bathroom party at Folly Bridge, Sarah Rothschild, straight from the cover of *Vogue*, William Stormont, fresh from his escapade at Westminster Abbey and reproved by our host for "upsetting Ma'am for pinching her chair". There was champagne and coffee, muffins and oysters with Guinness, the latter for show rather than consumption. In the inner sanctum our host lay sprawled in a large four poster bed, his arm round a hostile raven-haired beauty who did not speak when she was spoken to. Nancy Gillespie.

"Don't worry about her" said Julian, "she's from the Gorbals. A bit out of her depth."

"No, she's not" interjected Anthony "Daddy's conservative agent for Cheltenham. She'll speak as soon as she's mastered the Scots dialect."

I refused an oyster but ate a muffin. The tiny Baron interrogated me about my ancestors. The party was going swimmingly when there seemed to be an altercation near the door. Hardly raising his voice Desmond said "Oh buzz off Nicoloudi, you're not invited."

"I depart with pleasure" said His Serene Highness "I do not respect new money. Especially the Beerage"

Later than morning the charmers and I stumbled into the Botanic Gardens, wondering what to do next. Somewhere behind the greenhouses we came upon the disconsolate Prince of Greece swathed in his Dracula cloak and huddled on a wrought iron bench.

"Don't take it too hard" said kindly Julian. "It wasn't much of a party anyway."

"Nothing like the orgy we'd been hoping for" added Anthony.

Nicoloudis held his head in his hands and groaned. "I am deeply disappointed in this proletarian university" he said. "I see nothing but the riff raff and the bourgeois. A few merchants, tradesmen and brewer's offspring. There's not a lady I can invite to a Commem. Ball. I can't dance with a commoner"

"Oh, come on Nick" said Anthony, "there's Mariga (though she's already spoken for), there's Ginny Waldegrave, there's Caroline Cavendish..."

"*I'm* marrying Caroline Cavendish" interrupted Julian.

"So you are, are you? There's Antonia Pakenham...mad father, but no! Lady Magnesia Freelove would hardly suit..."

I had an idea. "Make yourself a famous eccentric and they'll all run after you. You'll get thousands of invitations."

I went to the Magdalen Commem with Anthony de Crespigny. We shared a table with Julian David and a rather stout grumpy blonde. So this was the famous Caroline Cavendish, whose existence I had started to doubt. I was enchanted when, late in the evening, His Serene Highness Prince Constantine waltzed slowly past us, dancing with a teddy bear.

For a time Constantine Nicoloudis was transformed from pretentious nuisance to charming eccentric. Seen as the embodiment of the *Brideshead* dream he was invited to dozens of parties. Unfortunately, many of them involved gambling and gambling far beyond his means. Having exhausted his modest fortune he resorted to stealing from his friends. Sitting one morning in the Botanic Gardens he told me that he had been arrested and charged with forging one of Desmond Guinness's cheques. He was on bail and due to appear at the Old Bailey (sitting as the City of London quarter sessions) the following month.

"But I'm not guilty" he assured me. "I have an alibi. At the time they allege I was cashing a cheque at Coutts in the City of London I was in fact back in Oxford. In bed with Nancy Gillespie."

Half in pity half in amusement the charmers and I decided that we must attend the trial. We took our places in the public gallery and saw His Serene Highness enter the Court and walk up the steps into the dock. There he handed his hat to one prison officer and his Dracula cloak to the other, before bowing deeply to the judge.

Alas Miss Gillespie did not turn up to give evidence for the defence. It took the jury less than thirty minutes to find him guilty. The judge gave him ten months imprisonment and off Nicoloudis went to Wormwood Scrubs.

"Poor, poor little Nick the Greek" said the charmers. Then forgot all about him.

I decided that I wanted to become a publisher. I borrowed a hundred pounds from my father and with an undergraduate from New College named Richard Cox, set about trying to create a magazine which would be really glossy, which we named *Couth*. Looking back, I think that a more suitable word would have been 'pretentious', that certainly matched the mood of the time. I wrote to Evelyn Waugh asking him to contribute an article.

He wrote back. "My dear young person, when you have reached my venerable age you will realise the enormity of your suggestion."

Despite this rebuff, Richard and I pressed on with our endeavour. We managed to persuade Cecil Beaton to donate a sketch for the first cover. Snobbish undergraduates were eager to contribute to *Couth* although obtaining advertising proved to be more of a problem.

In order to avoid the possible consequences of a mass climb-out-of and back-into, our Oxford colleges, we decided to obtain a legitimate weekend's leave and launch the magazine at a party in London. We borrowed a house from someone's trusting parents. I made myself an amazing frock, taking a nightdress made of layers of red and black chiffon and cutting it to knee length in what was called at the time the 'baby-doll' style. I then sewed pink carnations all round the hem. We invited the world's press and those whom we thought the world's press would consider to be the cream of Oxford society, that is to say the ghostly European aristocrats and the Beerage. Alas, neither category turned up or indeed bothered to answer our kind invitation.

Nevertheless, the loyal Bottom Table attended in force as did Ned Sherrin and my two charmers, Anthony Champion de Crespigny ennobling himself for the occasion. As for the world's press a solitary stringer from the *Daily Express* gossip Column 'William Hickey' attended. I feel that it is worth reproducing his rather splendid piece in full:

SO 'GUSTING' AT THE 'COUTH' PARTY

It was a literary party. In a tiny, but smart house in South Eaton place. You went up narrow stairs into a small sitting-room. Nice pictures. Pleasant furniture. About 50 people there. All standing. Drinking dry martinis. Smoking. Talking.

It was a party to launch a new Oxford magazine called Couth. The dominant personality is a girl called Nemone Lethbridge, who hopes to take a degree this summer.

"It was my idea," she said, looking most appealing with her large eyes and dark hair. "You see, 'couth' is a fashionable Oxford word. It means the opposite of 'uncouth'. I want the magazine to express Oxford's exquisite approach to life.

"An exquisiteness towards life with an underlying seriousness. I feel Oxford has become a 'red-brick' university in recent years."

By red-brick she means that it has become like the provincial universities – Manchester or Durham, for instance.

And Nemone – you pronounce it like anemone without the "a" – feels it her duty to save Oxford from that fate.

"Have you any other new, smart words at Oxford?" I asked Nemone.

She fluttered her eyelashes. An effective trick. Her eyelashes are long.

"Well," she said, "there's 'gusting'. That's about a fortnight old."

"I see," I said, "and that's the opposite of 'disgusting'."

"Yes," she said with the smile that one gives a backward child who has unexpectedly shown a spark of intelligence. "That's right."

"Any more?" I asked. I felt this matter of new words might lead to something.

"There's 'pellent'" she said thoughtfully. "There's 'pulsive'."

"I can imagine what they mean" I said. I was catching on.

"You're rather gusting," said Nemone.

I had another dry martini on that.

HARD-UPNESS.

A tall young girl came up – rather beautiful, with enormous eyes.

"I'm Jenifer Weston"," she said with the assurance of a film star.

"Jenifer Weston!" I said, "You're last year's Oxford idol, aren't' you?"

"Yes," she said, with the natural pride of a girl who has called Oxford "a sequestered shambles."

Of course Jenifer is hard up. All undergraduates are hard up. But like all undergraduates Jenifer has the money for the luxuries of life. She is flying to Greece later this month. To study Greek inscriptions. She is taking a degree in Greek and Latin in the summer. "Greats" they call it at Oxford.

I had another martini. The room was so thick with people now that there wasn't room to drop the ash of your cigarette on the carpet.

"I'm the Comte de Vierville." Said a handsome young man with a deep red waistcoat. "I'm Nemone's cousin."

I should call him a "pellent" young man. He has already taken a degree at St Andrews in Scotland. Decided to come to study philosophy at Oxford.

HORRID PHILOSOPHY.

I think he finds it quite gusting. But we agreed philosophy at Oxford is rather horrible.

I had another martini by now – and started to tell him about an extraordinary tutor I had who I used to hope, would electrocute himself with his attempts to light his pipe with bits of paper stuck into an electric fire. A little voice inside me told me that I was being more repellant than gusting. The tutor, who had a reputation for frightening young girl undergraduates by hiding under his table, has, I learned with sadness, left Oxford. Apparently he has become a professor at some university in Scotland.

"I hope to go into the Foreign Office," said the comte.

JENIFER'S ODE.

"I've got a poem in this magazine," said Jenifer Weston. She picked up Couth. I looked at the verses. They started
My hair, the grass, entangled is.
And I the earth in clods disposed –
By my own iron sown, by his
Co-habitation decomposed.
"I'll read it later," I said. "I think it unfair to say anything after only a quick glance at a party."

Another young man came up. "I'm Richard Cox," he said. Another "couth" type. Good-looking. Well-dressed. He is, in fact, the business manager of *Couth*.

"If it sells 2,000 copies," he said "we shall be all right. The cover drawing is by Cecil Beaton. He was very agreeable. He let us have it free."

"How much advertising have you got?" I asked in a severely practical way. "Five pages," he answered, "It's difficult, that. Only five out of 40 pages."

I understood. And the price is 3s a copy. A high price. I feel a bit sorry for them.

CASH SECRET.

"How much money did you have to put up?"

"£200"

"...Did Nemone put up her share?"

"Oh, yes."

I turned to Nemone, who was signing first copies of the magazine as if they would be as valuable as first editions of Jane Austen.

"Where did you get the money from?" I asked her.

"I can't tell you," she said. "If I did my father might be furious."

He is Major-General John Lethbridge who is Chief of Intelligence, Rhine Army.

THE RIGHT IDEA.

I didn't pursue the matter any further. In fact, I felt it was time to leave.

Enormously stimulated. Delighted to meet the couth, gusting, pellent, pulsive types. Hoping against hope that the magazine would not be the failure that it probably will be.

But confident that all these young people will make their mark in life. They have the right idea about Oxford.

We were all buzzing at the success of the party. Onward and upward! This was the life! Nothing could possibly go wrong. Jenifer Weston was thrilled to find herself a published poet. Shortly after the party she obtained another weekend's leave. Her father was, at the time, CEO of Shell Tankers. In order to cement relations with a Danish shipping consortium, the young Shell princess was invited to launch the latest of the Danish oil fleet at Odense on the Baltic coast. Jenifer invited Wendy Woodhouse and me to go with her, as her maids of honor. So off we went, Jenifer in a stupendous Dior dress and garden party hat, Wendy and I tagging along behind her in our little Marks and Spencer frocks.

Jenifer duly smashed a bottle of champagne on the bow of the tanker *Dorthe Maersk* and we all adjourned for some serious Scandinavian celebrations. Onward and upward! This was the life. Nothing could ever go wrong.

Trinity term still had a couple of weeks to run. Then the summer would end with Commemoration Balls and general debauchery. I still had one dinner to eat at Grays Inn in order to fulfill my student obligations. I got leave of absence for one more night and duly dined in hall. Dinner must have ended early – sometime after nine o'clock I recall. I telephoned the Flying Dutchman and told him that I was footloose and fancy free. Perhaps we could go to the 400?

The Dutchman picked me up from the Henekeys pub next to the Gray's Inn entrance.

"Where are we going?" I asked.

"We're going home. No argument" he said. "I want to hear all about Denmark." I could feel my heart thumping with terror. I wished that I hadn't rung him. Back at Shepherd Street, Anthony opened a bottle of wine and poured two glasses. It was suffocatingly hot in the tiny sitting room. He flung up the sash windows.

"Listen to this frighteningly boring man," he said, "I rather like him." A busker was singing in the Square below "Vous, qui passez sans me voir." Anthony threw a handful of coins out of the window. Then "Come here," he said. He took me by the shoulder and started to pull down the zip at the back of my dress. I was shaking uncontrollably.

"Oh, for God's sake woman! Stop trembling! Go away and don't come back until you've grown up." He pushed me to the top of the stairs and slammed the door after me. Weeping bitterly, I walked through the long dark streets to Paddington station. There I caught the milk train back to Oxford.

It was breakfast time. I didn't go into hall but went straight up to my room. Some kind person had collected my post from the previous day and placed it on my pillow. Among the letters was one from my mother. It appeared that my father (who had been moderately unwell for some time) had now been diagnosed with lung cancer. He was to undergo surgery at the London Hospital later that week.

Against all the odds and the statistical evidence, my father survived for ten years. Yet his recovery was only partial, a black depression descended on him and changed his character. While in his eyes Peter could do no wrong, for Cherry and me he became a figure of fear. It was as though the ghosts of the Somme, the atrocities of Afghanistan, the dreadful revelations of post-war Germany, rose up and overwhelmed him. I remember silent family meals where no one dared speak in case they became victims of his cosmic rage. It was not until the final weeks of his life that we were able to re-establish our friendship. I continued to see the Flying Dutchman from time to time at the opera or on other public occasions. The silly incident at his flat was never mentioned and he seemed content to introduce me to his friends, a flower in my hair.

Then one day he said "I'd better tell you that I'm getting married. Gina arrives on Monday." So she did, and within two weeks he had married Regina de Souza Coelho from Brazil.[2]

And what of the two charmers? Shortly after we had come down at the end of our final term, Anthony de Crespigny wrote to me: "I thought I'd better tell you about my marriage to Caroline Cavendish.Look after poor Julian for me. He's bound to be a bit sad for a couple of days. C.C. and I are off to South Africa. Fascinating political experiment taking place there." (This was, of course, the early days of apartheid.) "Chatsworth in the townships, what, what?"

Couth folded after three issues.

CHAPTER SIXTEEN

NEMONE

My mother said: "You have betrayed everything your grandfather stood for. You have closed your mind to common sense. You have sold out."[1]

I felt dreadful at having hurt her so much, yet, at the same time, triumphant, having made up my own mind and been true to my word. I had promised not to do anything irrevocable until I came down from Oxford and I had kept my promise. However, as soon as I came down at the end of Trinity term I embarked on a course of instruction in the doctrine of the Catholic Church. That autumn I was received into the Faith. The ceremony took place in the modest Church of Saint Catherine of Alexandria in Frome. The local dentist and his wife were my sponsors: they were the only Catholics I knew in Somerset.

After the ceremony we went back to their house and drank some whisky. "It must be amazing to see the Faith through fresh eyes" said the kindly dentist. "I can hardly imagine it".

I felt delirious. The blood-stained ghosts of Henry VIII, founder of the Church of England, of the two terrible Cromwells, Thomas and Oliver, who had haunted my childhood, disappeared into the distance; the grim little Ebenezer chapels which lined the hilly rain-swept streets of Frome, the embarrassing muscular Christianity of Bet Bouncer, PE Mistress of Tudor Hall, who had troubled my adolescence, faded into irrelevance and troubled me no more. I was embraced by the warmth, intoxicated by the ancient glamour of Rome and Constantinople, of

Lalibella and St Catherine of Alexandria. St Catherine spoke to Joan of Arc; perhaps she would speak to me.

It was some years before I was fully reconciled with my mother. Then one day she gave me a brooch: a dragonfly with turquoise wings and ruby eyes, a Mizpah brooch she called it. Then she, the militant Agnostic, quoted from the Old Testament: "The Lord watch between thee and me when we are absent from one another"[2]

JIMMY

Jimmy was having the time of his life. Seated at the bar of the upstairs room in the Star Tavern, he became famous as a raconteur, for his gallows humour, his tales of Parkhurst and Princetown, of villains and madmen. Paddy Kennedy encouraged him because he knew that he drew in the big-spending crowds. He became the recipient of lavish hospitality, from Gerry Albertini and Bob Hope at the races, from Judah Binstock or Sam Norman in the South of France. The Carlton at Cannes became his second stamping ground. Jimmy regarded his new friends with an innocent, an uncritical eye. The rich were, to him, all lovely people. It never occurred to him that they might be as flawed, as treacherous, as the old lags in Dartmoor or the wheeler dealers of Warren Street or Portobello Road. For a time he almost forgot the injustice he had suffered. He was happy living on his own legend.

NEMONE

I came down to London alone. Xanthe and Audrey were to stay on at Oxford for another year; Xanthe because she was reading Greats, which involved a four-year course, and Audrey because she had to re-take a couple of papers towards her law degree. It was agreed between us that as soon as possible we would re-assemble the Bottom Table in part at least and share a house together. I was going to have to do my Bar finals, a course organised by the Council of Legal Education, a course I found to be of the most stupefying boredom. Meanwhile I searched for and found a room through the small advertisements on the front page of *The Times*. £3 a week. It was in a beautiful old house, now a somewhat upmarket tenement, on the north side of Clapham Common, fronted by a wide paved courtyard with a wrought iron gate, and a magnificent magnolia tree which, in spring, was covered with waxy white blossoms. It was said that Christopher Wren had lived there while supervising the construction of St Paul's, hence its name, Wren House. It belonged to Betty Stucley an eccentric lady of statuesque figure who took in lodgers. She was a member of an old Devon family well known to my own. She ran a somewhat bohemian boys' club and wrote a book about it called *Teddy Boys' Picnic* which, alas, sold few copies.

I shared the attic with another law student, Kathleen O'Brien from Northern Ireland. She was a committed Protestant who used to write splendid speeches which she tried out on me addressed to her 'Loyal Orange Lodge'. I made no secret of my Catholicism and displayed a large picture of the Assumption over my bed. Nevertheless, we felt no tension between us and became firm friends. It is only now that it occurs to me that had we been living in Belfast, rather than in London, such a friendship would have been unlikely, if not impossible.

My centre of gravity had shifted from Somerville to Gray's Inn. Most northerly of the four ancient Inns of Court, still responsible for the care, education and discipline of law students, it occupies a site between Holborn and Theobalds Road. Entering through a low stone arch and a long dark passageway - you pass through a series of courtyards and squares into a sombre green garden, flowerless, but dominated by a magnificent Catalpa tree. It is so old that, having reached its magnificent height, it has started to grow down again. Wherever its arthritic branches touch the ground they spring up again as young trees. The old patriarch stands, in the middle of a dark London square, surrounded by his vigorous children.[3]

The Inn had suffered extensive bomb damage during the Blitz and, during my time there was still undergoing re-building. Happily, only days before the bombs fell, the magnificent carved screen from the hall and the collection of portraits, including that of my childhood demon, Thomas Cromwell, had been taken out and spent the rest of the war hidden, so I was told, deep in a cave in Wales.

The members of the Inn included, at the highest level, Law Lords and judges. Next in the pecking order came Queen's Counsel and junior barristers. Finally came a group of men (let it be noted no women) who enjoyed the convivial dinners, the facilities of a club in central London, but who did not have the aristocratic connections to join the grand old clubs of St James. Neither did they have any intention of practising at the Bar. Some did not even take the bar exams. They joined the Inn for the fun of it.

Among them was Dennis Braithwaite, wealthy son of a Conservative MP, a northern industrialist. He lived in a splendid flat in Eaton Square. Despite all this, when he called at Wren House, Betty Stukely, who despised money made in trade, took an instant dislike to him and christened him 'the Loathely Sausage King'. Poor Dennis! He was a nice man and didn't deserve the insult.

Before one could be called to the Bar, in addition to passing the Bar exams, one had to dine in hall, thirty-six times. The senior members, or Benchers, sat at the top table, the junior bar and students at long tables at right angles to their seniors. We dined in groups of four. Towards the end of dinner everyone rose to their feet and toasted the members of their immediate group. It was a good way to learn names and make new friends.

I had joined Gray's Inn (in preference to one of the other Inns) because someone had told my father than it was the kindest to its students. Certainly during that student year I enjoyed more parties and drank more champagne than I have done before or since. Because there were few of us, the girl students were spoiled rotten. Dinner often carried on into the small hours, in a nightclub or someone's flat. On one occasion when dinner was finished Dennis Braithwaite said "Let's go gambling." This was, at the time, strictly against the law, except on the racecourse. The obvious solution was to the leave the country. So, in the wee small hours, a group of us drove down to Lydd, in Kent, where Dennis happened to keep a small aeroplane. We flew to Le Touquet – at the time the nearest place to Gray's Inn where one could gamble with impunity – where Chemin de Fer was the game of choice. Forty-eight hours later, poorer if not wiser, with dreadfully sore heads, we were back at our books in Chancery Lane.

The Benchers of the Inn decided to entertain the Queen. Someone found, in the library, the script of a masque, addressed in somewhat sycophantic terms, to Gloriana, the first Queen Elizabeth. Robert Atkins, veteran of the Old Vic, was to declaim the spoken part, the young barristers and students to dance. Unfortunately, the young men seemed unable to master the geometric manoeuvres of the sixteenth century entertainment and, after several embarrassing rehearsals, they were sent home. Who was to partner the girls? In the end a group of splendid young chaps from the corps de ballet at Sadler's Wells were engaged. My partner was called Ron. He danced like a dream. We became friends. He asked me whether I had any erotic daydreams.

"Of course" I said.

"I'll tell you what I dream of doing" said Ron. "I'd like to go into a baker's shop, take off all my clothes, jump into a tray of cream buns and ROLL".

After the show we were presented to the Queen. About thirty at the time, she was a remarkably beautiful woman. I don't know whether Ron shared his erotic fantasy with her, but certainly when it was my turn to make my curtsey, HM said, rather wistfully I thought, "You must be having the most tremendous fun." I felt my stern republicanism fade away like morning dew and I curtseyed like a silly debutante.

There were occasions called Grand Nights when a special menu was served and entertainment enjoyed. Women were barred from these, for reasons which were never explained. I was outraged. I resolved to go to one of these mysterious events. With the collusion of one of the junior barristers, I crept into hall before dinner began and sat under one of the tables. I enjoyed the first half hour, rejoicing in my wickedness and hoping that something disgraceful would happen. It never did. One old boy sang "Drake's Drum" but that was it. After two hours I was feeling cold, cramped and miserable among the black shoes and trouser legs, longing for my warm bed and wishing that these idiots would go home.

Clarissa Dickson-Wright, who joined the Inn a couple of years later, wrote in her memoir that I had gate crashed the Grand Night dressed as a lion.[4] Dear Reader, this story is apocryphal. What is true however, is that, as a result of this debauchery, I failed my bar exams and to my embarrassment and fury, had to re-sit them all.

The year was 1956. Xanthe and Audrey had arrived in London. Xanthe, who had achieved a double first, passed effortlessly into the Foreign Office. Audrey, who was thoroughly disillusioned with the law thanks to Mr Davidge of Wadham, went to manage the Ballet Minerva. As agreed, they had found the first of a series of flats which we shared together.

I had to break it to Betty Stukely that I was leaving Wren House and going to live with my Somerville friends. I thought that she would be upset; she had formed a motherly affection for me and had taken a strong, if critical view of my gentleman callers. I found her, huge apparition seen through clouds of steam, in the kitchen, "cod and cockles" she roared. "Absolutely delicious. Come and have some". Obediently I took a plateful of the fishy concoction and stammered out my message. Surprisingly she didn't seem to mind.

"Don't worry about it darling" she said "I'm getting rid of all the lodgers – well, for the time being. I'm getting married. You can be my bridesmaid."

So, Betty married Johnny Northmore, an old admirer from her debutante days, in the Anglican church on Clapham Common. I was happy to be her bridesmaid and to wish her a long and happy life thereafter.,

I had eaten my thirty-six dinners. I had scraped through my bar finals. I had been called to the Bar by Gray's Inn in May that year after a splendid dinner, wearing a black taffeta crinoline I had made myself. It was now time to look for a pupillage. I was fortunate that, until his illness, my father had been Chief of Intelligence of the British Army of the Rhine. He had worked closely with Sir David Maxwell Fyfe (later Lord Kilmuir, Lord Chancellor) who was senior prosecuting counsel for the British team at the Nuremburg war crimes trials. At my father's request he arranged for me to do six months pupillage with Mervyn Griffith Jones, a member of his team. So my first step on the professional ladder was achieved not on merit, but by nepotism.

Later that summer I went home briefly, to Black Dog. My father, his cancer temporarily in remission, had retired early from the Army and was away working as Commandant of the Civil Defence Staff College at Sunningdale. My mother was head down in the herbaceous border. The place seemed oddly silent. Peter was away at Agricultural College, Cherry was up on Tyneside as a novice in an Anglican convent of Poor Clares. Oh, my poor mother! How her daughters tried her stern agnosticism! I spent my time reading: Dickens, my beloved Brontës and the grim historical novels of Harrison Ainsworth. Then, one afternoon, looking for something new, I fell upon my grandfather's collection of orange-yellow paperbacks, Gollancz publications on Orwell, the Webbs and Arthur Koestler. Sitting on the back stairs I read Koestler's *Reflections on Hanging* from cover to cover in one afternoon. I felt sick. I felt faint. I leaned against the banisters. I swore to myself that I would stop playing silly buggers. I would grow up. I had found something serious to do with my life. I would strive to put an end to this atrocity.

Arthur Koestler, Victor Gollancz and Canon John Collins had resolved to see an end to capital punishment within ten years. They would work to raise public consciousness so that, in the end, sheer revulsion would make its continuation impossible. The 1955 Homicide Act had divided the crime of murder into categories, those such as the killing of a police or prison officer or that committed in the course of an armed robbery and those committed, for example, in the course of a domestic dispute. The first category carried the death penalty, the second did not. To value the life of a policeman above that of a child seemed to many to be so absurd that capital punishment was suspended while the matter was debated in Parliament. This was exactly the time that I started my first pupillage. Had the death penalty not been suspended during those months I do not think that I could have survived.

It was nine o'clock of a fine Autumn morning that I climbed the shallow steps which led up to the Temple Place from Temple Underground Station, made my way east for a few hundred yards along the banks of the Thames, and turned left again into Middle Temple Lane. There can be few walks in London more evocative than that which leads under the great arch of Temple Gardens between high buildings which give, from time to time, a glimpse of a pleasant green lawn or brilliant herbaceous border, up to a fortress gate, forever locked and barred against the vulgar world outside, which stands between the Temple and Fleet Street. My first port of call that day was 2 Harcourt Buildings which stands on the right of the lane soon after one has passed from the embankment into that hallowed ground which is the Temple.

I presented myself at the chambers of JD Roberts at 2 Harcourt Buildings. 'Khaki' Roberts, head of chambers through seniority rather than forensic skills, had captained the English rugby team and was bluff and affable. Mervyn Griffith Jones, as his second in command, was intimidating; immaculately dressed in black jacket and striped trousers, he never left chambers without his bowler had and furled umbrella. His shoes were polished to a brilliant shine. I was told that he had a pair for every day of the week and that his old batman from his army days (during the war he had served in the Welsh Guards) came in once a week to polish them and to do his ironing.

Henry Twelftree, the senior clerk and George Woolf, his junior, were already in the clerk's room when I arrived. Henry, himself an intimidating figure, wore a brocade waistcoat stretched over his ample stomach and, like his employer, never left chambers without his bowler hat and umbrella. He greeted me with a kind of chilly courtesy, then looking me up and down said "the nail varnish will have to go. This is the Temple not the Palladium. George, do the necessary." George was sent up to Boots in Fleet Street to buy some varnish remover. Then, in my black dress, black seamed stockings and black court shoes, I was deemed sober enough to go to court.

Mervyn Griffith Jones arrived. He enquired after my father and told me that I could use his Christian name. This I found almost impossible to do. He was the most terrifying man I had ever met. Together we drove in his black jaguar to the Old Bailey, ten minutes or so away. He was to prosecute a murder. As first junior Treasury Counsel, murders where the staple of his practice. At lunchtime he took me up to the Bar mess and introduced me to some of his colleagues. Courteous and correct in every particular, I could still see that he was acutely embarrassed by my presence. I was the only female in the room.

Sometime later, Robert Harman, one of the junior tenants at Harcourt Buildings, told me that, when the letter from Sir David Maxwell Fyfe arrived, asking him to accept me as a pupil, Mervyn had been inclined to refuse. It was Henry Twelftree who intervened, saying "Sir, this is a Royal Command. Regard it as an experiment which is never to be repeated." It was several years before another woman crossed that patriarchal threshold.

For six months I trotted round behind my master like a little dog. In Court I sat behind him and took long, hand-written notes of the evidence as it was given. In Chambers I was set to work drafting indictments. At that time there were no lectures or seminars for pupils on the art of advocacy; one learned by watching and listening. One was thrown into the forensic waters at the deep end. Mervyn never told me how to do my job: he must have thought that I should work it out for myself.

It was Henry Twelftree who, seeing me shaking with fear on the occasion of my first appearance at the Old Bailey, said "Remember that you have the _right_ of audience". I had only been called for a few weeks. Today that right of audience cannot be exercised until a barrister has completed a full twelve months of pupillage.

Mervyn did however give me one piece of advice: "If you want to succeed at the Bar" he said, "you should join the Inns of Court Conservative and Unionist Association and learn to play golf". Of course I disregarded it. Had I taken it, my life would have taken a somewhat different course.

History has judged Mervyn harshly. I think unfairly. One ill-advised remark, made in opening the Lady Chatterly prosecution ("is this the kind of book you would allow your wives or servants to read?") had burned itself into the public memory and is all that many people remember of him. The truth is that Mervyn was essentially a Victorian. Had that question been asked a hundred years earlier, it would scarcely have raised an eyebrow. In fact Mervyn was a fair prosecutor, temperate in his arguments, who never cut corners. When later he sat as a judge at the Old Bailey, he was regarded as merciful and just.

Christmas Humphreys, who was at the time First Senior Treasury Counsel, attracted my admiration. He prosecuted the high-profile cases such as that of Ruth Ellis and Craig and Bentley (he was higher in rank than Mervyn who at that stage in his career was stuck with the second tier homicides). He had taken on a woman pupil, Jean Southworth, and kept her on in his Chambers as a tenant. She was a remarkable person who has never received the recognition she deserved (I think because she was born a generation too early). Serving in the Wrens during the war, she later worked at Bletchley Park as a codebreaker and, in time, became an outstanding prosecuting counsel and Old Bailey Recorder. She had a beautiful contralto speaking voice and a formidable presence. Some wag christened her *HMS Southworth* and the name stuck.

Back to Christmas Humphreys. He was a Buddhist by religion, which puzzled Mervyn's Victorian values.

"Curious fellow" Meryn said to me one day "doesn't believe in the death penalty".

I plucked up my courage to speak. "Well, do you?"

"Yes, just think about it. What could be more hideous than a life sentence?" I was too intimidated to argue.

I revert to the case where Henry Twelftree had tried to stiffen my trembling resolve. It was my first. My client, an elderly recidivist suffering from a terminal illness, was charged with arson with intent to endanger life. The offence carries a maximum sentence of life imprisonment. The case was listed before the Recorder of London, Sir Gerald Dodson, a terrifying old judge. It was totally inappropriate that so junior and inexperienced a barrister as I should have been let loose on such a case and before a judge with so fearsome a reputation. I should have cut my teeth on a shoplifter in the Magistrates' Court, but, to the bureaucrat in the List Office, my client must have seemed to be a human being of little worth, hardly worthy of better representation. In the event he pleaded guilty. I made my trembling little plea in mitigation of sentence and he was sentenced to seven years imprisonment. "My Lord" he said after sentence, "I'm a dying man. I'll never do it". "Just do your best" said the Recorder, "Just do your best".

I felt privileged during those months to hear some of the greatest advocates of their generation in action, Jeremy Hutchinson with his elfin humour, Victor Durand in his measured baritone. The company of my fellow pupils was a delight; Ann Curnow who was my exact contemporary, was a pupil of John Buzzard, achingly clever Treasury Counsel who was entrusted to prosecute the heavy frauds, Audrey Jennings, later a Stipendary Magistrate, Gerald de Basto, of Portuguese-Australian ancestry from Macau who later invited me to join his chambers in Hong Kong. The young bloods teased us quite unmercifully, taking the Davidge line on women barristers. Michael Corkery, later a serious prosecuting silk, asked us out in turn but said "none of you can ever make it, with your little squeaky voices. After all the BBC doesn't even allow a woman to read the news".

During my final month of pupillage Mervyn unbent a little. He even told me a story about an eccentric old aunt who used to ride a tricycle around Sloane Square. I decided to unbend a little myself. At this time no chap left home without his bowler hat and no girl without her gloves. My mother had given me a beautiful pink kid pair for my birthday. One day, I was sitting in the front passenger seat of his black Jaguar as we drove to Court, my hands crossed demurely in my lap when Mervyn looked down with a basilisk stare and said "Pink gloves Nemi, at the <u>Old</u> Bailey?" Well goodbye, tiny rebellion.

My time was up. I had paid Mervyn the obligatory fifty

guineas for the privilege of my pupillage. I had said my goodbyes at Harcourt Buildings. I was living at the time with Xanthe and Audrey in a rented flat in Cornwall Gardens, South Kensington. I decided to invite Mervyn and his wife Joanie for a farewell drink to meet my father, who wanted to thank him for his kindness to me and perhaps to exchange a few memories of Nuremburg. The Griffith-Jones seemed somewhat out of place in our student flat, but we managed to make stilted conversation and drink some sherry. They my aunt Buffy bounced in. My father was delighted. She'd been his favourite dancing partner when she was the prettiest of the Jakko Monkeys – my mother and her sister Buffy were known as the Jakko Monkeys in their debutante days, in Simla in the dying days of the Raj. "Well, here's a welcome breath of fresh air from the slums" he roared as he hugged her tight. I could see Mervyn flinch and then stiffen while Joanie's hand tightened on the stem of her glass. She was, of course, wearing immaculate, long white kid gloves.

A hundred yards or so up Middle Temple Lane from Harcourt Buildings stands Pump Court. To pass from the Victorian formality of the former into the genial atmosphere of the latter was to move from winter into spring. This was partly due to the fact that the head of Chambers, Ewan Montagu QC had broken with tradition and admitted as a tenant a woman.[5] I had heard Rose Heilbron at the Old Bailey when she defended a murder case which Mervyn was prosecuting. I was enchanted by her sympathetic and informal style (which also won over the jury). She became my heroine. I decided that, by hook or by crook, I must wrangle a second six months' pupillage in the Chambers of which she was a member.

This I succeeded in doing. I became pupil to Norman Brodrick, who practiced in family law and medical negligence. He was a member of the Western Circuit and sat as Recorder of Penzance. Norman was a lovely man, kind and informal, who treated me like a member of his large and boisterous family. There was something of a family atmosphere too at 3 Pump Court. At half past four, when the courts had risen, everyone, regardless of seniority or status, would adjourn for tea in Ewan

Montagu's room.

There was Rose Heilbron, the object of my admiration, a beautiful woman with crisp curly grey hair and scarlet lipstick, who was always kind to the pupils; there was Geoffrey Howe, later Chancellor of the Exchequer, in his carpet slippers, who had a great fondness for a cream bun. There was the great man himself, Ewen Montagu, who presided over the tea trolley and each afternoon regaled the members of chambers with an account of what he had said and done that day in court which was sometimes pretty shocking. He was, at the time, Chairman of Middlesex Sessions, which sat in the neo-gothic building in Parliament Square which now houses the Supreme Court. Although he was the most delightful man and an excellent head of Chambers it was universally agreed that he was a terrible judge. He could not resist doing what judges are supposed never to do, that is, to descend into the forensic arena and join the fight. He must have realised that he often overstepped the mark because he passed such lenient sentences that no one thought it was necessary to take him to the Court of Criminal Appeal. It was said that while justice must be seen to be done, in Ewen's court it had to be seen to be believed.

It was during my months at Pump Court that I had my first experience of life on the Western Circuit. This was the time before the Crown Courts Act established permanent courts which sat in every significant town or city in the country. They replaced the ancient system of Assizes of "oyer, terminer and general gaol delivery" where judges travelled the country and dispensed justice locally at regular intervals. This system had existed since medieval times. On the Western Circuit the Assizes visited the great Cathedral cities such as Winchester, Dorchester and Exeter and ancient boroughs such as Bodmin or Devizes. In each Assize town the principal hostelry was designated as 'the Bar hotel' where the Bar gathered the night before Assizes began and where the barristers stayed for the duration. Each hotel had a fine wine cellar, reserved for the exclusive use of the Bar, and among the staff who travelled with the Assize was a professional wine waiter.

The first time I dined in the Bar mess in the ancient Clarence Hotel in Exeter I was enchanted when, early in the proceedings, the wine waiter came up behind my chair with a bundle of papers and whispered "Miss Lethbridge, would you take the case of Smith in the morning?" and handed me the prosecution brief. This was the way it was done in those days. The junior prosecutions were all in the wine waiter's gift and the custom is commemorated in the title The Soup List. Few now recall its origins.

Norman Brodrick had a substantial practice in the field of family law. This was the time when the concept of a no fault divorce was still something on the distant horizon and a Petitioner had to prove adultery, cruelty, or desertion in order to win a decree. Many divorces were bitterly contested. The Respondent was supposed to be whiter than white – if it was found that he or she had offended, the Queens Proctor could step in between decrees nisi and absolute and block the divorce. The only way to avoid this was to serve a 'discretion statement' admitting adultery.

Just as in Harcourt Buildings, I had been set to work drafting indictments, here at Pump Court I was busied drafting discretion statements. Norman told me that the test of a successful one was that it would reduce the reader to sympathetic tears. So off I went. "Mr Smith always listened to my troubles and was a shoulder to cry on. Gradually our friendship deepened into something more intimate and adultery took place in a caravan at Leamington Spa."

One day I was entrusted with a defended divorce of my own. The allegation was adultery. The couple had six children. I was appalled to find that three were to give evidence for the father and three for the mother. I swore to myself "never again". I would go back to crime, somehow it seemed much cleaner.

Nevertheless, those months were among the happiest of my life. It was with sorrow that I left Pump Court and with trepidation that I made the next part of my journey, all of a hundred yards up Middle Temple Lane.

CHAPTER SEVENTEEN

<u>NEMONE</u>

Right at the top of Middle Temple Lane, just before the great fortress gate which gives on to Fleet Street, lies Hare Court. A somewhat dingy flight of stone steps leads up to Number 3 where I was to spend the five years of my first tenancy.

I made my way up the steps and into the narrow passage which led to the clerks' room. A man in workman's overalls gave me a cheerful "good morning, miss" as he looked up from his work. He appeared to be attaching a Yale lock to one of the closed wooden doors in the passage. I thought nothing of it, until later. In the clerks' room, which is the hub and engine room of every chambers, a bright coal fire was burning in the grate and a kettle whistling on the hob. Charles, the senior clerk, greeted me in the friendliest manner and offered me a cup of tea. He showed me where to hang my coat and the place where the kneehole desk my father had bought for me would go as soon as it was delivered. He showed me the shelf where my papers (when I had any) would be kept. He introduced me to Jean, who doubled as junior clerk and typist, a pleasant Cockney girl with sausage curls in the style of Rita Hayworth. As we drank our tea and Charles explained the rules of the house to me, the chap I had seen in the passage earlier came in through the open door.

"All done and dusted, guvnor" he said and plonked a handful of Yale keys on the desk.

"What's the damage?" asked Charles.

Money changed hands and the locksmith departed. Charles looked at me with slight embarrassment.

"The guvnors have decided that they don't think it suitable for them to share the – ahem – <u>facilities</u> with a lady" he said.

"Yeah, there's a key for every member except for you "Jean interjected with a laugh "you'll just have to go up Fleet Street and use the Kardomah caff." I hardly knew whether to laugh or cry.

This state of affairs continued for the next four years. It only came to an end when chambers took on as tenant Margaret Puxon, an alarming lady who was already qualified as a doctor and had practised as a consultant gynaecologist. No one dared argue with her. Two new keys were cut.

The twelve tenants of Hare Court received me, if not warmly, with a degree of courtesy. Barristers do not, by tradition, shake hands with one another, so I was greeted by each of the twelve members with a slight cough and a clichéd salutation such as 'welcome on board' was told to pay my rent, thirty-three guineas a quarter, direct to the head of chambers, Jack Ellson-Rees. It was explained to me that, because chambers depended largely on prosecution work which was in the gift of the Scotland Yard solicitor, who did not like women, I would not share in the chambers pool of work but would have to go out and find my own.[1]

"Why not pop down Sessions and try for a dock brief?" suggested Charles. Down I went to the London Quarter Sessions at Newington Causeway. I took my place among the other unemployed barristers in Court 1. At the start of the day's work defendants who had no counsel were brought up from the cells and invited by the Clerk of the Court to choose someone to represent them. If one was lucky, down one went to the cells to take instructions. Most of the defendants pleaded guilty which was just as well, as one had no solicitor to prepare the case for hearing. The pay was two pounds four shillings and sixpence (two guineas for oneself and two shillings and sixpence for the clerk). I once asked a client why he had chosen me when there had been other barristers available who were obviously older and more experienced than I. He replied "I wanted the other geezers to see I'd got the dolly bird in my peter"*.

I found Friday evenings in chambers somewhat depressing. The shelf where the briefs were kept would be stacked high with papers, tied in white tape for prosecution cases, pink for defence. I would watch sadly as the other members collected their work for the following week and went off home for the weekend. Even humble traffic cases, the mainstay of the junior tenants, were forbidden me. However, on this momentous Friday, Charles said "Miss Lethbridge, would you pop along to Arbour Square for me in the morning? The boys (as he used to call the two youngest men in chambers) are going to Twickenham for the big match and can't make it."

"Of course, I'll go, I'd love to."

"Very well, Jean will make you a nice little brief".

Jean duly typed up:

In the Arbour Square Magistrates' Court.
Police v Mr R Kray and Mr R Kray
Instructions for the Defence.
Lincoln and Lincoln, Solicitors.
London E.

She folded the paper, put a few blank sheets inside "to give it substance" and tied it up with a piece of pink tape. That was it. Nothing to indicate what the Messrs Kray were charged with. Jean could sense my discomfort.

"Alright then, I'll give you some instructions."

She typed: "Counsel will use her best endeavours" and slipped the note into my home-made brief.

Saturday morning. I duly made my way to Arbour Square Magistrates' Court, a small Victorian building in a cul-de-sac off Stepney Green. Although the court would not sit until half past ten at nine o'clock, when I arrived, the entrance hall was already buzzing with activity. A little woman wearing a floral pinafore, head scarf and curlers approached me. She was pulling a basket on wheels which appears to be full of dirty laundry.

"I'm their mum" she said. "They're innocent". A young man apparently escorting her, introduced himself. "Definitely innocent.

I should know. I'm their right hand man" interjected a small elderly man wih a rosy complexion.

"Gofer, more like" said brother Charles

"Redfaced Tommy! Go for this Go for that! Grinned the little chap.

"I'm brother Charles. Yeah, they're definitely innocent."

"It's a bleeding fix up innit" said another rather scary individual. "I should know, I'm their driver. The Jaguar. The white one."

A tall, elderly man with an unsuccessful shave detached himself from the crowd and announced "Patrick Pakenham. Lincoln and Lincoln Solicitors. I'm your chaperone for the day.

Let's go and meet our heroes. We'll soon find out what they haven't done."

The gaoler handed us the charge sheet. Paddy shook his grizzled head. "Sad really. Bit unworthy - Being a suspected person loitering with intent". Some copper must be a bit desperate. Or ambitious."

The gaoler unlocked the door and ushered us into the cell. "Let me introduce your clients, Sir and Madam. Show them the proper respect. Mr Ronald and Mr Reginald Kray."

The brothers sat, side by side, on the low shelf which served as a bed, at the end of the room, identical twins, silent and solemn as owls. They did not look like men who had spent a night in the cells. Their long pale faces were freshly shaved, their thick black hair Brylcreemed to glossy perfection. Their dark Montague Burton suits (Savile Row was in the not-too-distant future) were without a crease, their freshly laundered shirts white and dazzling. The cell was filled with the musky aroma of expensive aftershave.

Paddy said "Gentlemen, I'm sorry to see you in this situation."

"It's a fix up" said Ronnie "Is the Pope a Catholic?" answered Paddy, "Mr Lincoln sends his salutations but, as you know, can't come to Court on a Saturday. He's a frumer.[3] Has to do his religious duty. But he's sent you this lovely young lady in whom he has the utmost confidence (in fact I'd never met Mr Lincoln). She'll get you some bail today and then Mr Lincoln will come in person and do the trial for you on a day which suits."

The brothers stood up and shook my hand, bowing stiffly. I sat on the bed to take their instructions, writing on my knee, filling up a couple of pages of the brief which Jean had typed up for me. It was alleged that, between the hours of ten and eleven o'clock on Friday evening, the twins had been seen walking along Whitechapel High Street trying the handles of parked cars with the intention of stealing – though whether the intention was to steal the cars or their contents was not explained. There was one witness, a DC Powell. The twins were outraged. Such petty crime was far beneath them.

"We happen to be very wealthy businessmen" said Ronnie. "We happen to own three clubs which make a fortune. We're starring in the film of our life story, set in the Double R club. It's directed by Joan Littlewood and co-stars Barbara Windsor."

"That's absolutely brilliant" I said "I shall certainly go and see the film. But – (rather timidly) "I have to explain to the Court what you were doing on Whitechapel High Street last night."

"We was putting out flyers for our new enterprise, the Regency Club. As businessmen we can't never have too much publicity."

"This copper has the needle with us" interjected Reggie. "He's picked on us before for nothing."

"Yeah" said Ronnie "wants to get promotion."

"Nothing new under the sun" said the philosophical Paddy." Gaoler!"

Paddy and I went into Court. The usual Saturday morning collection of drunks, derelicts and misfits was processed in less than an hour. Then the twins were called. With their sharp suits and shining morning faces they looked like creatures from a different world.

"Good morning, Sir" they greeted the Bench, speaking in unison and bowing stiffly. The Magistrate regarded them with amusement almost.

"Who prosecutes?"

"I do, Sir" replied the fresh-faced young Detective Constable.

"Oh, DC Powell. We've met before. Once or twice."

The charges were put to the twins. They pleaded not guilty. I rose with a thumping heart to make my bail application. Out tumbled the clichés. When I got to "strong community ties" I heard brother Charlie, who was standing not far behind me, say sotto voce "Nice one", then, when I got to "respectable", he thumped a bundle of flyers for the Regency Club on to the railing in front of him. (The Magistrate could not have failed to see them.) When I got to "Charitable activities" Charlie said, audibly this time, "Nice one!" DC Powell glowered.

A date was set for the trial. The twins thanked me, formally and politely, and departed with their family and supporters. Paddy said "Come on, let's go and sample the wine of the country!"

This was the first of several Saturday morning appearances at Arbour Square Magistrates' Court and of a fruitful relationship with the firm of Lincoln and Lincoln. Before long I graduated to weekday appearances for clients recommended by the twins. I got splendid results. I began to think that I was the cat's whiskers as an advocate: it did not occur to me that my success had anything to do with the presences of the large scar-faced men standing at the back of the Court.

One afternoon I returned to chambers after a successful day at Arbour Square. In the clerk's room, warming himself by the welcoming fire, stood a stout jolly little man wearing a Homburg hat.

"This is the famous Mr Lincoln" said Charles.

"I'm very happy to make your acquaintance young lady. I've heard great things of you. My clients and very good friends the Kray siblings want you to take on the defence of a young protégé of theirs, Frank Mitchell, at present, alas, incarcerated in Her Majesty's holiday camp at Wandsworth. A charming fellow, nothing to fear. I've arranged a conference for Saturday morning at the prison. My man Pakenham will be there to see fair play."

"Thank you Mr Lincoln, I'd love to do it. What's our client charged with?"

"Attempted murder. Nothing to it really. It's another set up. Just tell them the tale."

Charles interjected "It's very good of Mr Lincoln to entrust you with such a heavy case."

"Oh yes, I realise that. I'm really thrilled."

"Don't worry your pretty little head. This is just the committal. Brother Ashe can take over at the trial if anything goes wrong."

"Brother Ashe", was Mr Lincoln's elder brother. He was in silk (a QC) widely respected for his war service in the Royal Navy and a founder member of AJEX, the Association of Jewish Ex-servicemen.

I was excited. Looking back, I realise that I got above myself and behaved disgracefully. I asked whether I could bring my sister to the conference, as my pupil.

"Of course, my dear. Bring who you like. Bring the Dagenham Girl Pipers."

Cherry, my little sister, a novice at an Anglican convent on Tyneside, the Franciscan order of Poor Clares, was taking a short break with me in London. I was worried about her vocation and wanted to widen her experience. What better chance than a visit to a maximum-security prison to meet a desperate criminal? Jean had already typed a letter of introduction for me addressed to the prison governor. She added to it "Miss K.C.P. Clare". This was my private joke: Cherry's baptismal names were Katharine Charmian, "P. Clare" were added for my own amusement. To do such an outrageous thing today would be impossible: to enter any penal establishment one has to produce evidence of identity – a passport or credit card.

We entered Wandsworth without problem and were shown into a conference room. After a couple of minutes our client arrived and his handcuffs were removed. In later years Frank Mitchell was demonised by the tabloid press as the Mad Axeman and depicted as a figure of terror. He was huge, alarmingly so, but apart from his size, there was nothing intimidating about him. At first glance one could have taken him as someone suffering from mild Down's Syndrome, with his big smiling innocent face. He seemed thrilled to see us.

"Did Ronnie and Reggie send you? They're my friends you know. They've been good to me. Ever so good to me. They give me a wireless you know. And a watch, a real Swiss watch. It cost a lot of money you know. But the screws took it off me. Maybe they'll give it back when I go home."

The conference was hard going. I tried to explain to Frank what the charge meant and the consequences which would follow if he was found guilty, but I was wasting my breath. All he would say was "It's a stitch up you know. The judge will chuck it out. That's for sure. He knows it's a stitch up." Then he'd revert to the twins and their kindness to him, ending with "And now they sent two beautiful young ladies to see me! Wait till I tell my mates." He seized Cherry's hands and mine and kissed them repeatedly.

"Leave off, Frankie" said Paddy, "you can't marry them both, you know. Come along ladies, our time's up. Frankie, we'll see you in Court. The twins will be there."

"Nice one" said the Mad Axeman.

Later I learned something of Frank Mitchell's history. His first encounter with the law had been when, at the age of ten, he had stolen a small child's cycle. He had been taken into care and sent to an industrial school. There he'd got into trouble for fighting. He'd been in trouble again for much the same kind of thing at his next institution. And again, and again. Now, in his mid-thirties, he hadn't seen daylight since he had ridden off on the little bicycle.

Because of his enormous size and limited intelligence Frank would be blamed for everything which went wrong in the institution in which he was held at the time. His family had long given up on him. Apart from the twins he had no visitors. To me he seemed more victim than villain, victim of a deeply flawed penal system.

A serious criminal case goes through the system in three stages: *charge*, when the nature of the offence is defined and put to the defendant; *committal*, when it is determined whether there is a case to answer; *trial*, when it is decided by a jury whether the offence has been proved. At that time the prosecution had to produce witnesses at committal and tender them for cross-examination. (Today committal can be achieved by a paper exercise.) So Frank was going to face twelve fellow prisoners and two prison officers from Wandsworth prison who had already made statements saying that, walking round the yard on exercise, they had seen him stab another inmate in the back.

The committal proceedings were to be held at the South West London Magistrates' Court. The Stipendiary Magistrate, Glenn Craske, had a fearsome reputation for rudeness and bad temper, in marked contrast to the affable fellow who sat at Arbour Square.

As Paddy and I arrived at the Court, the Krays' driver was parking the white Jaguar while the twins were striding into Court, glossy and immaculate, Redfaced Tommy trotting after them like a little dog. A whole day had been allocated for the hearing of the case. The Court had no other work. I was somewhat dismayed to find that the prosecution was to be conducted by a barrister from Six King's Bench Walk, a blue-chip prosecution set with a reputation for taking no prisoners. The authorities were obviously hoping for their pound of flesh.

The twins took their place in the public gallery, silent and expressionless. I could see security looking at them nervously, but their conduct was impeccable. They did nothing which could have led to their being asked to leave the Court.

Prosecuting counsel opened the case. Forty men, residents of 'B' landing, had been taking their daily exercise in the prison yard supervised by two prison officers. Among the prisoners was Albert Gibbs, the victim in this case, a man of five foot six in height and slight in build. Close behind him walked the defendant, Frank Mitchell, who was conspicuous for his height and build. In fact he towered over the victim by a good twelve inches. There was no one on exercise who approached his appearance. All of a sudden, the victim fell to the ground uttering a series of gasps and groans. Inmates who crowded round him found him to be covered in blood which was pouring from a wound in his back. Conspicuous by his absence from this group attending the victim was Frank Mitchell who had run to the far end of the yard. The victim was taken to hospital where he was found to have a laceration six inches deep in his back. His left lung collapsed, he spent five days in intensive care, but was happily now on the road to recovery. He will tell the Court that Frank Mitch-

with a long table, covered with a cloth of Honiton lace. We sat at the table, Ronnie at one end, Reggie at the other, various acolytes standing like footmen behind the chairs where Paddy and I took our places next to brother Charles.

Violet brought in the tea on a tray. There was a bone china tea set, biscuits in a silver barrel, cake on a three-tier cake stand. Charlie stepped forward to pour the tea, milk in first. We drank it and ate what was offered us. We made stilted conversation about the weather and the traffic on Mare Street and the Cambridge Heath Road. Then all of a sudden Ronnie rose to his feet.

"Miss Lethbridge" he said "we sincerely appreciate all you have done for one and all of our family. Also, for our poor friend Frank. On behalf of one and all of our family I would like to give you this small token of our appreciation." With this he handed me a thick wad of five-pound notes.

I was embarrassed. I said "I'm awfully grateful: it's really sweet of you. But I get paid by Legal Aid. I'm not allowed to take anything else."

Reggie was gesturing to his brother. "Use your loaf, Ron" he said, "you know the rules."

"Got you" replied the dominant twin. "All out." The acolytes left the room. Someone closed the door.

"Sorry Miss Lethbridge. I shouldn't have done it in front of witnesses. Here we go" and he handed me the money again.

"I'm terribly sorry" I said "but I'm simply not allowed to take gifts, but I do appreciate the kind thought."

Ronnie shook his head either in puzzlement or disbelief. He arranged for his driver to take Paddy and me back to chambers We said our slightly embarrassed goodbyes. I saw Paddy mutter something to Ronnie before we left and heard Ronnie say "got you."

On the ride back to Temple I said "Oh God, I hope I haven't blown it with the twins. We'll probably never see them again."

"On the contrary" replied Paddy, "I've arranged for them to get you a nice crocodile handbag. I'll work it down to you."

"I don't want a crocodile handbag! Can't you understand? I

don't want anything! Except of course their work."

Strangely the twins did not appear to have been offended by my odd behaviour. I continued to make my Saturday morning trips to Arbour Square and gradually work increased in quality. My first appearance at the Old Bailey, on the recommendation of the twins, came as a result of their interest in the film 'Sparrers Can't Sing'. Brother Charlie had fallen desperately, hopelessly in love with Barbara Windsor, the archetypal Cockney sparrow with her huge blond beehive as she teetered through the film on her six-inch heeled white court shoes. When misfortune struck, Charlie was there to help in any way he could.

Barbara's husband, Ronnie Knight, a sleek young villain from the East End, was charged, along with others, with robbing the Lots Road Power Station and stealing money amounting to several hundred thousand pounds. Ronnie had been committed for trial at the Old Bailey and I was instructed (by Lincoln and Lincoln) to apply for bail. Down I went and made my little speech, no easy task where the allegation was so serious. "Substantial surety, settled address, strong community ties – indeed, married to a famous actress". This last had not been in the public domain. The boys in the press gallery went wild. Who? When? How? There were plenty of people in the supporters' club present who were ready to name names and soon Barbara's secret was out. Despite my efforts, the judge refused bail.

Afterwards Barbara came up to me, I thought to discuss going to the High Court to renew Ronnie's application. But no. "You fucking little cow" she shrieked, "Fancy telling them that! You won't be able to sell me in this business with a pound of sugar after this."

Disconsolate, I thought that that would be the end of the Kray brothers' recommendations. But no. Ronnie was acquitted at his trial. All was forgiven and ever more substantial work continued to flow in my direction. As for Barbara, the story did her no harm whatsoever. It raised her profile, and she became, in the eyes of the press, something of a heroine, the loyal wife, the brave little Cockney sparrow who though thick and thin stood by her man.

As for the film which the twins had mentioned at that first

debated the Homicide Act) was re-introduced by an order in Council. I was appalled by this retrograde step. Ludovic Kennedy had already written *10 Rillington Place* about the Timothy Evans case which made clear what must have already been apparent to anyone with an ounce of intelligence, that is the danger of a miscarriage of justice where the principal witness in a case is dead. I had nightmares about the hideous decapitations following the Nuremburg Trials.

*   *   *

The Chambers at 3 Hare Court were flourishing. Sir Ian Percival, later Solicitor General, took over as head. A number of new tenants joined the set, including Margaret Puxon who came down from Birmingham and, married to a solicitor, brought in a swathe of family work. There was Sir Lionel Thompson, affectionately known as the bad baronet, who had been a Spitfire pilot in the Battle of Britain and was delightfully carefree and eccentric. He did a little light prosecuting but, if truth be told, he was more at home on the racecourse than at the Old Bailey. He was welcome in Chambers mainly, I suspect, because of his handle, but also because he added to the gaiety of nations. Unlike the young stuffed shirts in chambers, he was not embarrassed by being seen with me in public. We enjoyed a close, but chaste friendship while he went through various domestic problems.

One evening Lionel invited me out for a drink. After a short session in El Vino's, we made our way to Belgrave Mews and the Star Tavern. I had never been there before, but Lionel treated it as his local. We were welcomed by Paddy Kennedy and went straight upstairs to his special bar. It was packed. Lionel obviously knew everybody; I knew no one. I was introduced to a thin beautiful girl sitting alone on a bar stool "Christine Keeler" he said. We exchanged a few words and moved on. A group of men stood at the bar roaring with laughter. Lionel took me over. At the centre of the group stood someone who looked like a cartoon Irishman, lantern jawed, curly grey auburn haired, broad shouldered, worldweary.

"I want you to meet the most fascinating man in London" he said, "Jimmy O'Connor". We shook hands. "Come on you old scoundrel, tell Nemone your life story".

"I'm sure the young lady don't want to hear about Sunny Devon" he replied.

"I'm sure she does. And all about your friend Mr Pierrepoint

So it was. I was mesmerised. Like Desdemona at the feet of Othello at their first meeting. At the end of the evening, as time was called, Jimmy said "Would you have dinner with me sometime?"

Before I could answer Lionel butted in. "No James, that's a liberty, she's my woman. For now, anyway. Nemone, let's go."

The following Sunday I was coming home from the 6.30pm mass at St Mary of the Angels, Moorhouse Road. There was Jimmy, standing on the doorstep of my house. We were both embarrassed. Then he said "I wish you was my wife".

go home. To India."

Xanthe ran into her bedroom, slammed the door and locked it. To my eternal shame I turned my back on her and returned to my own problems. But Audrey was concerned. She rang Xanthe's mother in Derby and asked her to come down to London.

A few days later I was alone in the house when Lady Wakefield arrived. A contemporary of my own parents in Simla, her husband had been, at that time, a distinguished mountaineer. He had named a pass in distant Nepal after his fiancée Lalage. Red haired, befreckled Lalage. Distinctly grumpy.

"I don't understand how Xanthe can be so selfish" she complained. "She knows I've got so much to do in the constituency now that Teddy's been promoted.[2] Of course she's depressed. Anyone would be depressed working for that appalling left-wing BBC. I always wanted her to do something with animals. It would have suited her. Especially dogs. She understands them. She can make the naughtiest puppy sit, just like that."

I made tea for the matriarch and tried to defend her daughter and her daughter's employer.

Later that evening Xanthe arrived home from the BBC. She seemed less than delighted to find her mother sitting in the kitchen, by now drinking a large gin and tonic. Mother and daughter adjourned to Xanthe's bedroom which, as usual, looked halfway between a jumble sale and a refugee camp. I tried to shut my ears against the shouting match which followed. After half an hour or so, Lady Wakefield burst out of the bedroom, weeping furiously.

"It's an absolute shambles' she shouted. 'She can't even tidy her room".

Red-eyed she glared at, or rather through, me. I know what she saw was not me, not the little kitchen, or even the chaotic bedroom at Monmouth Road, but that nursery with its cot crushed in the Quetta earthquake some thirty years before.

"Why did it have to be Imogen?' she howled. 'Why Imogen?".

* * *

It was only a couple of weeks after our momentous meeting at the Star Tavern that Jimmy left his kindly widow in Paddington. He took a flat in Ladbroke Gardens, a leafy square off Kensington Park Road. There were high cool rooms, white marble fireplaces and a cast iron fronted balcony which ran the length of the first floor. Standing on it one was less than an arm's length from the pink and white blossoms which covered the chestnut trees rising from the garden below. Jimmy started to attend auctions to buy antique furniture. He cultivated demolition contractors: from one, who was taking down the old Polish embassy, he bought a crystal chandelier.

"You'll enjoy living here when you're my wife" he said.

"Don't be ridiculous" I snapped. "I'm not going to be your wife".

Jimmy told me about his case: about George Sewell and the watch and chain. He told me about the incompetence of his lawyers. "If only you'd been there to defend me" he said. "I'd have walked out of it."

"Don't be so stupid" I answered, "I was only nine years old at the time."

"But you can still do my appeal."

"Are you trying to bully me?"

"No. You could pull it off."

"In your dreams" I said ungraciously. "Anyway, you'll have to wait another thirty years to get your papers from the Home Office."

"Thirty years, forty years, it don't matter. You and me are going to be together for ever."

"I don't think so."

Ann Curnow was fast becoming my closest friend. Handsome, clever, dark eyed Ann, a graduate of King's College London and my exact contemporary at Gray's Inn. She lived in Ealing with her mother, a feisty humorous woman who supported herself and her daughter by playing the stock exchange on the telephone and who took no prisoners. Although her husband, while a prisoner of war of the Japanese, had died working on the notorious Burma-Siam railway, she was devoid of self-pity. I admired her.

Ann was pupil to John Buzzard, then second junior Treasury Counsel at 6 King's Bench Walk in the Temple. He recognised the contribution she could make to his Chambers and, when her pupillage was complete, offered her a tenancy. She remained in those Chambers for the rest of her life. She took silk in the eighties and married Neil Denison, a fellow tenant and the nicest judge at the Old Bailey. At the time of which I am writing Ann and I (who were both usually slimming) would, when not in Court, meet for 'no lunch' in Fleet Street to dissect the criminal justice system and put the world to rights.

Ann met Jimmy and adored him. She found him a refreshing change from the young stuffed shirts in her chambers who despised her non-Oxbridge degree and suburban address.

"Jimmy is a wizard man" she would say. "If you don't marry him, I'll snap him up myself."

"But my parents..." I was afraid. Still terribly afraid.

"Don't worry about your parents, once they know him they'll come round to him. Everybody does. He'll make them laugh."

Together we plotted my marriage. One of my great fears (which turned out to be well founded) was that the tabloid press would make a meal of it. We thought that the 'yellow press', as it was often called in those days, would be unlikely to publish anything in the absence of documentary proof of a wedding. The broadsheets would not be interested. In that I was wrong. I felt that while nothing appeared in the public records, then held at Somerset House, we would be safe. Jimmy took it all in his stride.

"I knew you'd come round to it" he said, "sooner or later".

I bought myself a pale green satin shirt-waister frock and, from Christian Dior, a little hat in the shape of a rose. I booked three airline tickets to Dublin in the names Mrs Curnow, Miss A Curnow and Miss B Curnow. Jimmy made his own arrangements. When I arrived at the Gresham Hotel with my party, I found him in the bar with Jack Fishman and two jolly car dealers from Warren Street, attacking the wine of the country.

15 August 1959. It was the feast of the Assumption and also the anniversary of my parents' wedding in Simla some thirty-odd years before. I chose the date because, despite their absence, it gave me some feeling of connection with my mother and father. I should have been happy, embarking upon this strange adventure and making what I hoped was a bold political gesture, but, as evening drew in over the darkening River Liffey, I felt nothing but an overwhelming sense of guilt, apprehension and

remorse.

I had fixed the wedding for eleven o'clock the following morning, but at a quarter to twelve the Curnows and I were still driving in a taxi round and round the Dublin Pro-Cathedral. Jimmy and his party were standing on the steps smoking like chimneys and waiting for the preceding Mass to finish. I saw a young altar server approach them, probably to explain or apologise for the delay. It was a holy day of obligation and masses would have been booked back-to-back.

"Tell your guvnor" I can imagine Jimmy saying "he's got too many runners and riders on the card."

Shortly after this accommodation was reached between the cathedral authorities and the wedding party. We were called inside, our ceremony tacked on to the back of an Italian Sodality Mass. So we enjoyed the benefit of the Latin and of glorious music. While both Ann and her mother were Anglicans, none of Jimmy's guests had been in a Catholic – indeed any – church before.

"When the geezer came round with the little sweets" complained one of the car dealers afterwards, "why don't he give me none?"

After a long liquid lunch at the Gresham, Ann and her mother left to catch their flight back to London. I suppose that I had imagined that I would take centre-stage, but it was Jimmy who occupied that position, entertaining his guests with jolly tales of Pierpoint and sunny Devon. After two or three hours, sulky and mortified, I took myself off to bed. It was not until the small hours that Jimmy stumbled upstairs. I doubt that my absence had been noticed.

Late the next morning we said goodbye to the hotel staff, all of whom were by now Jimmy's best friends and hired a car.

"Where d'you want to go?" Jimmy asked

"It doesn't matter" I replied. "Just point it west, steer by the stars and see where we land up."

We drove west across the damp green heartland of Ireland until we reached a long pale beach bordered by the crashing Atlantic. Omey Races. Skinny dark horses streaked up and down the beach, farmers drank Guinness from tankards, bookmakers shouted the odds. We stayed long enough to lose a little money, then, in the nearby town of Creggan, found a boatman to take us to the island of Inishboffin.

This lies about ten kilometres out into the ocean. Nothing between it and Nova Scotia, it is an emerald green lump appearing and disappearing between gigantic blinding waves. Our boatman directed us to Mrs Day's boarding house, the only hostelry on the island, a modest white-washed building where we ate lobster three times a day, huge white mushrooms and soda bread which Mrs Day baked daily before crack of dawn.

The only other guests were a doctor and a vet from the mainland. Neither seemed particularly pleased to see us.

"We come here for the peace and quiet" said the doctor, " but we never seem to get it."

"One eejit arrived here on his bicycle" said the vet, "he'd raced all the way from Poland – Why?"

"Don't worry about them' Jimmy said to me, 'just a couple of irons."[3]

No one could tell me where the exquisite Chippendale style furniture came from. It must have arrived during the bad old colonial days. Mrs Day didn't like it. It needed too much dusting. She would have preferred something more modern. I just gazed at it in envy and admiration, Jimmy wondered how to get it back to Ladbroke Gardens.

It was with a sense of apprehension that I arrived back at Ladbroke Gardens some three weeks later. I had half expected to find the place crawling with paparazzi or my father on the doorstep with a horse whip. As it was, peace and tranquillity reigned. Kindly neighbours greeted us with a bottle of champagne. I was entranced by the high cool rooms, the sparkling chandelier, the chestnuts outside just turning from their summer emerald to autumnal brown.

In chambers little had changed. I announced my marriage, but no one asked me to whom I was married. Except Lionel, who simply said "You're a silly girl Nemmers. You could have done much better for yourself" and went on to tell me that he was taking out the beautiful Bella Maharaj, a barrister from Trinidad. A trophy date. Charles, the senior clerk, simply asked me whether I wished to retain my maiden name.

The autumn was set to pass peacefully. Jimmy and I

were happy. I resolved to tell my parents when the time was right. Which was not yet. I was kept busy enough with work for Lincoln and Lincoln very often on the recommendation of the Krays. Jimmy joined forces with Jack Fishman to engage in a number of lucrative property deals. We were relatively prosperous.

On several occasions we went to Sunday lunch at Monmouth Road. Xanthe seemed happier and calmer. She commissioned me to do one or two short pieces for 'Tonight', a current affairs programme. She helped me to lower my voice by half an octave so that I sounded less like the Queen. Audrey was her usual sweet unselfish self, totally preoccupied with other peoples' problems. All seemed set fair. A calm sea and prosperous voyage.

Shortly after our return from Ireland I met Ann for our habitual 'no lunch'. In the event the occasion seemed to call for more than that, so we booked a table and sat down to a modest smoked mackerel salad at a restaurant in Fleet Street. At a table nearby we saw two men who had lunched rather more lavishly than we. To our embarrassment we saw them call a waiter across and pay our bill. They then drew up two chairs and, uninvited, joined us.

"Dowagers for dons and sweet girl graduates in the High" said the one.

"And lovely lissome nymphs in Middle Temple Lane" said the other. He had some difficulty articulating the word 'lissome'.

The second man, tall, fair and haggard, said "May I introduce my friend, Patrick Leigh Fermor? He lives in a rabbit hole in the Troodos mountains."[4]

The first, dark in complexion and somewhat weather beaten, interjected "And this maniac is Anthony Holland. Brought up at Eton. Lately head boy at His Imperial Majesty's holiday camp on the River Kwai."

Ann said stiffly "Thank you for paying for our lunch but as you're both obviously mad and rather offensive so I'm back to Chambers. Come on Nemone."

We rose to go.

"Nemone is it?" said Leigh Fermor. "Farsi or Greek? Don't go. Well, not until you've been for a walk under my celestial brolly. Open it up and you can see every constellation in the heavens."

Ann was getting annoyed.

"My friend's not going anywhere. She only got married last week."

"Married! It's impossible!" shouted Holland, "So virginal, so pornographically beautiful! I absolutely forbid it!"

Ann and I scuttled off down Middle Temple Lane to the sanctuary of our chambers. It would be some time before we ventured out to Fleet Street to eat no lunch again.

Some days later Patrick Leigh Fermor telephoned me in chambers. He apologised and in particular asked me to forgive Anthony Holland. "No one emerged from the River Kwai quite right in the head." He said "before the war the poor man was quite normal."

I explained that Ann's father had died on the Burma-Siam railway. He was mortified. "Even so, can't you bring yourself to come for a little walk under the celestial brolly?"

It was with some regret that I said I was quite sure. He seemed a lovely man.

Some days later I was making my way home from chambers at about seven o'clock in the evening. As I entered through the front door of our building I heard a loud bang from the vicinity of our flat on the first floor. As I went up the stairs I was appalled to see Anthony Holland outside our front door, a revolver in his hand. I turned and fled out into the street and raced down Kensington Park Road. He followed me, shouting obscenities and firing randomly into the air. Happily he tripped and fell, giving me the chance to turn into Elgin Crescent where I took refuge in a chemist's shop. Police were called and my attacker arrested. After a while I crept home and told Jimmy what had happened. He was totally unsympathetic.

"Blame yourself" he said, 'you must have encouraged him." It was our first big quarrel.

I expected the police to call and interview me. No one came. I expected to see headlines in the morning papers along the lines of "War veteran barrister arrested on firearms charge" but nothing. Only a small item on an inner page 'Anthony Holland, a clerk, pleaded guilty at Bow Street Magistrates' Court to a charge of being drunk and disorderly.' I never saw him again.[5]

Jimmy and I made up our quarrel. We spent a pleasant Autumn. Ian Percival, Conservative Solicitor General, took over as head of Chambers. 3 Hare Court prospered. I shared a room with Margaret Puxon, who, despite her alarming presence, became a good friend. She had retained her medical status and whenever she felt it necessary would liberally dose us with prescribed amphetamines. With her affable solicitor husband, Maurice Williams, Jimmy and I would often dine, or go to the Establishment (our cabaret of choice) or the theatre. It was a vigorous period for the stage, lively and innovative. Brendan Behan's 'The Hostage' opened in the West End, an adaptation of the Brecht/Weill 'Threepenny Opera' (billed as 'A Soho Opera'), brought John Gay's rogues and charlatans back to the nineteen sixties. Above all the genius of Joan Littlewood dominated the London Stage.

I was still in frequent contact with the Krays who, via their runner, Red-Face Tommy, pushed many an East End scoundrel my way. The twins had recently opened a new club in Knightsbridge 'Esmerelda's Barn' but still dominated their home territory in Tower Hamlets, Chaucer's 'Stratford atta Bow'. When it was announced that Joan Littlewood was to open her groundbreaking production 'Oh What a Lovely War' at the Theatre Royal, it seemed to me a good opportunity to introduce them to Jimmy. I was curious to see what he made of them. Being of an older generation he had not at that time met them but simply referred to them as "These new people". I suggested to them that they might attend the first night, having already established a friendly relationship with Joan Littlewood at the time she directed and they appeared in 'Sparrers Can't Sing'.

On the first night the brothers attended in force with their associates. They took the whole of the dress circle, splendid in their dark blue suits, George Raft style dark glasses, square cut pocket handkerchiefs and sparkling cufflinks. At the interval we all met up in the bar and Ronnie made one of his formal speeches "On behalf of one and all of all the family" before paying for every drink in the house. However, when the lights went down for the second act, the Krays were nowhere to be seen. More pressing business must have intervened. Later I asked Jimmy what he made of them. The answer was: not very much. "Fucking cheap suits" he said.

At the time the comedy of manners was giving way to an older, earthier tradition. Frank Norman wrote his autobiography *Stand on Me*, an unashamed incursion into the vernacular. The appointment of Sir Hugh Green as Director General of the BBC and of Sidney Newman as head of drama liberated a great swathe of working-class talent which under the austere regime of Lord Reith would never have seen the light of day. The young Turks James MacTaggart, Tony Garnet, Roger Smith and later Kenith Trodd, revolutionised the production of television drama. Plays were commissioned from Dennis Potter and David Mercer. Ken Loach introduced an entirely new style of directing for the small screen as ground-breaking as that of Joan Littlewood in the theatre. Jimmy's centre of gravity shifted from the Star Tavern to the BBC bar at White City. His hour was about to come.

CHAPTER NINETEEN

Our first Christmas together. Jimmy and I decided to spend it in Paris. Despite the glory of midnight mass at Notre Dame it seemed oddly quiet and dark: the houses shuttered, and the streets deserted. It poured with rain. I missed Black Dog, the blazing fires, the earthy smell of roasting parsnips, the benevolent presence of aunts, the secret Appomattox jelly, the silly games.

We came home to Ladbroke Gardens to receive appalling news. Returning home from a family Christmas in the Wirral, Audrey was alarmed to find the house at Monmouth Road cold and dark. Xanthe's bedroom was locked and there was no sign of her. Eventually, after making a telephone call to the Wakefields in Derby, Audrey found a ladder and climbed through Xanthe's bedroom window. There she was, lying in bed, stone cold, the pillow dark with dried blood, empty pill bottle on the bedside table. No sign of a note.

There was an inquest. The kindly coroner returned an open verdict. "I blame the dreadful left-wing BBC' said Lady Wakefield. The dreadful left-wing BBC mourned as did everyone who knew her. Ned Sherrin who danced with her, Donald Baverstock who nurtured her talent, the loyal Bottom Table. There were obituaries. My mother wrote to me:

I was shocked to see Xanthe's death in the paper. Wondered so much after what you told me whether she had done away with herself. If so I feel so desperately sorry for her mother in particular. Poor Lalage! What a terrible waste of a brilliant young person, and I wonder why she couldn't get on with life? It seems such a shame and such a sad thing and I can't stop thinking about it. It is frightening to think how little one can help people who are in despair. I expect you will find out what happened and I should like to know as I was always interested in Xanthe.

The Somerville girls asked why. Jimmy was angry and perplexed. Perhaps I was wrong, but I thought I knew the answer to the tragedy. The smell of dust and marigolds. The eternal snows. The Quetta earthquake. Imogen.

There was worse to come.

At this point I will fast forward my narrative by a year. Audrey did not have the energy to reassemble our Somerville ménage. She returned the keys of Monmouth Road to the owner. Paul Rowland had taken a seven-year lease on a small flat in Maida Vale. She moved in, alone. One evening I received a telephone call from Paul.

"I'm convening a meeting of the Somerville Bottom Table survivors" he said. "Audrey is very ill, although she doesn't know it. She mustn't be alone at this time". I knew that she had been to see a doctor called Shirley Sherlock, but I didn't, at that stage, know why.

"I can't move in with her myself for reasons you'll appreciate."

"I don't appreciate, you swine." I said under my breath.

"I want you to form a rota so that she's never alone until the end. There's a spare room."

I found out that Shirley Sherlock was Professor of oncology at the Royal Free Hospital. Audrey was suffering from an aggressive cancer of the oesophagus. "Six months maximum" we were told. I had no difficulty in assembling a rota of carers. Dear girls! How I remember your steadfastness, your love. Every evening one of us would arrive, cook dinner, stay the night, and give Audrey breakfast before departing for our various daily employments. Every evening Paul Rowland would arrive at six o'clock, pour stiff whiskys or gins for everyone present, then stay on for a couple of hours complaining about the government or the mismanagement of the Exchequer before going home to his wife. Sometimes we would watch the 'Tonight' programme and talk about Xanthe. Audrey's illness was never mentioned. After three or four months her parents came down from the Wirrall and stayed in a hotel nearby, arranged for by Paul. Every evening Mrs Briscoe would brush her daughter's hair, once thick and golden, now thin and depleted by chemotherapy. She would put on her lipstick and say "We'll make you pretty for Paul." Having been chatty and polite and always concerned with other people's problems, towards the end Audrey became hostile.

"Why are you all whispering?" she asked on one occasion, "I'm not going to die today".

No one knew how to answer her. I felt that we were insulting her intelligence but did not have the courage to confront it. I regret to this day the way we handled the whole tragic affair.

One evening I was standing in the passage outside Audrey's room. She was, by this time, bedridden. Nowadays I suppose she would have been moved into a hospice. Quite suddenly the whole area was filled with the scent of flowers, roses, lilies and twelve-week stocks. Five minutes and the scent was gone, to be replaced by the homely smell of tomato soup heating up in the kitchen nearby. That night Audrey slipped away, without a tear, without a goodbye, without a word to those who had loved her.

Paul Rowland wept. We girls blamed ourselves.

Mrs Briscoe blamed Xanthe. "I blame that wretched girl a hundred percent" she said "she put too much on to Audrey. It was utterly selfish to kill herself like that. She should have known better".

After the funeral we went our various ways. I saw much less of my Somerville friends than before. I never saw Paul Rowland again although I know that he kept in touch with Audrey's parents. Xanthe, Audrey and I had long before agreed to go up to Oxford to take our MA degrees together. Now I did not have the heart to go. I've never been back. Oxford became for me a luminous glow, just over the horizon, like Jude's Christminster, a dream, the relic of happier, more hopeful times.

My father had retired. His cancer had been in remission for ten years and he and my mother looked forward to the peaceful life together which they had so far been denied. They decided to sell Black Dog Cottage. Their obvious destination was the County of Devon considering the strong connections on both sides of the family. My father scrutinised the Ordnance Survey map and chose the area which seemed least likely to fall victim to the developers or to have a motorway driven across it.

The place he chose lies between Dartmoor and the Bristol Channel. It is an area of small subsistence farms Thomas Hardy would have recognised, impoverished by bracken and gorse, of bluebell coppices and glass-clear streams which rise from the bleak granite tors at the county's centre.

The local people, many of whom belong to that dour patriarchal sect the Plymouth Brethren, do not take kindly to strangers, even those bearing ancient Devon names. It was twenty years before they would acknowledge my mother's existence with a chilly "good morning". They practice adult baptism by total immersion in the deep dark waters of the Torridge or Taw. I remember one wicked old misogynist riding his Dartmoor pony into Okehampton market, his unfortunate wife trudging after him on foot; a rope around her neck. Jeremy Thorpe, at that time MP for North Devon, described his constituents as "sleeping on straw and eating raw meat".

Egregious as it was, my parents fell in love with the place, with the old pink-washed cottage, with the neglected woodland bisected by the trout-rich river Taw. Here, in the spring, one would see the salmon, returning from the Atlantic, leap the weir at Eggesford and then shoulder their way upstream to the moorland pools where they had been spawned, would themselves spawn the next generation and die. All his life my father had dreamed of having his own water to fish in. Now he had it: glass clear, ice cold, legendary, a mile, both banks, of the Taw.

With the assistance of two old woodmen, Bill and Frank (members of a gentler sect than the Plymouth Brethren) they planted hundreds of trees, some conifers but, in the main, native hardwoods. This little forest my mother later donated to the Woodland Trust.

My father made a vegetable patch, aiming to make the family

self-sufficient, he had already arranged for the removal of six beehives from Black Dog to Clapper Cottage. My mother made a stone garden from the remains of a derelict cottage, 'Betty Piper's Garden' she called it after the old crone who had once lived there. She planted thousands of bulbs and enormous rambling roses, banksia Lutea and filipes 'Kiftsgate', which flung themselves forty feet or more over the trees which lined the riverbank. "Them's ain't never roses" said Bill or Frank. The place had the makings of an earthly paradise.

Cherry wrote to me from her convent on Tyneside. She was having grave doubts about her vocation and wanted to come to London while she thought things out. Could she come and stay with me? Well, of course she could. But I knew that I could not involve her in my deception. When I told her my secret, she simply said "I never thought you'd have the courage to marry him". She and Jimmy became the best of friends. I had to come clean and tell my parents that I was married, and that Cherry would be staying with their new son in law.

I wrote to them. They replied. Not in anger, not with recriminations, but inviting me to bring Jimmy down to Black Dog, which they were in the process of closing up before they moved to Devon.

It is a long, long drive from West London to Somerset. I doubt whether I have ever felt as terrified as I did when Jimmy and I made our way west that day. I don't know which I found more alarming: the prospect of my father's anger or my mother's tears. In the event everyone was on his or her best behaviour and the meeting went surprisingly well. I had wracked my brains for something which Jimmy and my father had in common, something to talk about. Then I had a brainwave: shipwrecks. At the end of the First World War my father left France by sea to return to his regiment in India. The route was via the eastern Mediterranean and the Suez Canal. Somewhere off Malta his ship, SS *Cameronia*[1], was struck by a torpedo and sank in a matter of minutes. After several hours in the water my father and other survivors were picked up by a fishing vessel and put ashore on the island. Strangely my father had never spoken to me about the shipwreck. But then he rarely mentioned the First World War and we children learned not to mention it. But the two men spoke about this and the sinking of the *Lancastria*. The ice was broken.

Later my mother took Jimmy round the garden, pointing out her most treasured plants and speaking of her sadness at having to leave them behind on the move to Devon. In particular she mentioned the row of amelanchier which bordered the lawn and led down to the orchard. In spring they would be covered with translucent white blossom, in summer by small green-gold leaves.

Jimmy and I had taken a room in nearby Frome. After eating a homely supper with my parents, we retired to our lodging for the night. Relieved by the fact that the introduction had gone so well I slept deeply and long. When I woke in the morning, I found Jimmy's bed empty and his car gone from the hotel car park. Somewhat grumpily I walked the four miles to Standerwick. There I found him in his shirtsleeves digging up the amelanchier trees. These he loaded on to a lorry which he had hired earlier that morning. My parents looked on with amazement. Jimmy then studied the road map and drove the precious cargo down to Devon. There, with the help of Bill and Frank, he planted the trees along the riverbank. I hope they flourish there today. After this, in the eyes of my parents, Jimmy could do no wrong.

Life returned to normal. I was kept busy defending various London scoundrels. Jimmy, who had been commissioned by the Wednesday Play team at the BBC, started work on 'A Tap on the Shoulder', a comedy about commercial and political corruption. Ken Loach was to direct it: the first of six plays written by Jimmy and produced by the team. Lee Montague was cast in the principal role. Cherry returned to the convent on Tyneside but for reasons romantic rather than religious. Peter, who had graduated from Harper Adams Agricultural College and who had been working as manager of the home farm at Stourhead in Wiltshire met and married a tall Scottish beauty, Mary Wallace. The family later pooled its resources and bought him a farm at

Mortehoe on the North Devon coast. All seemed set fair. In fact, it was too good to be true.

My father's cancer had returned. Without warning and with terrible rapidity. He was briefly admitted to the London Hospital for assessment but after a short conversation with his consultant declined all further treatment and took the train home. Clapper Cottage was hardly the place to nurse a terminal invalid: my parents had been so obsessed with the forest and the garden they had left themselves little time to civilise the house. There was no central heating, no washing machine, I washed the sheets, now disfigured with terrible brown stains, in the river. Margaret Puxon, eager to help when I told her of the various problems, engaged a nurse who would move in and stay for as long as it took. Furiously my mother sent the poor woman packing. "I can deal with this myself" she said. She asked the local doctor (who lived a mere twenty miles away) about pain relief. He said there was a range of heavy-duty analgesics available but that they would cause some blurring of the personality. "Then we'll do without them" she said. My poor father continued with a regime of codeine and paracetamol.

I returned my work, took leave of absence from Hare Court and moved down to Clapper. Peter came over from Mortehoe every day as soon as he had fed his livestock. Jimmy drove down from London at frequent intervals. After a few weeks Cherry came down from Tyneside to join us. My father never complained, never mentioned his illness or its prognosis. It was gardening and fishing (he had made a collection of trout flies out of silk thread and feathers which was his pride and joy and which we still treasure). Later his mind wandered back in time and he would ruminate about Alexander's march from Greece to the Indus, about the Mughal emperors, about his own trips to Spiti and the high Himalayas. He hardly spoke about the First World War: it was as though he had never been to Ypres or in the trenches of the Somme. Germany and the horrors he uncovered while Chief of Intelligence working towards the Nuremburg trials, he never mentioned at all. It was in the last few weeks of his life that he found himself back in Afghanistan during the war of 1919.

On the last night of his life it was with terrible clarity that he recalled and recounted an incident he had never mentioned before. A group of Afghan guerrillas had captured a British Tommy and arranged a party to celebrate. They killed an antelope and lit a fire of brush wood on which to roast it, using their kukris as kitchen skewers. Having eaten their barbecue washed down with home-made hooch, the guerrillas danced around the fire, inviting their captive to dance with them. Suddenly one of the Afghans, having heated his kukri red hot in the fire, struck a mighty blow, decapitating the captive. He then laid the kukri on the stump of the Tommy's neck, causing some bizarre neurological reaction. The captive rose to his feet and danced round the fire with his captors, to their enormous merriment.

After that my father lapsed into silence. My mother sent Cherry and me to bed. I slept until nine o'clock when I went downstairs leaving Cherry still asleep. My mother was sitting by my father's bed which had been moved to a position by the living room fire. "Daddy has just died" she said, dry eyed. "You'd better telephone Mrs Ford. I'm going for a walk." I did as I was told. Mrs Ford was the little woman from the village who traditionally laid out the dead. She arrived soon after, on the back of an old Massey Ferguson tractor, a stout little figure like someone from one of Shakespeare's histories. I walked down the river where I cut armfuls of Himalaya balsam, purple like the rhododendrons at Chakrata, to lay beside the coffin.

I returned to the cottage. Mrs Ford had done her work well. Someone had already delivered the coffin and she sat by it, her hands folded in her lap. She was joined by my mother and Cherry. The coffin was open, just a piece of gauze over my father's face. He looked very well. The years had rolled away and with them the lines of pain and confusion. I thought what a handsome man he was. Jimmy, arriving late that evening said, "He was the bravest man I ever met". Major General John Sydney Lethbridge CB, CBE, MC had been in the house of his dreams with its mile of river for less than a year. He had never cast a trout fly in the water.

CHAPTER TWENTY

Cherry was going to be married. During her stay at the convent on Tyneside she had met a young Church of England curate who was working in the parish. Her vocation had melted away like snow in the first spring sunshine. They had been drawn to one another until finally he proposed marriage. No one could have been more different to Jimmy than Julian Eagle, or more of a relief to the older members of the Lethbridge and Slater clans; Protestant, descendant of a professional military family, educated at public school and Cambridge. If this description gives the impression of someone conventional and dull that impression is wrong. Julian was charming, tactless and funny, a perfect consort for my little sister.

The wedding took place in Exeter Cathedral. Cherry was given away by our father's younger brother Bob, a colonel in the Indian Army. The union, ideal as it seemed, was eccentric enough to attract a certain amount of comment and, of course, attention from the press. Few of the guests at the reception realised that the swarthy chap in a dark blue suit, lavishly Brylcreemed, who charmed the old ladies as he interrogated them, was Peter Earle from the *News of the World*. The following day I took a telephone call from a reporter on the *Daily Mirror*. He asked me about the newlyweds but even more about Jimmy and myself. I was appalled. In panic I rang Cecil King, at that time owner-proprietor of the paper and begged him not to publish the story, saying that it would ruin our lives. He was polite and sympathetic and the story was put on hold for several days. However, the genie was out of the bottle and could not be stuffed back in.

The morning the story was finally published I was in the middle of a trial at London Sessions. I was late for Court, an almost unforgivable sin. The judge, Reggie Seaton, said, when I stumbled in, "Miss Lethbridge you are late. I do not seek to know the reason. In fact, I would prefer not to know it. I consider that you should go home and consider your position."

"The whore's son" said Jimmy when I arrived back at Ladbroke Gardens. I rang chambers to ask for a short leave of absence while I took my mother out of the line of fire. I imagined the paparazzi swarming over Clapper Cottage and frightening her to death.

Charles was severely practical and made me an offer for my wig and gown. "I'm not selling them" I said furiously, "I'll be back in a couple of weeks".

"I doubt it" said Charles.

I went up to the local travel agent and bought two airline tickets to Greece. I then took the train to Devon and collected my mother.Two days later we arrived in Athens together, where we signed up for an archaeological tour of the Peloponnese. As we drove south along the western coast, I felt the recent madness in London slip away to be replaced by a welcome sense of peace and calm.

At Kalamata we stayed in a modest tavern in the renowned olive grove. It was early autumn and the first pressing of the harvest was taking place. As the pale green oil began to trickle from between the great millstones used for the process, locals rushed in, each with a loaf of bread to dip in the magic emulsion. Our tour guide pointed out a house on the far side of the olive grove. "The house of a war hero" she said, "an Englishman, Mr Paddy Leigh Fermor". I wondered whether he still walked under his celestial brolly. It would have been good to have joined him.

It was almost a month later that we arrived back in Athens where Jimmy joined us. During the time we had been away we hadn't listened to the radio or seen a newspaper. Now we found out that while we were circumnavigating the Peloponnese the world had very nearly come to an end. Earlier in the year exiles from Fidel Castro's regime had mounted an unsuccessful invasion of Cuba at the Bay of Pigs. Now it appeared that nuclear weapons had appeared in the Caribbean and threatened the United States. Only some very neat footwork by President Kennedy had avoided cosmic catastrophe. It certainly gave my own small troubles a sense of proportion.

We had three days left before our airline tickets expired. We went down to Piraeus and decided to get on the first boat out. This turned out to be the *Naias*, making her twice weekly trip to the islands of Syros, Tinos and Mykonos. This last island is close to the archaeological site of Delos, in legend a floating island which anchored itself so that the goddess Leto could give birth to Apollo. That sounded good enough for us, so we boarded the ship.

Mykonos presents a low treeless, austere landscape, a chunk of Salisbury Plain dropped into the middle of the Aegean. There is a fine north-facing harbour, deep, sapphire clear, a little town built in the cubist Cycladic style and painted dazzling white, a row of windmills on the skyline. We stayed the night in the one hotel, the Leto, recently built with post-war Marshall Aid. We dined on red mullet and retsina. Jimmy said "I like this place. We'll come back next year and maybe stay a bit".

Back in London there was a pile of mail waiting on the door mat. First letter: from Sir Ian Percival, my head of chambers at 3 Hare Court.

> *"Dear Nemone,*
> *For reasons which you will appreciate but which I feel disinclined to explore I have today instructed the clerks to return your rent for this quarter and to remove your name from the door. I am sorry that matters have reached this sorry pass but I cannot risk further the reputation of 3 Hare Court.*
> *Yours etc..."*

I telephoned Margaret Puxon, hoping that she would intercede on my behalf. She refused to accept my calls. Later Anne Curnow told me that Ms Puxon had rung her and advised her to sever all contact with me.

There were several more letters in the same vein from members of the Bar, including old dancing partners. Then one from Jenifer Wates – the Somerville Shell Princess.

> *"Dear Nemone,*
> *I'm sorry that you've been getting a lot of publicity lately. From now on between you and me there will be a great gulf fixed but I hope that from time to time we'll be able to shout across it.*
> *Best love,*
> *Jenifer"*

I started doing the rounds, trying to find new chambers. I had no success. The only two barristers who were not ashamed to acknowledge me were Ann Curnow and Jean Southworth. I love and honour them both.

My final endeavour was to approach Gerald Gardiner, Lord Chancellor of the Callaghan government. He had the reputation of being enlightened and liberal in outlook. Surely a <u>Labour</u> Lord Chancellor would help me out. He received me warmly when I visited him in his chambers. "My dear" he said, "I think you've done a wonderful thing. I really admire you for it. Unfortunately, I can't help you. We don't accept women in these chambers."

Although I was over thirty, I was childishly naïve. I was astonished by Gerald Gardiner's behaviour. I believed firmly that left was good, right bad. How could a Labour Lord Chancellor be so anti-feminist? My simplistic belief was shattered when a letter arrived at Ladbroke Gardens.

From the Mayor's parlour.

> *Dear Mr and Mrs O'Connor*
> *Congratulations on your marriage. The Lady Mayoress and I wish you good fortune and every happiness in your future together. I was delighted to discover that you are among my constituents. I would be delighted if you would join us for drinks etc: etc*
> *Yours Sincerely*

J Elliott Brooks
Colonel (retired) Mayor of Kensington and Chelsea.

Wow! I said to myself. A Tory! So sympathetic and so kind!

We accepted the invitation and a couple of weeks later Jimmy and I found ourselves drinking whisky in the Mayor's parlour.

The Mayor, a large corpulent fellow boomed at us. His small, subdued wife said very little. Jimmy tried to put her at her ease. In spite of his history, she really shouldn't be frightened of him.

"I'm not going to eat you darling" he said.

Meanwhile our host was, as they say, trying to chat me up. "I knew your father by reputation. A most distinguished soldier. Unfortunately, by the time he arrived in Burma I was already a guest at his Imperial Majesty's elite holiday camp on the River Kwai".

"It must have been awful for you" I said.

"It had its moments."

Later the Mayor said, "My spies in the Temple tell me that you've been having a little local difficulty."

"That's to put it mildly."

"Well, happily I'm in the position to help you there. I'm senior partner in Theodore Goddard. Have you ever considered changing sides?" (Theodore Goddard was at that time a leading firm of solicitors in the City.)

"I could fix you up with articles. If young Jimmy here agrees. I'll take you to lunch next week and give you some essential reading on trust accounts".

So it was. We arranged to meet at a restaurant near the Bank of England one day the following week. I was just leaving Ladbrook Gardens to catch the tube when I received a telephone call.

"I'm sorry, my dear, but I've double booked myself. I quite forgot that I've promised to meet an old girlfriend of mine. We'll make it a threesome at her place. She is a nice girl. You will like her."

So, as instructed, I took the underground to Sloane Square where I found the Mayor waiting. He kissed me as though we were old friends and walked a couple of hundred yards to a block of flats where my host rang the doorbell. A somewhat faded blonde came to the door. She was wearing a dressing gown and fluffy pink slippers. We took the lift up to a small flat where the Mayor made the introductions. After a short interval a courier arrived with lunch in a plastic box. A very mediocre lunch.

We consumed the meal and made stilted conversation. Evidently the lady had spent the morning at Peter Jones's sale but had failed to find the bargains she has hoped for. With lunch finished the Mayor took a cane from the umbrella stand in the hall.

"Nemone, he said. I'd like you to beat Flossie now. She won't mind."

Flossie had slipped off her dressing gown. She was wearing a pair of winceyette pyjamas. I was outraged.

"Why ever should I beat her? She hasn't done anything wrong."

"I ask you because it would give me the greatest pleasure to watch" Said the Mayor.

I made my furious way back home. I didn't tell Jimmy. I felt outraged. But I was also afraid and ashamed. For a moment I was nine years old again enduring the misery of Walton Elm School.

The following morning, I rang the man in his office.

"I rang to tell you that I think you're the most ridiculous man I have ever met. Not only have you insulted me but you're exposing yourself to blackmail. Not everyone is as forgiving as I am". The Mayor seemed unperturbed. He laughed and said,

"How can anyone blackmail me? Everyone in London knows about me already."

It was not long before he got his comeuppance. It seems he kept a cabin cruiser on the Thames. One fine afternoon he invited two office girls to join him on board for lunch. He invited them to beat each other. When they refused, he did the job himself then poured whisky onto the injuries he had inflicted. Unfortunately for him one of the girls had a boyfriend who worked for the The Sunday People. The Story of The Spanking Colonel made the front page and ended both his legal and political careers.

For the time being I gave up trying to get back to the law. I hung round the BBC, I found the Wednesday Play team so friendly and congenial after the judgmental idiots in the Temple: warm-hearted James MacTaggart, Brummie Tony Garnet – inventor of the wonderful phrase 'agitational contemporanity', dear Ken Loach with his radical philosophy and spectacles mended with sticking plaster. Jimmy was working on his masterwork, his anti death penalty play 'Three Clear Sundays'. I wrote some songs for the soundtrack, using traditional folk music learned at Tudor Hall.

Jimmy liked to recruit people from the "real life" as opposed to professional actors to appear in his plays when this was possible. He chose them for their faces. One such was John Bindon who he met for the first time in Esmerelda's Barn. He saw in him perfect material for one of his plays. "Biffo" as he was known was the archetypial social mountaineer. His career ran from a period as a petty criminal in Fulham to a spell playing rugby for the London Irish, to a time running errands for the Kray Twins (who he called R and R and of whom he was terrified) to holidays on Mustique with Princess Margaret of whom he was in awe. Jimmy cast Bindon in several of his plays, notably *"Thirty Stretch"* and *"Her Majesty's Pleasure"* alongside Bob Hoskins and Dereck Griffiths. He invited him to Ladbroke Garden where Jimmy made some disrespectful remark about the Princess. Suggesting that there might be some carnal relationship between the two *"Give her one Biffo?"* he grinned. Bindon was outraged. *"Don't never talk like that, Jim. She wouldn't do nothing like that. She is a most gracious lady".*

Jimmy took his protégé up to the BBC bar to meet the Wednesday Play team. Biffo caused a small sensation when he exposed himself there, dangling six beer glasses from his enormous member.

For several years Bidon lived with the daughter of a peer who sold her story to a tabloid newspaper. Finally, so legend has it, he died of AIDS.

One evening at the time that *"Three Clear Sundays"* was in rehearsal Jimmy and Ken Loach and I were sharing a drink in the BBC bar at White City. A little scruffy man pushed his way through the assembled drinkers and made his way to Jimmy. "'Ere, Ginge" he said "She's the one I'm looking for. The twins want a word. Where's she been hiding?" "Sorry Tom. She don't work no more. She's retired". "That's plain stupid!" said Red Faced Tommy. "I don't fancy telling that to Ron and Reg. They've got a big one coming up. They'll see her alright. She don't want to mess around with this load of comedians."

"Sorry Tom. She's with me now".

Red Faced Tommy did not speak to me or try to persuade me to overrule my lord and master. Tom was, after all, one of a long line of cockney misogynists. I confess that I felt a strong sense of regret. It would have been great to be back in court.

Time passed. Jimmy said "we'll go and have another butcher's at that Greek island".

One glass-clear windless afternoon we found ourselves back on Mykonos. There had been rain in September and the barren hillside had burst into bloom: all the flowers one expects to see in spring, miniature narcissi, crocus, tiny cyclamen. We sat on the harbour side drinking a glass or three of ouzo and enjoying the meze of black Kalamata olives and calamari. An affable man was fishing in the harbour. After a while he approached us.

"I'm Nick Fiorentinos" he said, "I'm a refugee from Joliet, Illinois, US of A. Who are you?"

We introduced ourselves.

"I've come back home" he said, "where my heart is. How long are you staying?"

"Only a few days"

"Why don't you stay forever?" said Nick Fiorentinos, "I'm going to".

"Well, I might just do that" said Jimmy.

Thirty years later he was still there.

Greece divides the far end of the Mediterranean in half. Looking from South to North, on the left lies the Ionian, gentle and chalky, embracing the leafy-green island of Corfu, on the right lies the Agean, its constant force-nine gales battering the austere Cyclades. Among those islands is Mykonos, treeless, bone dry, its slopes much paler than the overarching indigo sky

For centuries the north-facing harbour provided sanctuary for the pirate islanders who would dart out and rob the passing merchant ships en route East from mainland Greece to Turkey or Northwards to Odessa and the Black Sea ports. The labyrinthine streets of the little town provided refuge for the robber seamen returning home. The twenty or so windmills ground the corn which supplied the Russian navy commissariat.

This is where Jimmy and I made our home. We bought a piece of land on the hill above the harbour. There was a one-room cottage, a plot of land devoid of vegetation but surrounded by dry stone walls, a well bubbling with ample fresh water which gave the place its name 'Vrisi' meaning spring or fountain. Walking home at night one's path was lit by thousands of glowworms whose tiny lanterns illuminated the stony curb.

The two thousand odd islanders lived by fishing or subsistence farming. Many of the women wove brilliantly-coloured fabrics on ancient looms, just as Penelope had on Ithaca, centuries ago. There was a handful of expats, most of whom came to study the archaeological site on the adjacent island of Delos, mass tourism was a couple of decades away. Among the notable foreigners who built a house above the harbour was Yehudi Menuhin whom I saw for the first time standing on his head in Viennoula's knitwear shop on the main street in the little port. The locals acknowledged his genius but, on balance, said that they preferred the music of Petros Harapis who played violin or bouzouki at local festivals 'because Petros taught himself'.

Mihalis Koukas, the local builder, extended the little house at Vrisi for us, adding a pigeon house in the form of a tower, decorated in the traditional Cycladic style. He built a 'sterna', a reservoir to conserve our precious water, in the foundations. It produced a strange soft reverberation, like the lowest notes of a double bass, every time the donkeys trotted down the lane at the back of the house. Mihalis had no need of instruments to take measurements when designing the house: he did the whole thing by eye, like the builders of the Parthenon. He was a great ladies' man who would, on occasion, come to the house late at night and play the sambouna, the single-stem Cycladic bagpipes. Peggy Glanville-Hicks, Australian composer and protégé of Yehudi Menuhin, thought that he was Apollo reincarnate because he had been born in Delos and was so devilishly handsome.

We slipped easily into island life. My mother came to stay and planted vines and olive trees. Jimmy wore a blue fisherman's cap and drank ouzo with the old boys. I took Greek lessons from the local midwife. I wore a white cotton headscarf and behaved myself like an obedient Greek wife. We had an old Land Rover which gave us a certain prestige: because it was the only private car on the island.

I was almost reconciled to what I had lost in England. Well, how could it have been otherwise, there, on that earthly paradise? For a time, we were truly happy.

NOTES

CHAPTER 1
Jimmy's story
To write this part of the narrative I have drawn on Jimmy's own memoirs *The Eleventh Commandment*, published in 1976 by Seagull. I have relied obviously on hundreds of conversations with him, with Annie his mother, with Ted Rogers, Annie's boyfriend for the last twenty years of her life; with Maria Hill, his sister and James William, his eldest son now deceased; with Bill Butler aka Billie the Orphan, and a number of 'the Faces' from Paddington and Portobello Road.

    1.   British Nationality Act 1947
    2.   *The Men of Ness*, Eric Linklater, published by the Orkney Press.
    3.   *Forthrights and Meanders*, Katharine Lethbridge, published by Merlyn Books.

4. *Plain Tales from the Hills,* Rudyard Kipling.
5. *Kim,* Rudyard Kipling.
6. The Bayswater Road was known by Cockneys as 'the Holy Mile' because of the large number of prostitutes who worked there.
7. St Vincent's Orthopaedic Hospital, Eastcote, Pinner-on-the-Hill.
8. This was written of St George's Cathedral, Southwark, built during the same period.
9. Quex Road was at the heart of the Irish Ghetto. It was here, in 1974, that the Guildford Four were arrested in a lodging house and charged with terrorist offences.
10. *Forthrights and Meanders*
11. Rosa Lewis had been mistress to the Prince of Wales, later King Edward VII. The Cavendish Hotel was her reward for services rendered. She was immortalised by Evelyn Waugh as 'Lottie' in *Vile Bodies*. A fictionalised account of her life formed the subject matter of a television series 'The Duchess of Duke Street'.
12. The Eleventh Commandment
13. *Ecclesiastes* Chapter 9 verse 11

CHAPTER 2

1. This famous Cockney pub song was immortalised by Harry Champion.
2. The age of criminal responsibility was set at ten by the Children and Young Persons Act (1933). I was seven at the time, so would have avoided the most dire consequences of my act.
3. *The Men of Ness*
4. 'This is the place of my song-dream, the place music played to me' whispered Rat, as if in a trance. Here in this holy place, here if anywhere we surely we shall find Him!'

Then suddenly the Mole felt a great awe fall upon him, an awe that turned his muscles to water, bowed his head and rooted his feet to the ground. It was no panic terror – indeed he felt wonderfully at peace and happy – but it was an awe that smote and held him and, without seeing, he knew it could only mean that some august presence was very very near. With difficulty he turned to look for his friend, as saw him at his side cowed, stricken and trembling violently....

'Rat!' he found breath to whisper, shaking 'Are you afraid?' 'Afraid?' murmured that Rat, his eyes shining with unutterable love. 'Afraid? Of him? Oh, never, never! And yet – and yet – oh Mole, I am afraid.' Then the two animals, crouching in the earth, bowed their heads in worship.

The Wind in the Willows, Chapter 7: The Piper at the Gates of Dawn, Kenneth Grahame, 1908.

5. 'I heard among the solitary hills
Low breathings coming after me, and sounds
Of undistinguishable motion, steps
Almost as silent as the turf they trod
...Oh, at that time
While on the perilous ridge I hung along,
With what strange utterance did the loud dry wind
Blow through my ear! The sky seemed not sky
Or earth – and with what motion moved the clouds
...I dipped my oars into the silent lake
And, as I rose upon the stroke, my boat
Went heaving through the water like a swan;
When, from behind that craggy steep till then
Then horizon's bound, a huge peak, black and huge
As if with voluntary power instinct
Upreared its head. I struck and struck again,
And growing still in stature the grim shape
Towered up between me and the stars, and still,
For so it seemed, with purpose of its own
And measured motion like a living thing,
...Strode after me...
...huge and mighty forms, that do not live
Like living men, moved slowly through the mind
By day, and were a trouble to my dreams.'

The Prelude, Book 1 – William Wordsworth
    6.   The Eleventh Commandment: Chapter 3
    7.   'The Beggars Opera': John Gay 1728
    8.   *Suite Francaise,* Irène Nemirovsky
    9.   The Serpentine Lake in Hyde Park.

Jimmy, like many London children of his generation, had been forcibly taught to swim by his father, who threw him into the deep water by the bridge where poor Harriet Shelley had committed suicide.

    10.   1920

The *Lancastria* was built on the Clyde by William Beardmore and Company, a subsidiary of Cunard. She made her maiden transatlantic voyage on 19 June 1922. Originally named the *Tyrrhenia*, her name was changed after the crew irreverently called her 'The Old Soup Tureen'. She was 16,243 gross registered tons, 578 feet (178m) long and could carry 2,200 passengers. When she was sunk she was carrying more than twice that number of military and civilian refugees – some estimate the number as 9,000. *The Lancastria* was used as a cruise ship from 1932 until the outbreak of war, when she was requisitioned as a troopship.

When she went down, two weeks after Dunkirk, the loss of life was so great that, as mentioned, all record of the disaster was suppressed by the issue of a D-notice. Survivors and persons manning the rescue ships were forbidden to discuss the matter under threat of court martial. The story was eventually disclosed by the *New York Times* and later by the *Scotsman*.

The British government has consistently refused to designate the wreck site as an official maritime war grave or to issue a commemorative medal as a symbol of official recognition and acknowledgment for all those who had been aboard the *Lancastria*. (This is in contrast to the actions of the Scottish Parliament which approved the issue of a medal to survivors and the building of a memorial on Clydebank.) The disaster remains in the UK largely a forgotten tragedy. https://en.wikipedia.org/wiki/RMS_Lancastria

CHAPTER 3

1.   One hundred and ten survivors were put ashore at Plymouth. Others were disembarked further up the coast. *The Blitz*, Juliet Gardiner (chapter 15), published by Harper Press.

2.   In fact, by January 1940 60% of the evacuees had already returned. *The Blitz* (chapter 1) above.

3.   My mother took in four little boys from Bethnal Green. They lasted for less than two months. They were lonely and homesick: they also hated her food.

4.   Maynard, J. *The Russian Peasant – And Other Studies*. London. Gollancz. 1942

Maynard, J. *Russia in Flux*. London. Gollancz. 1946

5.   An extract from this letter is incorporated in the main text

Letters from East and West, ed Katharine Lethbridge, published by Merlin.

In his letters to his mother Bertie described Appomatox and its environs. It was not a great palace like Montecello or other mansions of the Old South but rather resembled a rambling English manor house:

'The house stands at the junction of two rivers (the James and the Appomatox) which meet on a well wooded promontory. There is water on three sides of it, sometimes steely, sometimes yellow with flood and steamers and barges pass up and down... The house is of wood, two storeyed and with verandas on two sides... here is a pretty garden with fine trees and a few flowers... just outside are the paving stones over which Pocahontas walked and in the garden stands one of the cabins which were put up for General Grant's officers when the place was occupied in the Civil War. There are several marks of bombardment on the woodwork of the house and the day we got home (from honeymoon) they dug up a cannon ball.'

6.   Our 'giant's rubbish dump' must have been one of the 'Starfish' sites. These were decoys intended to lure the bombers away from their intended targets and to drop their loads relatively harmlessly in the countryside. Other sites near Bristol were located in the Mendips and at Chew Magna where Peter and I went to school. *The Blitz* (chapter 14 et seq).

7. 'All children, loving her, thinking no innocent or pretty fancy ever to be despised.' Charles Dickens, *Hard Times*.

CHAPTER 4

1. Speiler: slang for a gambling club deriving from a German-Jewish surname meaning 'player'.
2. 'shovel' rhyming slang shovel and pick = the nick, i.e. prison.
3. A discount of about a third of the appropriate sentence to be passed for a particular crime where the defendant pleads guilty was, for decades, a matter of practice. It is now embodied in statute. (See Criminal Justice Act 2003.)
4. *The Eleventh Commandment* chapter 5
5. *The Eleventh Commandment* chapter 5
6. *The Eleventh Commandment* chapter 5
7. *The Eleventh Commandment* chapter 5
8. 'Her Majesty's Pleasure' – a play set in Broadmoor was produced by Granada TV in 1968, directed by Barry Davis. Tony Garnet was a member of the BBC TV team responsible for 'The Wednesday Play'. Jimmy wrote several plays for this series which were directed by Ken Loach.
9. Hector Hughes KC MP (14th August 1887 – 23rd June 1970) represented Aberdeen for many years. He was a published poet and wrote the national anthem for Ghana when it was granted independence in 1957. He campaigned against the death penalty and I like to think that the fiasco of Jimmy's case played some part in his thinking. His career came to an inglorious conclusion when he was convicted of shoplifting in WH Smith's in Waterloo Station.
10. It has long been a matter of practice for a defendant to sign his Counsel's brief when it has been decided that he should not give evidence. This is intended to help the barrister in the case where counsel and client fall out and the client makes a complaint.

11. No transcript of the trial exists, so we have no record of the judge's interventions. When Jimmy was released from prison in 1952 he went to work for *The Empire News*, a Sunday newspaper (now defunct) owned by the Kelmsley group. The paper mounted an investigation into his case. Mr Littnar, the jeweller from Bath, was interviewed. He recalled the burglary in 1942 and, when the watch and chain were described to him, said that at the time he had carried stock of that type.

'Jock the Fitter' was, <u>after</u> the trial, interviewed by DI Thorpe. He refused to confirm or deny that he had taken part in the Bath burglary.

CHAPTER 5

1. The Eleventh Commandment chapter 6.
2. I have this picture. I keep it in my old Latin (pre-Vatican 2) missal.
3. The Eleventh Commandment chapter 6.
4. Bishop Matthew later became an Archbishop and Papal Emissary to Ethiopia. His brother was Sir Theo Matthew, Director of Public Prosecutions (1944-64).
5. Sir Alexander Patterson, Prison Commissioner, was a man of liberal and humane views. He was an advocate of prison reform and an opponent of capital punishment.
6. Jimmy was outraged to discover, some months later, that his reprieve had come through via a telegram from the Home Office to the prison governor, some twenty hours before he was informed of it. No one bothered to tell him until the official document arrived, presumably by courier. The family learned the whole history of the reprieve when Jimmy's file was released by the Home Office some three decades later under the Thirty-Year Rule.
7. Peter: slang for a cell, possibly from Cockney rhyming slang Peter Pan= Can, another word for a prison cell.

CHAPTER 6

1. Dartmoor is a geological oddity. Formed of granite, the tumbled rocks of the Tors are evidence of some ice age catastrophe. The centre of the plateau is, in effect, a giant saucer, filled with rainwater which never drains away because of the impervious rocks. The water is invisible because of the thick layer of moss which covers the surface. This is what makes it so dangerous. There must be many bodies (of men and animals) preserved in its sterile, peaty waters.

2. The war of 1812-14 was fought over a dispute between the United States and the UK over the Canadian borders. Neither side claimed a conclusive victory. Over six thousand American prisoners were taken, of whom a thousand were Afro-American. The Treaty of Ghent provided for the repatriation of the white prisoners. The unfortunate Afro-Americans were sold by their masters to the British for $1,204,960. Many of the prisoners were incarcerated at Dartmoor gaol – the youngest was twelve years old. Those who died were buried in a graveyard known to this day as 'The American Cemetery'.

3. Nuphar Lutea

4. *The Water Babies,* Charles Kingsley.

5. Sir Aurel Stein, described by Peter Levi as "the greatest of all explorers of Central Asia" died at Kabul on 26 October 1943 and was buried at the Christian Cemetery at Gora Kabur. The inscription on his grave reads as follows:

MARK AUREL STEIN
OF THE INDIAN ARCHAEOLOGICAL SURVEY.
SCHOLAR, EXPLORER, AUTHOR.
BY HIS ARDUOUS JOURNEYS IN INDIA, PERSIA
AND IRAQ HE ENLARGED THE BOUNDS OF KNOWLEDGE.
BORN AT BUDAPEST 26 NOVEMBER 1862 HE BECAME
AN ENGLISH CITIZEN IN 1904.
HE DIED AT KABUL 26 OCTOBER 1943.
A MAN GREATLY BELOVED.

He always travelled with a fox terrier named Dash who went through seven incarnations. His travels on the Silk Road were the subject of a major exhib-

ition at the British Library in 2004.
6. 'Gooserwallah': Hindustani word for a grumpy child.

CHAPTER 7

1. Today this line, which fell victim to the Beeching cuts, runs only as far as Meldon Quarry, near Okehampton. It is used for the transportation of stone. Access to Princetown is by road.
2. *Four Quartets*, T. S. Elliot, from 'Burnt Norton'.
3. *The Rout of the Ollafubs*, Katharine Lethbridge.
4. Major General Yamamoto was my father's opposite number, as Chief of Staff to the Commander of the Japanese 16th Army, Lieutenant General Yuichiro Nagano.

5. John Buyan 17th writer and devout Protestant evangelist. Imprisoned at time of English Civil Ware in Bedford goal where he wrote "Pilgrim's Progress". He served 12 years for supporting the Parliamentary cause.

CHAPTER 8

1. My father threw all the resources available to him into this investigation. The Intelligence Division found Hitler's will, interviewed witnesses, collated information. The results formed the basis of Professor Trevor Roper's book *The Last Days of Hitler*. While making passing reference to the work of the Intelligence Division, my father is not mentioned, or thanks given. One is left with the overwhelming impression that Trevor Roper did the whole thing himself. The book became a bestseller. This rankled with my father (and the whole family). He used to brood on it when suffering from depression and the lung cancer which led to his death in 1961.

2. *Decision in Germany* published by Doubleday 1950.

3. I have read that travellers have experienced something of the same phenomenon crossing the Bermuda Triangle at the spot where slaves were thrown overboard from the slave ships when the traders found them too ill to be worth the trouble of transporting them any further towards the plantations. I have myself encountered the same overwhelming feeling twice: once in the Tower of London and once in the Coliseum in Rome.

4. *Inside the Third Reich*, Albert Speer, published by the MacMillan Company, New York, 1970.

5. *The Last Days of Hitler*, Hugh Trevor Roper (Lord Dacre) – Chapter 3

6. The full picture of the part played by the Goebbels family did not emerge until after the publication, on 1st November 1945, of 'The British Intelligence Report on the Death of Hitler.' It was this report which later was expanded and published as Hugh Trevor Roper's book *The Last Days of Hitler.* Further material emerged at the Nuremberg trial when Goebbels' 'Appendix to the Fuehrer's Political Testament' was produced in evidence. Albert Speer in his memoir *Inside the Third Reich* first published in 1970, describes a fascinating account of his farewell visit to the bunker on 29th April, including conversations with Eva Braun and Frau Goebbels.

7. At the time of the British Intelligence Report, it was thought that he had shot himself through the mouth. This cannot be correct as later his jaw was found intact and identified from dental records.

8. Henry Vaughan 1621 – 1695, *The Retreat*

CHAPTER 9

1. The fate of Martin Borman is still uncertain. One witness, who had fled the Bunker with him immediately after Hitler's suicide, said that he was killed

by a Russian shell on the outskirts of Berlin. Another said that, when he realized that escape was impossible, he bit the standard issue cyanide capsule. Neither account has been corroborated. The hunt for Borman as a major war criminal was formally called off in 1973.

2. *English History 1914 – 1945*, A.J.P. Taylor, Chapter XIV.

3. A.J.P. Taylor ibid

4. Unpublished letter from a member of the Control Commission.

5. *The Berlin Airlift,* Ann and John Tusa, Chapter 3, Published Atheneum, New York, 1986.

6. *Nothing for Tears*, Lali Horstman, Published Weidenfeld and Nicolson, 1958.

7. In those days our pets lived entirely off green stuff; in clement weather dandelions and cow parsley gathered from the hedgerows, supplemented by vegetable scraps from the kitchen. They did not need water. Today every self-respecting rabbit eats oats and bran and knows how to drink from a bottle. How did it learn?

8. *Barrack Room Ballads*, Rudyard Kipling.

9. *The Bible* (Authorised Version), Psalm 14 v 1; (Douai Version) Psalm 13.

10. 'Henry IV part II', William Shakespeare

CHAPTER 10
1. *The Eleventh Commandment* Chapter 8
2. *The Eleventh Commandment* Chapter 8

CHAPTER 11
2. After the Easter rising of 1916 Eamon de Valera (1882-1975) and his co-rebels were condemned to death. All were executed at Kilmainham Goal in Dublin save for de Valera, who was an American citizen. He was sentenced to life imprisonment. Part of this sentence was served at Dartmoor. He was Taoiseach

(prime minister) of Ireland on three different occasions between 1937 and 1959, and President 1959-73. Shortly after we were married Jimmy and I attended an exhibition of prisoners' art sponsored by the Arthur Koestler Foundation. Among the pictures was one of Dartmoor Prison, painted by Benny Pearsall. "There's me barrow" said Jimmy, delighted. We bought the picture and it still hangs on my staircase, with pride of place.

3. Bath High School was, at the time, part of the Girls' Public Day School Trust. It was later absorbed into the comprehensive system.

4. I am told that my mother, her sisters Buffy and Josephine, my sister Cherry and I all had voices which were indistinguishable on the telephone. In the late 1950s when I did some work for the BBC 'Tonight' programme, Xanthe Wakefield, a member of the production team, helped me to lower my voice by half an octave.

5. It is strange that Miss Blackburn did not realise Mary Berry's potential. Mary, millionaire and National Treasure, has of course, been a thousand times more successful than I.

CHAPTER 12
    1. *The Eleventh Commandment* – Chapter 10

CHAPTER 13
    Part (i)
    1. Ted and Annie never married but lived together in perfect harmony until Ted's death in 1970. Annie told me that "he gave me twenty golden years".
    2. Note on change in employment law.
    3. Lord Denning's comment on Birmingham 6
    4. *Eleventh Commandment* Chapter 11 page 147.

Part (ii)
    5. *French Provincial Cooking*: 'Alsace and Lorraine'

p35, Elizabeth David, published Michael Joseph, 1960

CHAPTER 14
1. *The Eleventh Commandment.*
2. *Jude the Obscure*, Thomas Hardy.
3. *Testament of Youth*, Vera Brittain.
4. Later married to historian Asa Briggs
5. Later CEO Royal Opera House

CHAPTER 15
1. The Programme was 'Terra Firma' a documentary magazine described by one critic as "Blue Peter for grown-ups". Donald Baverstock was producer, Ned Sherrin, Alasdiar Clayre (academic, fellow of All Souls) and I were presenters. It lasted for just eight months on BBC 2. It was felt that Manchester was not a suitable location for the production of important and expensive documentaries. Donald railed furiously at 'Londinium' and took in a big way to the bottle.
2. This marriage lasted for about five years. Then, after an intervening marriage, Anthony remarried Gina in the nineties and remained with her until his death.

Louise de Vilmorin ended up with Ali Khan; Anthony's first wife, Lady Ursula Manners (later D'Abo) with Paul Getty.

CHAPTER 16
1. My Grandfather stood for a kind of high stoic Agnosticism. His attitude to religion was largely influenced by Sir James Fraser's *The Golden Bough*.
2. 'Genesis' chapter 31, verses 41 – 49 tells of the quarrel between LabaN and Jacob, his son in law, which was resolved at a place they named Mizpah.
3. I was broken hearted when walking recently through Gray's Inn Garden to find that the Catalpa tree

is no more. Shame!

4. *Spilling the Beans*, Clarissa Dixon-Wright, published by Hodder and Stoughton.

5. Ewen Montagu served during the war in Naval Intelligence. He was responsible for the brilliant piece of counter-intelligence later known variously as 'The man who never was', 'Operation Heartbreak', and formally as 'Operation Mincemeat'.

6. The body of a homeless man who had died of pneumonia was dressed up as that of a soldier who had drowned. In his pockets were put documents giving misinformation about the Allied landings in Southern Europe in the latter months of the war. These were seized and acted on by the Germans. It is said that the deception shortened the war by several months.

CHAPTER 17

1. Ronnie formed a friendship or 'business association' with Lord Boothby, to the delight of the tabloid press.

2. Tom Lehrer, American academic, wrote and sang satirical songs. For a time, their import into the UK was prohibited.

3.

CHAPTER 18

1. One day in the early 1990s I was on my way to Knightsbridge Crown Court. Mt attention was drawn to a small crowd which had gathered in the Brompton Road. It seems that a pedestrian had been knocked down by a passing motor vehicle and severely injured. A grey haired man dressed in a formal dark suit was kneeling by his side. Out of curiosity I approached the two and was astonished to hear the grey haired man intoning in Latin what I recognised to be the last rites. He looked up at me. I recognised him. "Francis!" I said.

He smiled. "Once a priest always a priest" he said. It turned out that he was now a barrister and was on his way to court to prosecute a case which i was instructed to defend.

2. Sir Edward Wakefield was now Conservative Chief Whip.

CHAPTER 19

1. My father and other survivors of the SS Cameronia later served together at Army Headquarters at Simla formed the Cameronia Society – see "Forthrights and Meanders" my mother's memoir page 67.

Dramatis Personae

1. Banwell, Susan (Lady Briggs)
Born & Educated Wiltshire
St Ann's College Oxford
Married historian & academic Asa Briggs
https://en.wikipedia.org/wiki/Asa_Briggs

2. Bindon, John
Born and bred Fulham. Minor villain. Discovered as actor by Jimmy. Played in 3 of Jimmy's plays. Social mountaineer.
https://en.wikipedia.org/wiki/John_Bindon

3. Broderick QC, Norman
Leading member of Western Circuit. Recorder of Penzance
https://www.independent.co.uk/news/people/obituary-judge-norman-brodrick-1533421.html

4. Brookes, John Elliott
Solicitor. Colonel 14th Army. Prisoner of the Japanese on Burma Siam railway. Mayor of Kensington and Chelsea.
https://london.wikia.org/wiki/John_Elliott_Brooks

5. Briscoe, Audrey
Educated Merchant Taylors School, Liverpool.
Somerville College, Oxford (Hon school of Jurisprudence). Later ran Ballet Minerva.

6. Curnow Ann
Educated Anglican convent Whitby, King's College London.
Barrister, QC Bencher Gray's Inn. Married Neil Dennison "nicest judge at the Old Bailey". https://en.wikipedia.org/wiki/Ann_Curnow

5. Eagle, Julian
Educated Sherbourne & Cambridge
Anglican priest: industrial Chaplin to South Hampshire. Honorary canon of Winchester Cathedral. Married Cherry Lethbridge.

6. Eppes, Alfreda Horner
Ninth child of Dr Eppes of Appomatox Manor Jamestown Virginia USA. Married Herbert John Maynard, grandmother of the Lethbridge children.

7. Fishman, Jack
News Editior of Kemsley Group Empire News
https://www.independent.co.uk/news/people/obituary-jack-fishman-1261416.html

8. Fraser, Antonia nee Pakenham
Educated Lady Margaret Hall Oxford
Popular historian
Married (i)Hugh Fraser MP (ii) Harold Pinter
Known as "Lady Magnesia Freelove".
https://en.wikipedia.org/wiki/Antonia_Fraser

9. Guinness, Desmond
Son of Diana Guinness, nee Mitford
Married Marie-Gabrielle von Urach
https://en.wikipedia.org/wiki/Desmond_Guinness

10. Griffith-Jones, Mervyn

Barrister, member of the prosecuting team at Nuremberg trials. Later Senior Treasury Counsel and judge at Central Criminal Court. Remembered as prosecutor in "Lady Chatterley" obscenity trial.
https://en.wikipedia.org/wiki/Mervyn_Griffith-Jones

11. Heilbron, Rose

Born and educated in Liverpool to a distinguished Jewish family. Rose to prominence during the war years. Joined chambers of Ewen Montague at 3 Pump Court. One of the first woman to take silk, appointed King's Counsel at the age of 34. Married to a doctor. Daughter, Hilary Heilbron who is also now in silk.
https://en.wikipedia.org/wiki/Rose_Heilbron

12. Holland, Anthony

Educated Eton. Barrister, prisoner of Japanese worked on notorious Burma – Siam railway.

13. Kray, Charles, Ron & Reg

East end gangsters. Larger in legend than in life. Remembered for films and iconic photographs taken by David Bailey and for friendship with Lord Boothby. https://en.wikipedia.org/wiki/Kray_twins

14. Lethbridge, Major General John Sydney CB CBE MC

Educated Uppingham, Jesus College Cambridge. Bengal Sappers – Royal Engineers. Married Katharine Greville Maynard.
Fought in World Wars 1 and 2. 3rd Afghan War. Father of Nemone, Peter and Katharine Charmian (Cherry).
https://en.wikipedia.org/wiki/John_Sydney_Lethbridge

15. Lethbridge, John Peter

Educated Uppingham. Harper Adams Agricultural College. Royal Engineers – served at Suez. Farmer at Damage Barton North Devon. Married Mary Wallace.

16. Lethbridge, Katharine Charmian – Cherry.

Educated Sherbourne Faculty of Speech Therapy, London University. Married Julian Eagle.

17. Lethbridge, Katharine Greville nee Maynard
Born India. Educated Sherbourne. Married JS Lethbridge. Author autobiography "Forthrights and Meanders" "Letters from East & West" and 3 Children's book. Mother of Nemone, Peter and Cherry.

18. Ken Loach
Born Warwickshire. Award winning film and TV director. Radical views. Directed 6 of Jimmy's plays. https://en.wikipedia.org/wiki/Ken_Loach

19. Logue, Christopher. Poet. Wrote English version of Iliad, translated by Xanthe Wakefield.

20. Lowenstein, Prince Rupert
Educated Magdalen College Oxford. Merchant banker: later financial advisor to The Rolling Stones. Married Princess Josephine, TV commentator on class and royalty.
https://en.wikipedia.org/wiki/Prince_Rupert_Loewenstein

21. Maynard, Sir John Herbert
Educated Merchant Taylors School. St John's College Oxford. Indian Civil Service. Linguist – 9 languages. Wrote extensively on Russian and post-revolutionary Russian. "Russia in Flux" and The Russian Peasant & other studies." Published Gollanz.
Married Alfreda Eppes, grandfather of Lethbridge children.
https://en.wikipedia.org/wiki/John_Maynard_(civil_servant)

22. Marreco, Anthony Friere
Educated Westminster School. Served Fleet Air Arm World War II. Barrister, junior to Sir Hartley Shawcross QC at Nuremburg trials. Later publisher at Weidenfeld & Nicolson Ltd, Lloyd's Name. Founding Director of Amnesty International. Farmer in Ireland.
https://en.wikipedia.org/wiki/Anthony_Marreco

23. Maxwell-Fyfe, Sir David, later Lord Kilmuir

Conversative Lord Chancellor, leading prosecuting counsel at Nuremberg trials.
https://en.wikipedia.org/wiki/David_Maxwell_Fyfe,_1st_Earl_of_Kilmuir

24. MacTaggart, James
Born and educated Glasgow. BBC drama producer & director. Produced Jimmy's and Nemone's plays for BBC. Memorialized by MacTaggart Lecture. https://en.wikipedia.org/wiki/James_MacTaggart

25. Mitchell, Frank
Frank "The Mad Axeman" Mitchell. Protégé if Kray siblings. Escaped from Dartmoor. Officially still "at large".
https://en.wikipedia.org/wiki/Frank_Mitchell_(prisoner)

26. Montague, Ewen
Barrister, Chairman of Middlesex Session. Head of 3 Pump Court Chambers. Wartime Naval Intelligence. Famous for "Operation Mincemeat" and wrote "The Man Who Never Was" 1953 an account of the operation.
https://en.wikipedia.org/wiki/Ewen_Montagu

17. Nicoloudis, Constantine
Prince Constantine of Greece.
Educated Trinity College Oxford. Imprisoned – at Old Bailey – sentenced to 10 months for forgery.
https://trove.nla.gov.au/newspaper/article/12645168

18. O'Connor, James
Born 1935. Eldest son of Jimmy and Mary (nee Davy) Educated Kilburn Primary. Mercantile Marine College. Merchant Navy (transatlantic liners). Served United States Air Force. US Citizen 1961 (veteran's fast trackentry) Married Eleanor Rose Bandon. Worked in container shipping industry Oaklands CA USA.

19. Sherrin, Ned
Born & educated Somerset, Exeter College Oxford.

Writer (with Caryl Brahms) Impresario, TV and radio producer & presenter. Wit and raconteur.
https://en.wikipedia.org/wiki/Ned_Sherrin

20. Puxon, Margaret
Educated Birmingham University.
Gynaecologist & barrister QC. Deputy circuit judge. Recorder. Tenant 3 Hare Court.
Married to solicitor Maurice Williams.
https://www.thetimes.co.uk/article/margaret-puxon-0m8v935kc3s

21. De Stempel, Baron Michael
Estonian heritage.
Educated Christ Church Oxford. Amateur historian and archivist.

22. Stein, Sir Aurel
Hungarian born naturalised British. Scholar & archaeologist. Explored silk road & central Asia. Wrote "With Alexander to the Indus" and other related works of scholarship. Nemone's godfather. https://en.wikipedia.org/wiki/Aurel_Stein

23. Thompson, Sir Lionel Bart
Barrister. Flew Spitfires in World War II. Tenant at 3 Hare Court.

24. Wakefield, Sir Edward (Teddy) Bart
Indian Civil Service 1933-1947.
Conservative MP for West Derby. Held various junior ministerial posts including Chief Whip. Married to Lalage. Father of Xanthe.
https://en.wikipedia.org/wiki/Humphry_Wakefield

25. Wakefield, Xanthe
Born in India.
Educated Wykham Abbey, Somerville College, Oxford (double first). Foreign Office.
BBC current affairs. Translated Iliad for Christopher Logue.
http://www.thepeerage.com/p60203.htm

26. Wates nee Weston, Jennifer
Educated Sherbourne, Somerville College Oxford (double first). Married Neil Wates of building dynasty.

27. Windsor, Dame Barbara DBE
Born & bred in North East London. Discovered as actress by Joan Littlewood. Married Ronnie Knight, East End gangster. Highly successful career with Theatre Workshop, in film "Carry On" series and television, notably EastEnders amongst many others. https://en.wikipedia.org/wiki/Barbara_Windsor

* * *

28. Percival, Sir Walter Ian
Conservative MP for Southport 1959 - 1987. Solicitor General 1979- 1983. Head of Chambers 3 Hare Court. Introduced private members bill (which failed) attempting to reintroduce death penalty. Expelled Nemone from Chambers when her marriage to Jimmy became public knowledge. https://www.wikiwand.com/en/Ian_Percival

29. Hector QC, Samuel James
Scottish Labour MP for Aberdeen North 1945-1970. Leading defence counsel for Jimmy at 1942 trial for murder. Political career ended in disgrace when he was arrested for shoplifting in WH Smith's book shop on Waterloo Station. https://www.dib.ie/biography/hughes-hector-samuel-james-a4141

Printed in Great Britain
by Amazon